THE *Best American Infographics* *2014*

THE BEST AMERICAN

Infographics

2014

With an Introduction by **Nate Silver**

Gareth Cook, Series Editor

MARINER BOOKS
HOUGHTON MIFFLIN HARCOURT
BOSTON | NEW YORK 2014

Contents

IV. INTERACTIVE
By Fernanda B. Viégas

Foreword

MANY YEARS AGO, at the dawn of the Powerpoint era, Stephen Kosslyn served as chair of Harvard's psychology department. One of his duties was to attend every talk the department sponsored, including those delivered by a long train of job candidates. As he sat listening, day after day, he started paying attention to the speakers' slides, and, specifically, how very, very bad they often were. One slide would be filled with text, which the presenter would then read; another would feature a long series of bullet points that failed to provide much clarity; and then, almost inevitably, the *pièce de résistance* — a complex graph that caused the audience to shift uncomfortably in their seats. Kosslyn recalls one particularly disastrous piece of Powerpoint artistry that moved him from frustration to action. The speaker had selected a template called "celestial": white stars dotted the black of space, and Saturn sat in the foreground, its proud rings sweeping across the frame. On this, the presenter had laid down blocks of tiny white type. The lines became difficult to read every time they hit a patch of stars and nearly vanished on encountering Saturn. "Here were these world experts in psychology," Kosslyn told me, "and they were making these unbelievable errors." Given all that is known about how the brain processes information, Kosslyn wondered, can't we do better?

Kosslyn, who is now the founding dean of the Minerva Schools at the Keck Graduate Institute, went on to write a series of articles and books about the dos and don'ts of visual presentation. Kosslyn and other scientists exploring the neuro-science of vision have discovered things that may surprise even some designers. Did you know, for example, that cobalt blue (a mixture of blue and red) is a bad choice for text, or thin lines, because of the way the eye brings these particular colors into focus? Yet the researchers have also been able to articulate broader principles: visual "rules" that elite designers already know by intuition. The mind does some things with shocking speed — grouping similar objects, say, or noticing the one item that is different — while other tasks, like reading small text on a background of a similar color, are slow and labored. Good design plays to our strengths of mind.

In some sense, then, the story of Powerpoint — and of infographics, and of all visual design — begins hundreds of millions of years ago. From the earliest days of vision, the advantage went to those creatures that could decode the patterns around them (predator, food, mate) and act. The brain has since been shaped by evolution over countless millennia to make quick sense of what it sees. Something like half of the brain is involved in processing images. This, fundamentally, is why infographics have become such a force in our increasingly visual media. Put information in the right visual form, and your audience will immediately get the gist. This also helps explain why the best infographics are so satisfying. When the pattern emerges and we see the point, we experience the same primal thrill as a hunter who sees an animal track in a line of broken grass. Yes, a poorly done infographic causes pain as the mental gears grind. But the good ones? The ones that bring flashes of clarity? These leave us feeling . . . *ahhhhh*.

The Best American Infographics is a celebration of the *ahhhhh* moment. The collection is divided into three subject areas. We start with "You," a celebration of the individual. Here a designer at *Time* tells you how to be happy—in the form of a board game. You will learn how to pair wine with food, how to decode the Empire State Building, and how to decide whether a creative project is worth the time—as determined by an "existential calculator" (which you'll need to find or make). Other infographics bring us into private worlds. Two women in San Francisco track their wayward cat with GPS. A man with synesthesia shows the flavors he associates with the names of stops on the London Tube. The stations on his map include "coconut," "ginger beer," and "Ritz crackers." To get from "apple pie" to "boiled cabbage" you'll want to transfer at "sausage and fried egg."

The collection's second part, "Us," covers people in the collective. How was Pope Francis selected? Where, precisely, are the boundaries of the Midwest? What are judges looking for in competitive surfing? Some of the pieces are determinedly light-hearted: a map of French kisses, or a deep look at the evolution of Justin Bieber, superstar. But many of the infographics here work as social commentary. The *New York Times* tracks what has happened with gun laws since Newtown. *Time* tells us how the NSA is listening in and what may be coming next. The *National Post* explains force-feeding at Guantanamo Bay, including enough about the workings of a nasogastric tube to make anyone a little bit uncomfortable. The section closes with a haunting work of remembrance for those who have died in armed conflict.

From there, we move to the world beyond people. Here are dinosaurs and bees and what is probably the most drop-dead gorgeous piece in this year's collection: a view of the perilous journeys taken by migrating birds. Fans of baseball and of bourbon will be rewarded. Cheese will be served. Some of the more moving pieces here succeed by the perspective they provide, such as the "present clock," which asks you to see time in terms of seasons, not hours—and asks that you wonder whether an infographic must appear in print to be an infographic. Or on a screen: At the end of the book are tributes to the ten best interactive infographics of the year.

Choosing what made this year's collection was a difficult job. Defining what is "best" in such a diverse art form is, honestly, impossible. I had tremendous help from my excellent brain trust and many thoughtful (even spirited) debates with friends and colleagues. I sought infographics that were excellent in some way, that showed the range of work being done, that were innovative, that captured the year somehow. For the tough calls, though, I often found myself going with feeling. As I looked at an entry, did I feel the gears grinding, hints of the feeling one gets from Powerpoint gone wrong? Or did I feel taken care of, that my mental effort was being rewarded, that I had seen something I had not seen before and was better for it?

All of the images in *The Best American Infographics 2014* were originally published for a North American audience, online or in print, during 2013. The top 10 interactive works were selected this year by Fernanda Viégas, who, with her professional partner, Martin Wattenberg, has done some of the field's most enduring work. Choosing the rest of the works fell to me. To nominate infographics for the next volume, see the rules at garethcook.net, or email me at contactgarethcook@gmail.com.

I'd like to thank Nate Silver and Carl De Torres for being a part of this project. Nate is one of the leading thinkers at the intersection of statistics and story, and Carl's work on the cover—an infographic about the power of infographics, and a thing of beauty—says far better than I could why it's been so great to have him on board. I'd also like to thank my brain trust for sending so much excellent work my way and for plenty of behind-the-scenes help. And I would like to thank my assistant, Emily Kent, as well as the team at Houghton Mifflin Harcourt, particularly designer Patrick Barry, permissions guru Mary Dalton-Hoffman, promotions master Michelle Bonanno, able editorial assistant Emma Rosenberg, and—lastly, most importantly—Deanne Urmy, whose idea this series was. All of them have worked unbelievably hard to make this book what it is.

GARETH COOK

Introduction

IF THERE WERE an Information Design Hall of Fame, its inductees might include Edward Tufte, the Yale statistician who rallied against the use of "chartjunk"—and Dona Wong, who studied under Tufte and went on to lead the graphics desk at the *Wall Street Journal.* It would have a shrine to Harry Beck, who designed the London Tube map, and to cartographers from Ptolemy to Mercator.

But when I think of information design, the first image is from another hallowed hall: the Baseball Hall of Fame in Cooperstown, New York. Somewhere in Cooperstown is the best infographic ever. It was designed by Ted Williams, the baseball player.

Williams's infographic consists of a display of 77 baseballs, arranged in a rectangular grid that mimics the dimensions of baseball's strike zone. At the center of the grid are baseballs in shades of vermillion and tangerine, with gaudy numbers like .400 and .390: the batting averages that Williams thought he'd hit for on pitches thrown in that part of the strike zone. At its margins are baseballs colored in sickly hues of plum and gray, on which Williams expected to hit no better than .230.

The strike zone display is brilliant not just because of its aesthetic appeal, or its meticulousness, or because it almost exactly anticipated graphics that would be generated by computers many years later. Rather, it is powerful because it gives us a window into Williams's mind and tells a story that *couldn't be told in any other way.*

The best infographics, like the ones you'll see in this book, do the same. Design has traditionally been seen as a field for "right-brained" types: those who think visually and spatially rather than with symbols like words and numbers. But modern information design is equal parts art and science, form and function, architecture and engineering. It combines the best of at least three fields of achievement: aesthetics, technology, and journalism.

By aesthetics, I mean all the usual things, but especially proportionality. For information designers, this quality is not so abstract as it might be in other mediums. Their goal is tangible: to convey as much information as possible given some set of constraints.

Traditionally, these constraints included the cost of materials, the designer's time, and a finite amount of printed or physical space. As design moved into virtual realms, some of these constraints were removed. But early attempts at information design on the web, and at web design generally, tended toward the cluttered, the indulgent, and the just plain ugly. (Think of the Myspace profile you had as a teenager.)

The community of information designers came to realize that there was another constraint: the viewer's attention. Tufte (and others) have long spoken to the importance of minimalism in information design. But it proved to be more important as design was translated onto the web, where attention spans are measured in seconds and the next graphic is but a mouse-click or hand-swipe away. More isn't always better: no more in information design than in poetry, or painting, or product design. A superfluous axis on a chart, an extra dimension of information, can distract from the focal point just as much as an extraneous word in a sonnet or an unnecessary button on a tablet. It can reduce the signal-to-noise ratio and leave the viewer less well informed.

Successful examples of information design can sometimes be highly intricate, but these cases usually involve a layered approach. The most essential elements of the graphic—the most essential parts of the story—jump out immediately. Peer a little deeper, and you'll discover a little more. Deeper still, and there might be a surprise lurking. But it's always proportionate to the reader's field of view. When looking at a map of the United States, you don't need to know whether Seventh Avenue runs north or south through Manhattan. When you're running late to a meeting in Midtown, you don't need to know what continent you're on. The best designers have the talent and the experience to strike the right balance.

Technology in the field of information design has come a long way from the days of Ted Williams. The job listing we posted for data visualization journalists at *FiveThirtyEight* blog asked for experience in HTML, CSS, Javascript, Raphael, D3, TileMill, QGIS, and TopoJSON.

But you'd be mistaken to assume that the men and women who work as information designers will have their places taken by computers anytime soon. By contrast, visual acuity is something that humans have honed after tens of thousands of years of evolution. Computers remain quite clumsy at it. In fields like weather forecasting, human beings use their eyes and their knowledge of geography to significantly improve on the work of supercomputers. Computers struggle to solve a CAPTCHA that distorts letters or images in minor ways, when a six-year-old could have the right answer in an instant.

Instead, information design represents one of the best marriages of men (and women) and machines. Computers provide the horsepower and enable thousands or millions of datapoints to be processed in the span of a second. Humans still need to guide the horse to water.

Great works of information design are also great works of journalism. Some information designers may not think of what they do as having any relationship to journalism. But when I began my three-year tenure at the *New York Times,* in 2010, I found that the information designers there were quite conscientious about identifying themselves as journalists. I thought they were a little stuck-up at first. I soon discovered that they had just the right idea.

At the core of journalism is the mission of making sense of our complex world to a broad audience. Newsrooms from the *New York Times* to *BuzzFeed* place emphasis on gathering information. But they're also in the business of organizing that information into forms like stories. Visual approaches to organizing information also tell stories, but have a number of potential advantages against purely verbal ones:

Approachability. Human beings have strong visual acuity. Furthermore, our visual language is often more universal than our words. Data presented in the form of an infographic can transcend barriers of class and culture. This is just as important for experts as for laypersons: a 2012 study* of academic economists found that they made much more accurate statistical inferences from a graphic presentation of data than when the same information was in tabular form.

Transparency. The community of information designers has an ethos toward sharing their data and their code — both with one another and with readers. Well-executed examples of information design *show* the viewer something rather than *telling* her something. They can peel away the onion, build trust, and let the reader see how the conclusions are drawn.

Efficiency. I will not attempt to tell you how many words a picture is worth. But surely visualization is the superior medium in some cases. In trying to figure out how to get from King's Cross to Heathrow Airport on the London Tube, would you rather listen to a fifteen-minute soliloquy from the bloke at the pub — or take a fifteen-second glance at Beck's map?

That information design is part and parcel of journalism also means that it inherits journalism's burdens. If it's sometimes easier to reveal information by means of a data visualization, that can make it easier to deceive. Trendlines plotted through a noisy landscape of data can give the impression of a clearer relationship than really exists. Bar charts unmoored from the X-axis can misconstrue a minor change as a paradigm shift. Spatial mappings can make Mitt Romney's win in North Dakota (population 700,000) seem more important than Barack Obama's in New Jersey (population 8.8 million).

These aren't easy questions: does an infographic that makes New Jersey appear larger than North Dakota do more to reveal or conceal? What one journalist thinks of as organizing information, the next one might call censorship.

But it's long past time to give information designers their place at the journalistic table. The ones you'll see in this book are pointing the way forward and helping the rest of us see the world a little more clearly.

NATE SILVER

* http://emresoyer.com/Publications_files/Soyer%20%26%20Hogarth_2012.pdf

THE *Best American Infographics 2014*

YOU   US   MATERIAL WORLD   INTERACTIVE

You

Who We Are

Understanding the people of the world, without percentages.

ARTIST Jack Hagley, graphic designer, London.

STATEMENT When I was a boy in the '90s, my mother had a printout of a chain e-mail pinned to the wall in our kitchen. It was called "The World as 100 People," and it was just a simple list. I never forgot it because it was a simple but clever idea — a child could understand it without knowing the concept of percentages. One day, I didn't have any other work to do and I was sitting in my studio. The idea and the method came to me very quickly. I knew that I wanted to make it round, like the world. I wanted to use colors that might remind people of flags. I made the first draft in the morning and it was on the Internet by the afternoon.

PUBLICATION *jackhagley.com,*
Courrier International Paris (May 2013)

The World as 100 PEOPLE

GENDER
50 female
50 male

CONTINENT
11 Europe
5 North America
9 South America
15 Africa
60 Asia

AGE
26 aged 0-14
66 aged 15-64
8 aged 65+

RELIGION
33 Christians
22 Muslims
14 Hindus
7 Buddhists
12 other
12 no religion

AREA
49 live in rural areas
51 live in urban areas

LITERACY
83 able to read & write
17 unable

LANGUAGE (First)
12 Chinese
5 Spanish
5 English
3 Arabic
3 Hindi
3 Bengali
3 Portuguese
2 Russian
2 Japanese
62 other

COLLEGE
7 have a college degree
93 do not

HOUSING
23 have no shelter
77 have a place to shelter

INTERNET
30 can access the Internet
70 cannot

NUTRITION
21 overweight
63 adequate
15 undernourished
1 starving

POVERTY
48 live on less than 2 US dollars per day

WATER
87 have safe water
13 do not

PHONES
75 have cell phones
25 do not

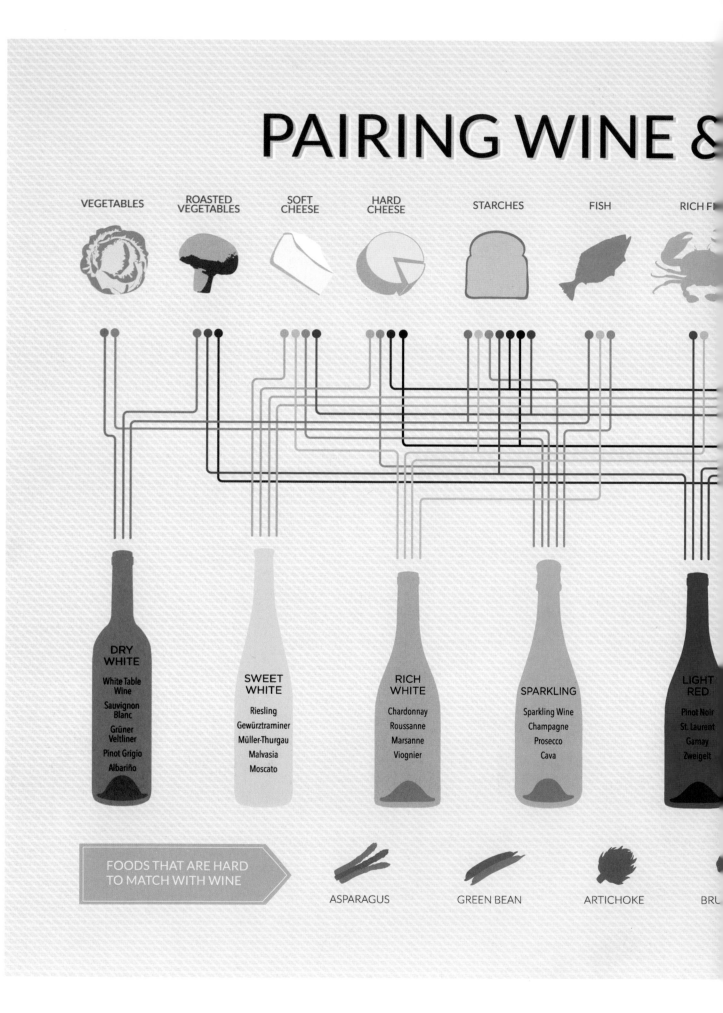

PAIRING WINE &

VEGETABLES ROASTED VEGETABLES SOFT CHEESE HARD CHEESE STARCHES FISH RICH FI

DRY WHITE

White Table Wine

Sauvignon Blanc

Grüner Veltliner

Pinot Grigio

Albariño

SWEET WHITE

Riesling

Gewürztraminer

Müller-Thurgau

Malvasia

Moscato

RICH WHITE

Chardonnay

Roussanne

Marsanne

Viognier

SPARKLING

Sparkling Wine

Champagne

Prosecco

Cava

LIGHT RED

Pinot Noir

St. Laurent

Gamay

Zweigelt

FOODS THAT ARE HARD TO MATCH WITH WINE

ASPARAGUS   GREEN BEAN   ARTICHOKE   BRU

FOOD

WHITE MEAT   RED MEAT   CURED MEAT   SWEETS

MEDIUM
RED

Red Table
Wine

Tempranillo
Sangiovese
Zinfandel
Grenache
Merlot

DESSERT

Late Harvest
Ice Wine
Sherry
Madeira
Port
VDN

learn about wine
winefolly.com
© 2013, Wine Folly

WINE
FOLLY

TROUT   CHOCOLATE

The Perfect Wine for the Meal

Just follow the lines.

ARTIST Madeline Puckette, designer and certified sommelier at Wine Folly in Seattle, WA.

STATEMENT My goal was to communicate how simple wine and food pairing is. Even though there are over 1,300 wine varieties, most can be segmented into just eight styles. Start with the food of choice and end with a wine that tastes great paired with it. The inspiration for this design was drawn from destination maps, such as train, subway, and city maps.

PUBLICATION *Winefolly.com* (February 2013)

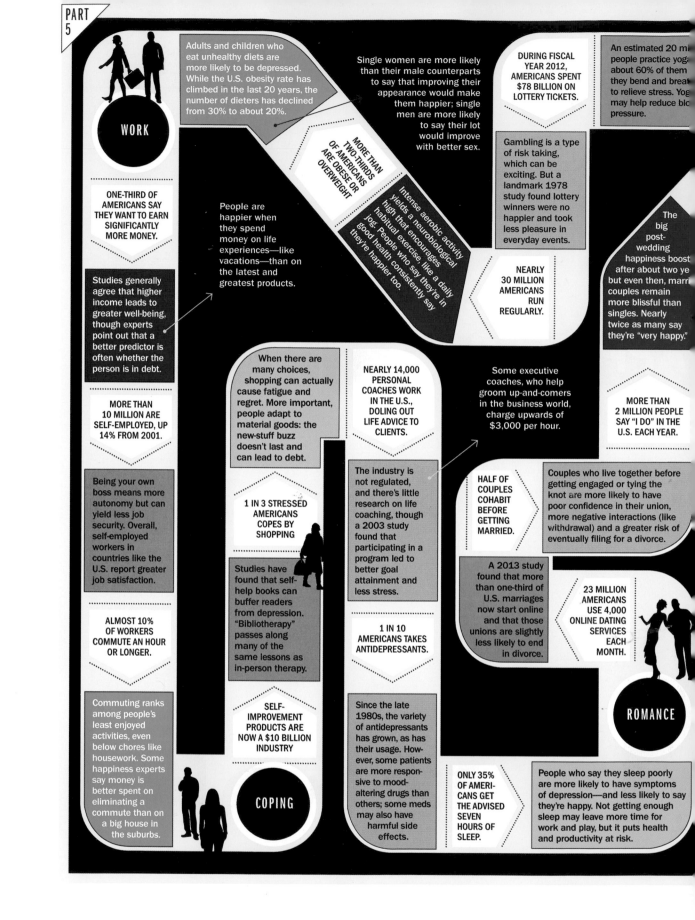

PART 5

How to Be Happy

Let science be your guide.

ARTISTS Heather Jones, infographics designer, and Katy Steinmetz, writer/researcher, at *Time*.

STATEMENT This was one of seven pieces in a special issue called "The Pursuit of Happiness," which explored why Americans are wired to be happy—and what that is doing to us. We had tons of stats to work with, so we chose the most surprising or powerful ones, and I designed them by age or stage in life, packing in as much of the deeply reported information as possible. The color key gave it multiple points of entry, and the figures helped make it playful to navigate.

PUBLICATION *Time* (July 2013)

The Secret to Success Is Starting Early

"Success begets further success," write Isabel V. Sawhill, Scott Winship, and Kerry Searle Grannis of the Brookings Institution. "Children who are successful at each life stage from early childhood to young adulthood are much more likely to achieve the American Dream." On the other hand, early failures set children on a path for future disappointments and a longer shot at getting into the middle class.

This graphic, based on the Brookings scholars' research, shows that the widest paths are those that lead from successs to success

and from failure to failure. Some children recover from failure, and some backslide from success, but those paths are rarer. That suggests the most-effective interventions are those that would steer off-track children toward success as early as possible.

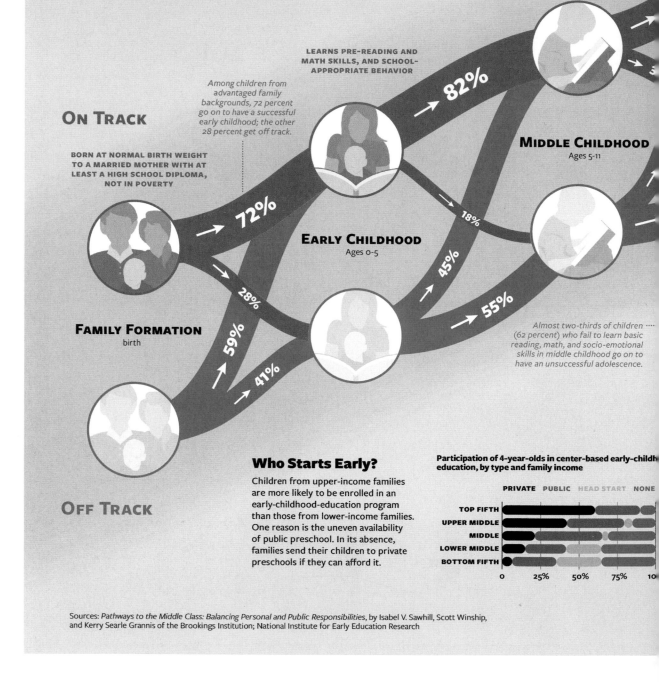

LEARNS BASIC READING AND MATH SKILLS, AND SOCIO-EMOTIONAL SKILLS

LEARNS PRE-READING AND MATH SKILLS, AND SCHOOL-APPROPRIATE BEHAVIOR

Among children from advantaged family backgrounds, 72 percent go on to have a successful early childhood; the other 28 percent get off track.

ON TRACK

BORN AT NORMAL BIRTH WEIGHT TO A MARRIED MOTHER WITH AT LEAST A HIGH SCHOOL DIPLOMA, NOT IN POVERTY

MIDDLE CHILDHOOD
Ages 5-11

82%

72%

18%

EARLY CHILDHOOD
Ages 0-5

45%

FAMILY FORMATION
birth

28%

59%

55%

41%

Almost two-thirds of children (62 percent) who fail to learn basic reading, math, and socio-emotional skills in middle childhood go on to have an unsuccessful adolescence.

OFF TRACK

Who Starts Early?

Children from upper-income families are more likely to be enrolled in an early-childhood-education program than those from lower-income families. One reason is the uneven availability of public preschool. In its absence, families send their children to private preschools if they can afford it.

Participation of 4-year-olds in center-based early-childhood education, by type and family income

	PRIVATE	PUBLIC	HEAD START	NONE
TOP FIFTH				
UPPER MIDDLE				
MIDDLE				
LOWER MIDDLE				
BOTTOM FIFTH				

0   25%   50%   75%   100%

Sources: *Pathways to the Middle Class: Balancing Personal and Public Responsibilities*, by Isabel V. Sawhill, Scott Winship, and Kerry Searle Grannis of the Brookings Institution; National Institute for Early Education Research

The First Steps Matter the Most

The early years shape a life.

ARTISTS Peter Bell, graphics director, and Stephanie Stamm, news artist, at *National Journal*.

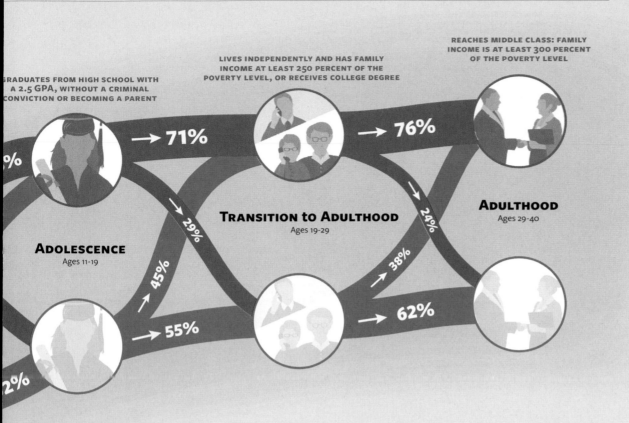

GRADUATES FROM HIGH SCHOOL WITH A 2.5 GPA, **WITHOUT A CRIMINAL CONVICTION OR BECOMING A PARENT**

LIVES INDEPENDENTLY AND HAS FAMILY INCOME AT LEAST 250 PERCENT OF THE POVERTY LEVEL, OR RECEIVES COLLEGE DEGREE

REACHES MIDDLE CLASS: FAMILY INCOME IS AT LEAST 300 PERCENT OF THE POVERTY LEVEL

→ 71%   → 76%

TRANSITION to ADULTHOOD
Ages 19-29

ADOLESCENCE
Ages 11-19

ADULTHOOD
Ages 29-40

29%   24%

45%   38%

→ 55%   → 62%

The Roads Less Traveled Are Bumpier

Not all paths to the middle class require a successful early childhood. Children who recover from early deprivation and succeed in middle childhood and adolescence have nearly as strong a chance of reaching the middle class as children who lucked out from the beginning—almost three in four, in fact. The catch is that only 8 percent of children take that route. Children who aren't well-prepared to start school face a harder, narrower path toward a middle-class adulthood than it is for those who succeed as youngsters.

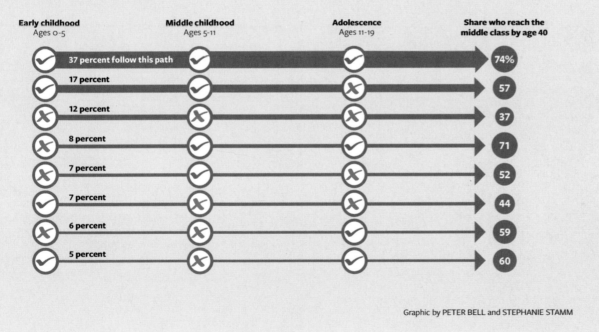

Early childhood Ages 0-5	Middle childhood Ages 5-11	Adolescence Ages 11-19	Share who reach the middle class by age 40
✓ 37 percent follow this path	✓	✓	74%
✓ 17 percent	✓	✗	57
✗ 12 percent	✗	✗	37
✗ 8 percent	✓	✓	71
✗ 7 percent	✓	✗	52
✓ 7 percent	✗	✗	44
✗ 6 percent	✗	✓	59
✓ 5 percent	✗	✓	60

Graphic by PETER BELL and STEPHANIE STAMM

STATEMENT Success and failure in life are cumulative. Children born into relatively advantaged circumstances are likelier than their disadvantaged peers to have a successful early childhood, and from there are likelier to go on to further success. For children who are born into poverty, or who don't hit those early developmental milestones, it's harder to get onto the success track. The work of Isabel Sawhill, Scott Winship, and Kerry Searle Grannis quantified for me the importance of early success. I wanted our graphic to do their research justice and bring it to a wider audience.

PUBLICATION *National Journal* (December 2013)

Taste Tube Map

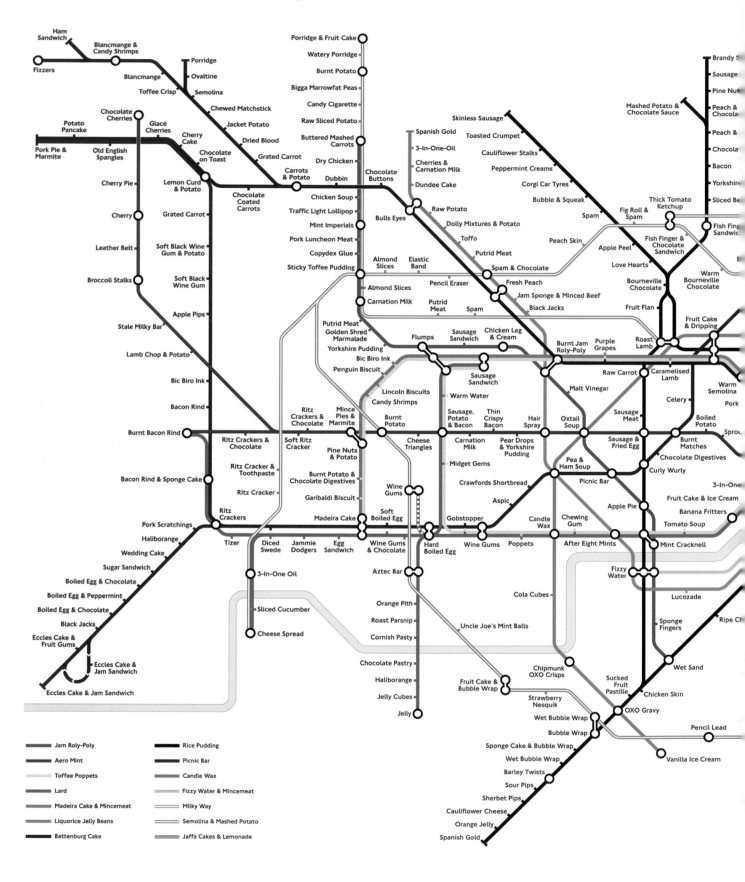

Legend:
- Jam Roly-Poly
- Aero Mint
- Toffee Poppets
- Lard
- Madeira Cake & Mincemeat
- Liquorice Jelly Beans
- Battenburg Cake
- Rice Pudding
- Picnic Bar
- Candle Wax
- Fizzy Water & Mincemeat
- Milky Way
- Semolina & Mashed Potato
- Jaffa Cakes & Lemonade

MAYOR OF LONDON

YOU   US   MATERIAL WORLD   INTERACTIVE

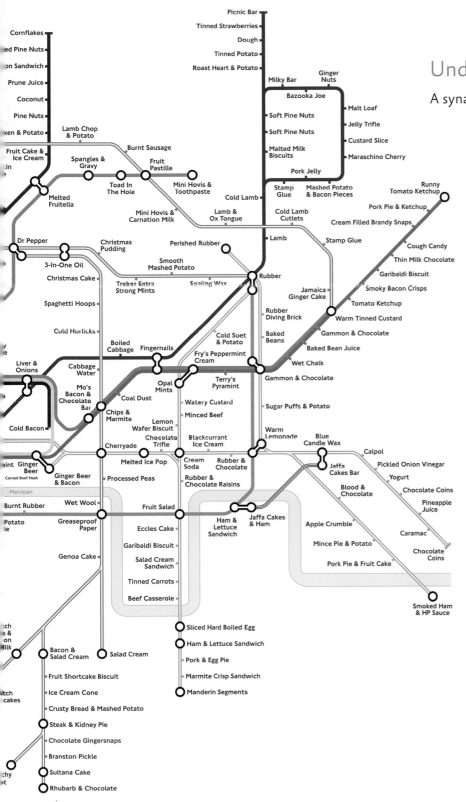

Underground Taste Map

A synaesthesia tour of London.

ARTIST James Wannerton, president of the UK Synaesthesia Association.

STATEMENT This map is a graphic representation of each of the tastes and textures I experience as I travel around deep beneath the streets of London. I have synaesthesia, a neurological trait that blends or mixes my sense of sound and sight with my sense of taste. Every time I stop at or pass through a Tube station on the London Underground subway system, I experience an involuntary taste and texture, a real mouthfeel, specific to that particular station name. Over five decades I visited every station on the network and made a note of the tastes and textures specific to each station name. The journey began in January 1964 at Dollis Hill, and reached the end of the line at Woolwich Arsenal in August 2013.

   This Synaesthesia Taste Tube map is a reworking of Harry Beck's iconic original 1931 Underground map design; it helps demonstrate that each of us perceives the space and world around us in different and unique ways that we sometimes take for granted. The Taste Tube Map graphic is reproduced by kind permission of Transport for London. Special thanks to David Ellis at TfL and Alan Foale at Pulse Creative for all their help and support.

PUBLICATION Online (2013)

Transport for London
UNDERGROUND
© Transport for London

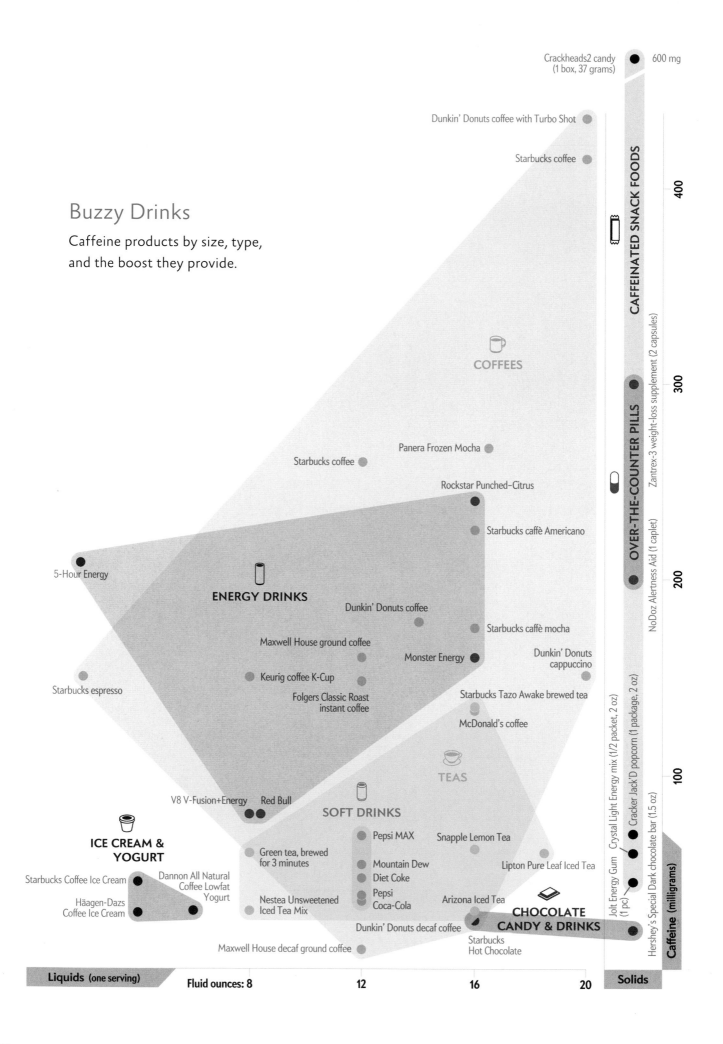

Buzzy Drinks

Caffeine products by size, type, and the boost they provide.

Crackheads2 candy (1 box, 37 grams) — 600 mg

Dunkin' Donuts coffee with Turbo Shot

Starbucks coffee

CAFFEINATED SNACK FOODS

Zantrex-3 weight-loss supplement (2 capsules)

COFFEES

OVER-THE-COUNTER PILLS

NoDoz Alertness Aid (1 caplet)

Panera Frozen Mocha

Starbucks coffee

Rockstar Punched–Citrus

Starbucks caffè Americano

5-Hour Energy

ENERGY DRINKS

Dunkin' Donuts coffee

Starbucks caffè mocha

Maxwell House ground coffee

Monster Energy

Dunkin' Donuts cappuccino

Starbucks espresso

Keurig coffee K-Cup

Folgers Classic Roast instant coffee

Starbucks Tazo Awake brewed tea

McDonald's coffee

TEAS

Crystal Light Energy mix (1/2 packet, 2 oz)

Cracker Jack'D popcorn (1 package, 2 oz)

V8 V-Fusion+Energy   Red Bull

SOFT DRINKS

Pepsi MAX

Snapple Lemon Tea

ICE CREAM & YOGURT

Green tea, brewed for 3 minutes

Mountain Dew

Diet Coke

Lipton Pure Leaf Iced Tea

Starbucks Coffee Ice Cream

Dannon All Natural Coffee Lowfat Yogurt

Pepsi
Coca-Cola

Arizona Iced Tea

Jolt Energy Gum (1 pc)

Hershey's Special Dark chocolate bar (1.5 oz)

Häagen-Dazs Coffee Ice Cream

Nestea Unsweetened Iced Tea Mix

CHOCOLATE CANDY & DRINKS

Dunkin' Donuts decaf coffee

Starbucks Hot Chocolate

Maxwell House decaf ground coffee

Liquids (one serving)   Fluid ounces: 8   12   16   20   **Solids**

Caffeine (milligrams)

400   300   200   100

ARTISTS Dirk Aschoff, senior art director, and Klaas Neumann, art director, of Golden Section Graphics, Berlin.

STATEMENT This shows the amount of caffeine in selected products on the US market in relation to their serving size, with the products grouped according to their composition (yogurt, soft drinks, tea). We found out that it was best to create a matrix of caffeine amount/serving size, then to add a second layer combining products of the same composition to create a "landscape" of caffeinated products. That gives the reader the ability to compare products within their category and to other categories and, of course, to compare whole groups of caffeinated products.

PUBLICATION *Scientific American* (November 2013)

Is the Author Human?

The signature of Twitter bots.

ARTISTS Cedric Kiefer and Johannes Poell of Onformative. Josef Reyes, designer, Lee Simmons, writer, and Sarah Fallon, editor, at *WIRED*.

STATEMENT This chart shows activity patterns for hundreds of Twitter users over the course of a day. It suggests a new approach to spam filters, weeding out corporate shills and robots just by analyzing their timestamps. Our graph is based on some lovely new work by neuroscientist Aldo Faisal and computer scientist Gabriela Tavares. They were after big game — universal laws governing human communications — and they'd collected piles of metadata from Twitter users for analysis.

We had to figure out how to tell the story visually. The algorithm was based on an elusive concept — the distribution of time lags between tweets — which would have needed explanation. Instead, we decided to look at the timing of tweets over the course of a day. Now, you wouldn't build a Twitter filter on this level of data — a clever spammer could easily game the rules. But this simpler, more intuitive image vividly conveys the idea, revealing clear differences between user types, sort of like temporal "fingerprints." More generally, it demonstrates the informational richness of communications metadata — a sobering thought, perhaps.

By the way, the researchers found their universal law: it turns out that humans are more predictable than robots. Those annoying tweets that arrive with machinelike regularity each day? Those are actually your friends.

PUBLICATION *WIRED* (October 2013)

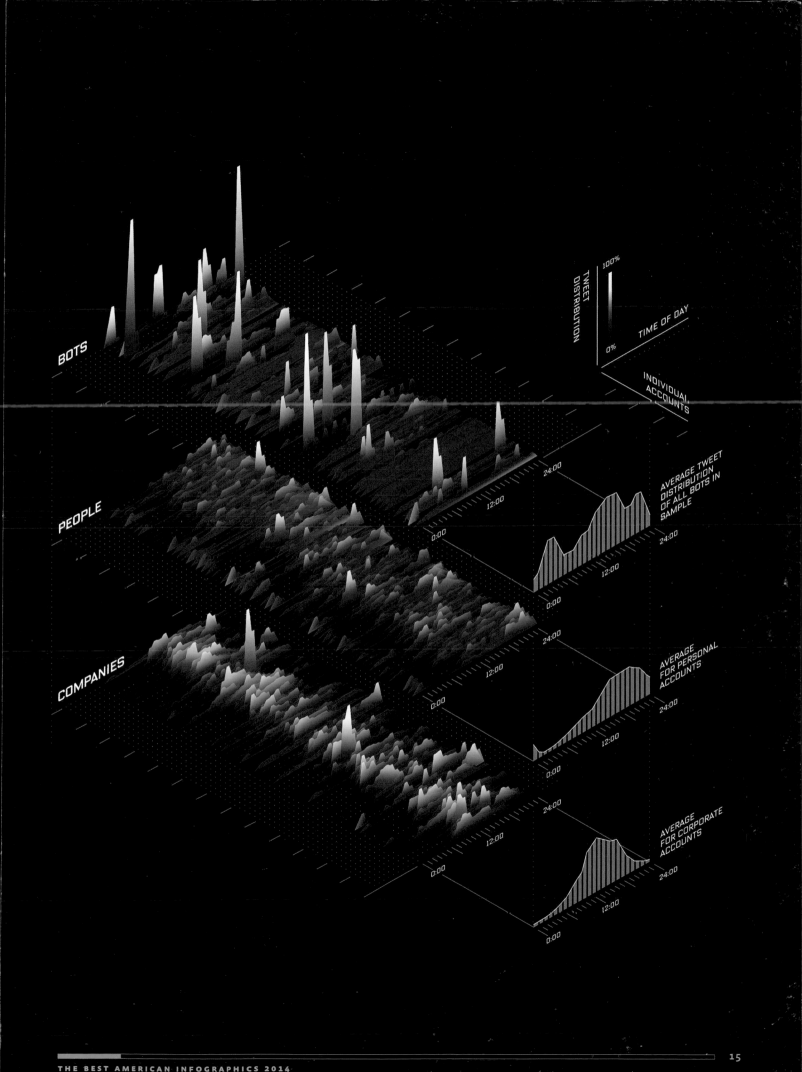

BOTS

PEOPLE

COMPANIES

TWEET
DISTRIBUTION

100%

0%

TIME OF DAY

INDIVIDUAL
ACCOUNTS

24:00

12:00

0:00

24:00

AVERAGE TWEET
DISTRIBUTION
OF ALL BOTS IN
SAMPLE

12:00

0:00

24:00

12:00

0:00

24:00

AVERAGE
FOR PERSONAL
ACCOUNTS

12:00

0:00

24:00

12:00

0:00

24:00

AVERAGE
FOR CORPORATE
ACCOUNTS

12:00

0:00

Windup
The necessity is balance. Standing on one leg, the pitcher shouldn't be leaning in either direction.

Elbow flexion
The angle of the elbow when the arm is cocked needs to be in the range of 90 to 112 degrees.

Shoulder rotation
As the front foot contacts the ground, the armpit angle created by the upper arm and torso should be 90 degrees. The shoulder will rotate at a rate of 6,350 to 8,300 degrees per second.

Upper-trunk rotation
Follows the pelvis in sequence and should rotate at 1,050 to 1,200 degrees per second.

Follow-through
Back of the throwing shoulder should appear to the batter and throwing hand should end up near the opposite knee, thigh or hip.

Bringing Heat

After studying digital imaging of hundreds of pitching motions, researchers now understand the most effective approach to maximizing a pitcher's velocity. Fortuitously, it's the same technique that can prevent injuries to the arm and shoulder. But throwing 100 miles per hour can still be hazardous to your health.

—*Mike Sudal*

Arm cocking
Shoulder rotates back 180 degrees.

Stride length
Distance between front of the pitching rubber to the front ankle should be 79% to 88% of the pitcher's height.

Pelvis rotation
Immediately after the front foot hits the ground, pelvis should rotate quickly at a speed of 500 to 650 degrees per second.

Knee angle
As the ball is released, knee should be at a 21- to 45-degree angle.

Clocking a Kinetic Chain
A series of body parts work in orderly symmetry to maximize velocity. This chart shows the rate of rotation: how quickly each joint would be spinning in one second, if the motion lasted that long and the joint could spin 360 degrees rather than be held in place.

6,000 degrees/second
4,000
2,000
0
-2,000

— Shoulder rotation
— Elbow flexion
— Upper trunk rotation
— Pelvis rotation

Leg lift   Stride   Foot contact   Arm cocked   Ball release   Follow through

A League of Their Own
Pitchers who throw at least 25% of their fastballs 96 mph or faster, by season:

60 pitchers
62
30
0
'03 '04 '05 '06 '07 '08 '09 '10 '11 '12

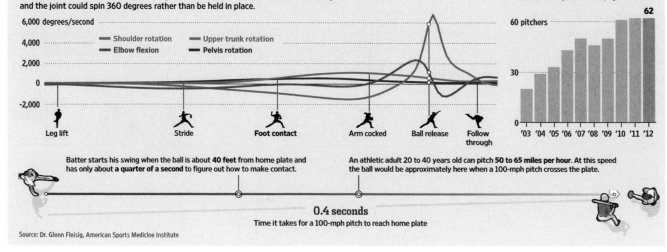

Batter starts his swing when the ball is about **40 feet** from home plate and has only about **a quarter of a second** to figure out how to make contact.

An athletic adult 20 to 40 years old can pitch **50 to 65 miles per hour**. At this speed the ball would be approximately here when a 100-mph pitch crosses the plate.

0.4 seconds
Time it takes for a 100-mph pitch to reach home plate

Source: Dr. Glenn Fleisig, American Sports Medicine Institute

Fastball Analytics

Inside one of the sports world's most violent moves.

ARTISTS Mike Sudal, graphics editor, Matthew Futterman, senior sports writer, and Seth Hamblin, graphics director, of the *Wall Street Journal*.

STATEMENT "Bringing Heat" illustrates the most effective approach to throwing a 100-mph fastball, and what the human body experiences while executing one of the most violent movements in all of sports.

   When we started this infographic, we only had the data from the American Sports Medicine Institute on the body's rate of rotation while throwing a 100-mph fastball. This in itself was fascinating to see, and it surprised us how hard the motions are on a pitcher's joints. We combined the data with a diagram showing exactly what the player's body does while throwing such a hard pitch, using research based on digital imaging of hundreds of pitching motions. The bottom of the piece shows just how fast a 100-mph pitch reaches home plate, compared to the pitch of an average athletic adult. We hope this addition gives the reader a real-world feel for how they would compare if stepping up to the mound, or standing in the batting box.

PUBLICATION *Wall Street Journal* (March 2013)

TOP TRENDS IN COSMETIC PROCEDURES

In 2000, only 300 American women had upper-arm lift surgery, but the operation's popularity has grown massively in recent years. According to new statistics from the American Society of Plastic Surgeons, 15,136 women and 321 men took the surgical route to buff arms in 2012. Below we take a look at some of the other trends in plastic surgery and minimally invasive procedures for women and men in the United States.

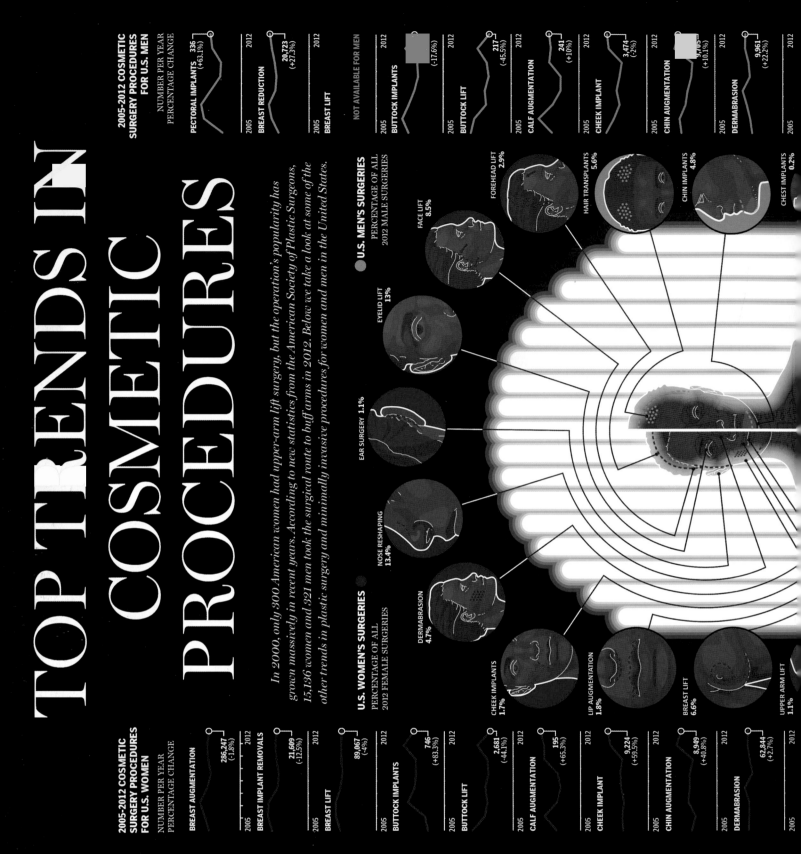

2005-2012 COSMETIC SURGERY PROCEDURES FOR U.S. MEN
NUMBER PER YEAR
PERCENTAGE CHANGE

PECTORAL IMPLANTS 336 (+63.1%) 2005 2012

BREAST REDUCTION 20,723 (+27.3%) 2005 2012

BREAST LIFT NOT AVAILABLE FOR MEN 2005 2012

BUTTOCK IMPLANTS (-17.6%) 2005 2012

BUTTOCK LIFT 217 (-45.5%) 2005 2012

CALF AUGMENTATION 241 (+10%) 2005 2012

CHEEK IMPLANT 3,474 (-2%) 2005 2012

CHIN AUGMENTATION 9,705 (+10.1%) 2005 2012

DERMABRASION 9,961 (+22.2%) 2005 2012

CHEST IMPLANTS 0.2% 2005

U.S. MEN'S SURGERIES
● PERCENTAGE OF ALL 2012 MALE SURGERIES

- FOREHEAD LIFT 2.9%
- FACE LIFT 8.5%
- HAIR TRANSPLANTS 5.6%
- CHIN IMPLANTS 4.8%
- EYELID LIFT 13%
- EAR SURGERY 1.1%
- NOSE RESHAPING 13.4%
- DERMABRASION 4.7%
- CHEEK IMPLANTS 1.7%
- LIP AUGMENTATION 1.8%
- BREAST LIFT 6.6%
- UPPER ARM LIFT 1.1%

U.S. WOMEN'S SURGERIES
PERCENTAGE OF ALL 2012 FEMALE SURGERIES

2005-2012 COSMETIC SURGERY PROCEDURES FOR U.S. WOMEN
NUMBER PER YEAR
PERCENTAGE CHANGE

BREAST AUGMENTATION 286,247 (-1.8%) 2005 2012

BREAST IMPLANT REMOVALS 21,609 (-12.5%) 2005 2012

BREAST LIFT 89,067 (-4%) 2005 2012

BUTTOCK IMPLANTS 746 (+83.3%) 2005 2012

BUTTOCK LIFT 2,681 (-44.1%) 2005 2012

CALF AUGMENTATION 195 (+65.3%) 2005 2012

CHEEK IMPLANT 9,224 (+59.5%) 2005 2012

CHIN AUGMENTATION 8,949 (+40.8%) 2005 2012

DERMABRASION 62,844 (+2.7%) 2005 2012

Body Sculpture

What people choose to change.

ARTISTS Richard Johnson, assistant managing editor for graphics and illustration, Mike Faille, graphic artist, and Michael Higgins, foreign editor, at the *National Post* in Canada.

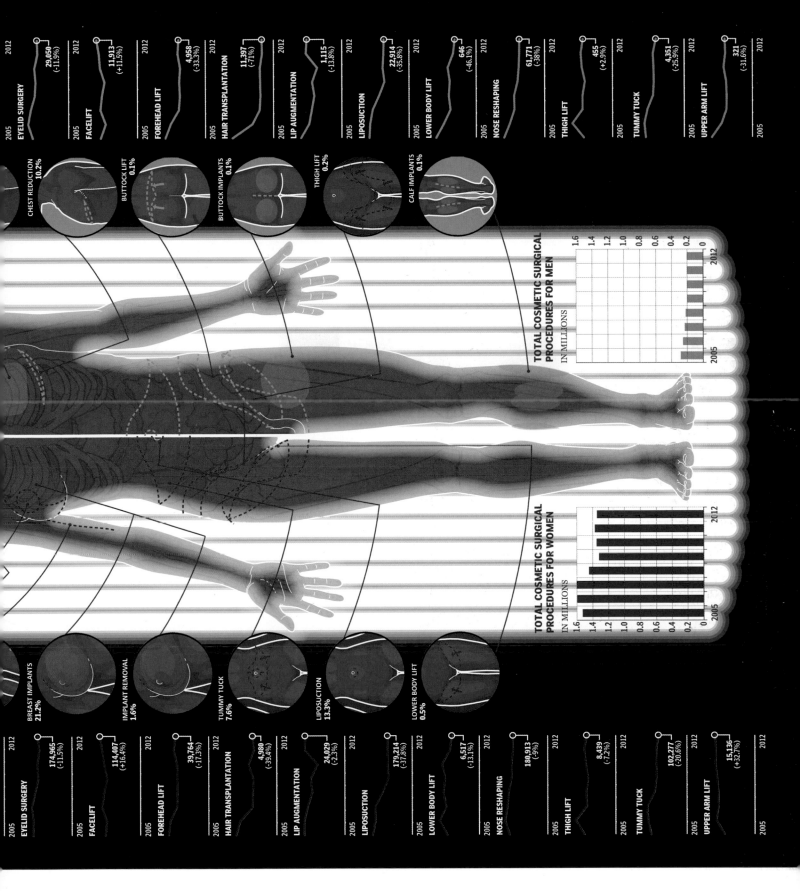

STATEMENT This graphic came out of an annual report by the American Society of Plastic Surgeons that detailed the most popular surgeries for men and women in the United States. It was interesting material that revealed the gradual shifts in body modification popularity by both sexes. For instance, the biggest growth area in surgery types was the removal of "bat wings" or underarm flesh. We decided to illustrate the procedures themselves in a minimal way.

PUBLICATION *National Post* (June 2013)

Lost Cat

Obsessed pet owners use GPS tracking to
uncover their cat's secret life.

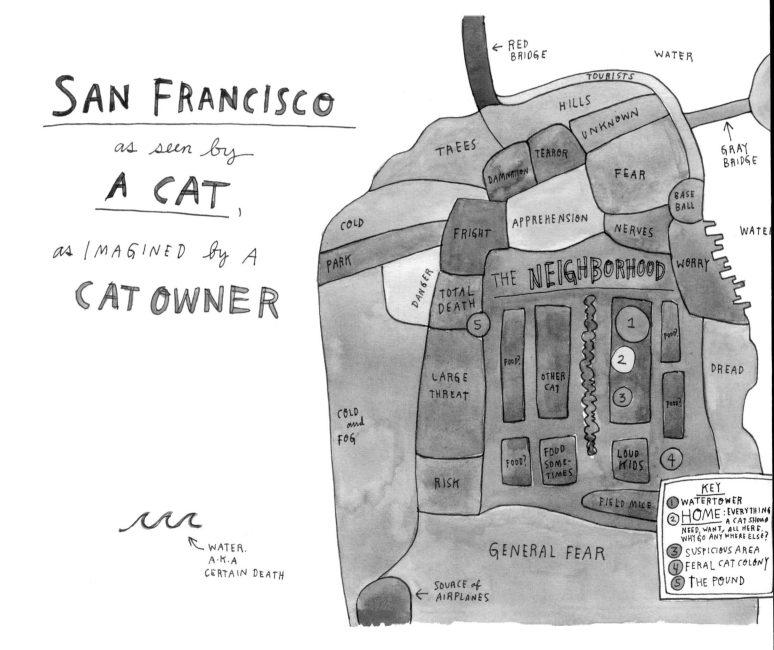

SAN FRANCISCO

as seen by
A CAT,

as IMAGINED *by* A
CAT OWNER

WATER.
A·K·A
CERTAIN DEATH

← RED BRIDGE

WATER

TOURISTS

HILLS

UNKNOWN

TREES

TERROR

DAMNATION

FEAR

GRAY BRIDGE

BASE BALL

APPREHENSION

COLD

FRIGHT

NERVES

WATER

PARK

THE NEIGHBORHOOD

WORRY

DANGER

TOTAL DEATH

5

1

FOOD?

2

DREAD

FOOD?

OTHER CAT

3

LARGE THREAT

COLD and FOG

FOOD?

FOOD SOME-TIMES

LOUD KIDS

4

RISK

FIELD MICE

GENERAL FEAR

← SOURCE of AIRPLANES

KEY
1 WATERTOWER
2 HOME : EVERYTHING A CAT SHOULD NEED, WANT, ALL HERE. WHY GO ANYWHERE ELSE?
3 SUSPICIOUS AREA
4 FERAL CAT COLONY
5 THE POUND

WE LIVE HERE

BLUE LINES = CAROLINE TESTING THE G.P.S.

WE LIVE HERE

● Outliers ●●● Concentration over time (earlier to later = darker to lighter)

ARTISTS Caroline Paul, writer, Wendy MacNaughton, illustrator, and Tibby the cat.

STATEMENT Our cat Tibby disappeared suddenly, and we were devastated. Then five weeks later he returned, fat and happy. We were overjoyed he was back, but where had he gone? We decided to strap a GPS unit to his collar and find out where he spent his days. The first image shows Tibby tolerating the GPS unit we strapped to his neck for weeks. The second is a map of what we imagined was our cat's view of the world.

The first map shows Caroline's movements during a test of the GPS (blue lines) and Tibby's actual movement over the course of one day (pink lines). The second map shows Wendy's attempt to uncover Tibby's travel patterns, and thus his secret life. Data analysis included layering multiple maps in Photoshop and identifying frequented areas over time. These images also effectively map our own emotional territory. As humans, and pet owners, we are much more lost than our cat.

PUBLICATION *Lost Cat: A True Story of Love, Desperation, and GPS Technology* (April 2013)

E-Mail: Not Dead, Evolving

by **Barry Gill**

Periodically you may hear digital hipsters claim that e-mail is dead. Don't believe them. People still spend half their workday dealing with it, they trust it, and overall they're satisfied with it, according to our 2012 survey of 2,600 workers in the U.S., UK, and South Africa who use e-mail every day.

E-mail is not dead, it's just evolving. It's becoming a searchable archive, a manager's accountability source, a document courier. And for all the love social media get, e-mail is still workers' most effective collaboration tool.

It's far from perfect: Three-quarters of all e-mail is junk, and we're wasting lots of time dealing with less important messages. But it remains the mule of the information age—stubborn and strong.

HBR Reprint F1306Z

WHICH ARE THE MOST EFFECTIVE CHANNELS FOR COLLABORATION?

When asked to select all the tools they trust for collaboration, respondents chose e-mail as the best, by far. Workers use 19 distribution lists on average. But 22% would like to see e-mail adopt a more social construction, using self-selected "followers" and "friends."

- 60% E-mail to individuals
- 34 E-mail to lists
- 23 E-mail to teams
- 19 Teleconferencing
- 15 Video/web conferencing
- 10 Instant messaging
- 8 Facebook
- 6 Business collaboration tool
- 4 LinkedIn
- 3 Twitter/microblog

HOW DO WE ACCESS E-MAIL?

The desk is still where we spend most of our time chipping away at the in-box, but some 40% of respondents access work e-mail outside the office during off hours. Here's the breakdown of how much of their e-mail workers access, on average, from each device.

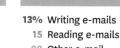

- 60% Work PC/laptop
- 11 Home PC
- 8 Mobile
- 5 Home laptop
- 3 iPad/tablet
- 13 Other

HOW MUCH TIME IS SPENT ON E-MAIL?

In a year workers spend, on average, the equivalent of 111 workdays dealing with e-mail. Most would like better search functions and document management, and there's good reason to make that happen: A 10% increase in efficiency would buy back more than two workweeks per year per employee.

- 13% Writing e-mails
- 15 Reading e-mails
- 22 Other e-mail activities (searching, archiving, managing)
- 50 Not spent on e-mail

HOW SATISFIED ARE WE WITH E-MAIL?

While people are satisfied overall, satisfaction is slightly lower for the searchability of e-mail, and significantly lower for archive management: Only 44% rate that highly. The lowest satisfaction is with mobile access to e-mail: Only 37% rate it highly.

- 25% Very satisfied
- 45 Satisfied
- 23 Somewhat satisfied
- 4 Somewhat dissatisfied
- 2 Dissatisfied
- 1 Don't know

WHAT DOES A YEAR'S WORTH OF E-MAIL LOOK LIKE?

Most of it is junk. Fortunately, workers see only a small portion of the malware, phishing scams, and promotional offers that bombard their accounts every day. Of the e-mails that make it into the in-box, 42% are essential or critical and just 8% are spam.

WHAT DO WE USE E-MAIL FOR?

Half of respondents believe that e-mail reduces the need for other file storage systems—meaning they are using it to archive important documents. Still, this function could improve. A third of users find e-mail search to be time-consuming and difficult to navigate. Average time to locate a document in e-mail is two minutes.

We asked respondents to list the tasks they use e-mail for. Note that communication between individuals—the original intent of e-mail—isn't even listed in the top five activities.

- **76%** EXCHANGING DOCUMENTS
- **69** SENDING INFORMATION TO GROUPS
- **61** IMPROVING COMMUNICATION ACROSS TIME ZONES
- **60** ACCOUNTABILITY
- **59** SEARCHING FOR INFORMATION

A Portrait of Your In-Box

E-mail, analyzed.

ARTISTS Bonnie Scranton, artist, James de Vries, creative director, Scott Berinato, senior editor, and Christina Bortz, articles editor, at the *Harvard Business Review*.

STATEMENT Is e-mail dead? Based on a survey from Barry Gill of Mimecast, this graphic shows that e-mail

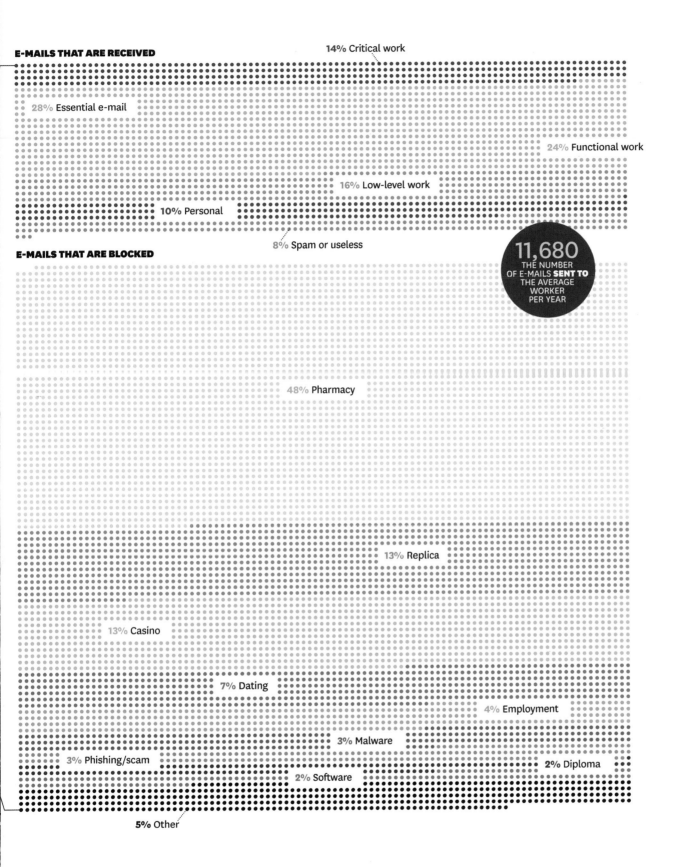

E-MAILS THAT ARE RECEIVED

14% Critical work

28% Essential e-mail

24% Functional work

16% Low-level work

10% Personal

8% Spam or useless

E-MAILS THAT ARE BLOCKED

11,680 THE NUMBER OF E-MAILS **SENT TO** THE AVERAGE WORKER PER YEAR

48% Pharmacy

13% Replica

13% Casino

7% Dating

4% Employment

3% Malware

3% Phishing/scam

2% Diploma

2% Software

5% Other

is just evolving. Scott Berinato, a senior editor, worked with James de Vries, the creative director at *Harvard Business Review,* to brainstorm the topic for the double-page information graphic called "Vision Statement." The monthly graphic we publish is usually based on a large data set from an outside source. Sometimes there is an existing, often poorly executed visualization to consider. Other times, like this, we just had some numbers. I came to the solution pretty quickly, creating a design that represented each e-mail as a dot on the page.

PUBLICATION *Harvard Business Review* (June 2013)

Empire State Building Decoder

What do the lights mean?

ARTISTS Karishma Sheth, designer, Thomas Alberty, design director, and Emma Whitford, writer, at *New York Magazine.*

STATEMENT Sometimes the most interesting info-graphics come from tackling the simplest questions. Most New Yorkers have had the experience of looking out at the Empire State Building and wondering what on earth those lights mean. The answer turned out to be both informative and visually satisfying.

PUBLICATION *New York Magazine* (April 2013)

Intelligencer

KNOW YOUR ILLUMINATION OPTIONS:

Halo · Top · Fins · Middle · Bottom

THE EMPIRE STATE BUILDING LIGHT-SHOW DECODER

BEFORE THE Empire State Building replaced its floodlights with computerized LEDs in November, changing the colors was a six-hour task and choices were limited to just ten. The new system allows for over 16 million color combinations. Organizations can request lighting programs, which also change for holidays and other milestones, though the meaning behind the hues is often lost on skyline watchers. Here, a guide to the new display's first four months.

EMMA WHITFORD

| 11/29/12 | 11/30/12 | 12/1/12 | 12/2/12 | 12/3/12 | 12/4/12 | 12/5/12 | 12/6/12 | 12/7/12 | 12/8/12 | 12/9/12 | 12/10/12 | 12/11/12 | 12/12/12 | 12/13/12 | 12/14/12 | 12/15/12 | 12/16/12 |

| 12/17/12 | 12/18/12 | 12/19/12 | 12/20/12 | 12/21/12 | 12/22/12 | 12/23/12 | 12/24/12 | 12/25/12 | 12/26/12 | 12/27/12 | 12/28/12 | 12/29/12 | 12/30/12 | 12/31/12 | | 1/1/13 | 1/2/13 |

MULTI-COLORED LIGHTS CHANGED ALL THROUGH THE NIGHT (12/31/12)

| 1/3/13 | 1/4/13 | 1/5/13 | 1/6/13 | 1/7/13 | 1/8/13 | 1/9/13 | 1/10/13 | 1/11/13 | 1/12/13 | 1/13/13 | 1/14/13 | 1/15/13 | 1/16/13 | 1/17/13 | 1/18/13 | 1/19/13 | 1/20/13 |

| 1/21/13 | 1/22/13 | 1/23/13 | 1/24/13 | 1/25/13 | 1/26/13 | 1/27/13 | 1/28/13 | 1/29/13 | 1/30/13 | 1/31/13 | 2/1/13 | 2/2/13 | 2/3/13 | | 2/4/13 | 2/5/13 | 2/6/13 |

LIT UP AFTER POINTS SCORED (2/3/13)

| 2/7/13 | 2/8/13 | 2/9/13 | 2/10/13 | 2/11/13 | 2/12/13 | 2/13/13 | 2/14/13 | 2/15/13 | 2/16/13 | 2/17/13 | 2/18/13 | 2/19/13 | 2/20/13 | 2/21/13 | 2/22/13 | 2/23/13 | 2/24/13 |

| 2/25/13 | 2/26/13 | 2/27/13 | 2/28/13 | 3/1/13 | 3/2/13 | 3/3/13 | 3/4/13 | 3/5/13 | 3/6/13 | 3/7/13 | 3/8/13 | 3/9/13 | 3/10/13 | 3/11/13 | 3/12/13 | 3/13/13 | 3/14/13 |

LIGHTS OUT FROM 8:30 TO 9:30 (3/23/13)

| 3/15/13 | 3/16/13 | 3/17/13 | 3/18/13 | 3/19/13 | 3/20/13 | 3/21/13 | 3/22/13 | 3/23/13 | | 3/24/13 | 3/25/13 | 3/26/13 | 3/27/13 | 3/28/13 | 3/29/13 | 3/30/13 | 3/31/13 |

11/29/12 Big East Championship football game (Rutgers vs. Louisville)   **12/1/12** (RED)/World AIDS Day   ···**12/4/12** Fifteenth anniversary of Disney's *The Lion King* on Broadway   ···**12/6/12** St. Jude Children's Research Hospital   ···**12/8–12/9/12** Hanukkah   ···**12/10/12** Human Rights Watch and Human Rights Day   ···**12/11/12** The European Union, for winning the 2012 Nobel Peace Prize   ···**12/12/12** The Robin Hood Foundation's Concert for Hurricane Sandy Relief   ···**12/13/12** PGA of America's announcement of the 2014 Ryder Cup captain   ···**12/14–12/16/12** Hanukkah   ···**12/21–12/27/12** Christmas   ···**12/28/12** New Era Pinstripe Bowl   ···**12/29–12/30/12** Christmas   ···**12/31/12** New Year's Eve   ·**1/1–1/6/13** Christmas   ···**1/14–1/20/13** Facebook vote for official standard ESB colors   ·**1/21/13** Martin Luther King Jr. Day   **2/1/13** American Heart Association's "Go Red for Women" campaign   ·**2/3/13** Super Bowl XLVII (Ravens vs. 49ers)   ·**2/4/13** World Cancer Day   ···**2/6/13** 36th annual Empire State Building Run-Up   ·**2/8–2/10/13** Lunar New Year   ·**2/11/13** Westminster Kennel Club   **2/13–2/14/13** Valentine's Day   ·**2/16–2/18/13** President's Day   ·**2/21/13** Anonymous partner   ·**2/25/13** International Corporate Philanthropy Day   ···**2/26/13** National Eating Disorder Week   ···**2/28/13** Swedish House Mafia's Black Tie Rave charity event   ·**3/1/13** Memorial Sloan-Kettering Cancer Center's Cycle for Survival   ···**3/7–3/8/13** Major League Baseball and the World Baseball Classic   ···**3/11/13** Tenth anniversary of New York City's 311 Call Center   ···**3/16–3/17/13** St. Patrick's Day   ···**3/23/13** The World Wildlife Fund's Earth Hour   ···**3/30–3/31/13** Easter

English by the Book

When new words were made.

WHERE WORDS CAME FROM

The *OED* traces the origins of words. Many arrived from other European languages or via global exploration.

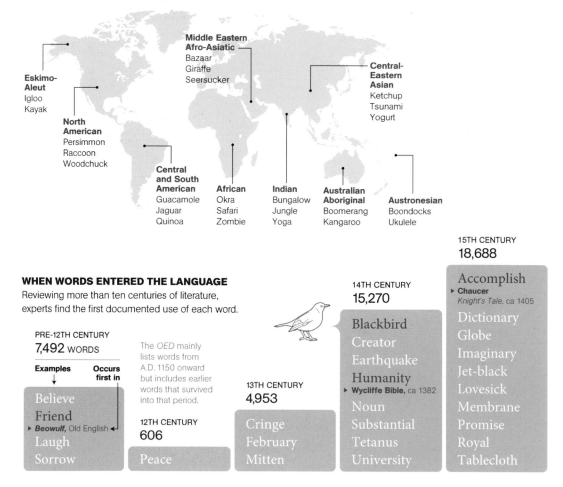

Eskimo-Aleut
Igloo
Kayak

North American
Persimmon
Raccoon
Woodchuck

Middle Eastern Afro-Asiatic
Bazaar
Giraffe
Seersucker

Central-Eastern Asian
Ketchup
Tsunami
Yogurt

Central and South American
Guacamole
Jaguar
Quinoa

African
Okra
Safari
Zombie

Indian
Bungalow
Jungle
Yoga

Australian Aboriginal
Boomerang
Kangaroo

Austronesian
Boondocks
Ukulele

WHEN WORDS ENTERED THE LANGUAGE

Reviewing more than ten centuries of literature, experts find the first documented use of each word.

PRE-12TH CENTURY
7,492 WORDS

Examples / Occurs first in

Believe
Friend
▶ *Beowulf,* Old English
Laugh
Sorrow

The *OED* mainly lists words from A.D. 1150 onward but includes earlier words that survived into that period.

12TH CENTURY
606

Peace

13TH CENTURY
4,953

Cringe
February
Mitten

14TH CENTURY
15,270

Blackbird
Creator
Earthquake
Humanity
▶ **Wycliffe Bible,** ca 1382
Noun
Substantial
Tetanus
University

15TH CENTURY
18,688

Accomplish
▶ **Chaucer**
Knight's Tale, ca 1405
Dictionary
Globe
Imaginary
Jet-black
Lovesick
Membrane
Promise
Royal
Tablecloth

ARTISTS Graphics by John Tomanio, senior graphics editor, and Alexander Stegmaier, graphics research editor, at *National Geographic.* Art by 5W Infographics.

STATEMENT The graphic shows when the usage of different words in the English language was first documented, based on the *Oxford English Dictionary.* Words like "believe" or "friend" (first used in *Beowulf*) predate the twelfth century. Others, like "supernova" or "clone,"

19TH CENTURY
75,029

The industrial revolution
and booms in scientific
research and publishing
contributed to the jump
in new words during
the 19th century.

Abuzz
▶ **Dickens,** *A Tale
of Two Cities,* 1859
Acid rain
Bicycle
Biosphere
Blueprint
Cello
Dwarf planet
Dyslexia
Feminist
Headphone
Immunize
Lunchbox
Mammal
Mascara
Mesmerize
Mom
Narcissism
Neonatal
Omnivore
Pasta
Photograph
Polarize
Purebred
▶ **Darwin** letter, 1839
Quartzite
Radicalism
Rain check
Rhinoplasty
Rickshaw
Rigor mortis
Rubber band
Smart aleck
Southerner
Statehood
Subliminal
Subway
Taxonomy
Thingamajig
Urbanization
Vegetarian
Vertebrate
Wordsmith
World war
X-ray

The *OED* is still
catching up with
words for 20th-century
technology and
innovation. As a result,
the number here is
low—but growing.

20TH CENTURY
36,233
AND COUNTING

Acronym
Brainwash
Clone
Database
Gazillionaire
Gorp
▶ *National Geographic*
May 1972
Icecapade
In-box
Lifestyle
Moped
Multiracial
Neurobiology
Nitpick
Oink
Postmodern
Racist
Recycle
Supernova
Techno
Vegan
Yeehaw

17TH CENTURY
51,076

Aboriginal
Americanize
Black sheep
Caribbean
Civilization
Free market
Geographic
Hand grenade
Hotel
Ice cream
Identify
Islam
Key chain
Ladybug
Magnetism
Mahogany
Mezuzah
Moccasin
▶ **John Smith**
Map of Virginia, 1612
Naive
Nincompoop
Orangutan
Ostracize
Palatable
Powwow
Prairie
Raspberry
Schoolteacher
Territorial
True blue
Volcano
Womanizer

Ventures abroad
helped feed a new
appetite for unusual
words in the 16th
and 17th centuries.

16TH CENTURY
37,047

Blueberry
Communicate
Dictatorship
Easter egg
Education
Heartbroken
Hellenism
Maritime
Mathematics
Mosquito
Nomad
Overpower
▶ **Shakespeare**
Richard II, 1597
Potato
Procrastinate
Quinoa
Reality
Redhead
Runaway
Terrify
Timeless
Useful

Fewer new words
were adopted in
an era that
emphasized
precise writing.

18TH CENTURY
24,980

Abolitionist
Bigwig
Capitalize
Dog-eared
Electrician
▶ **Benjamin Franklin**
letter, 1749
Handyman
Homesick
Millimeter
Neurosis
Optimist
Pervasive
Roommate
Terrorism

5W INFOGRAPHICS, ALEXANDER STEGMAIER AND JOHN TOMANIO, NGM STAFF
SOURCES: PHILIP DURKIN AND KATHERINE MARTIN, OXFORD UNIVERSITY PRESS

originated with the technology and innovation of the
twentieth century. The eighteenth century, which emphasized precise writing, brought far fewer new words
than the nineteenth century, when the industrial revolution and a scientific boom demanded new terms.

PUBLICATION *National Geographic*
(December 2013)

Haircuts: Brady vs. Manning

An untold element of the classic quarterback matchup.

ARTISTS Adam Duerson, senior editor, and Trevor Lazarus, associate art director, at *Sports Illustrated*.

STATEMENT This infographic was part of a larger seven-page package that celebrated the fourteenth meeting of two legendary NFL quarterbacks: Peyton Manning and Tom Brady, who by most measures are near clones. To buttress (and soften the blow) of a whopping, football-heavy essay, I wanted a few light supplements. I've always been a big fan of the aesthetic side of sports—uniforms and logos and absurd haircuts—and as I held these two guys up against each other, this one thing struck me: aesthetically, Brady has been through myriad looks representing just as many phases of his playing/dating career and maturation. Manning? Not so much; he's more of a Supercuts kinda guy. By visually stripping them down to this one element, I hoped to accentuate some personality differences that we tend to overlook when we view these guys as only their helmeted selves. Admittedly, some of this inspiration for this comes from soccer, a sport where players' domes go uncovered, allowing for far more pea-cocking and follicle flexing. I'm as much a fan of that sport, and I tend to keep a mental log of soccer's craziest hairdos. Here was a rare chance to simply take index of the hairdos in football.

PUBLICATION *Sports Illustrated* (November 2013)

BRADY   MANNING

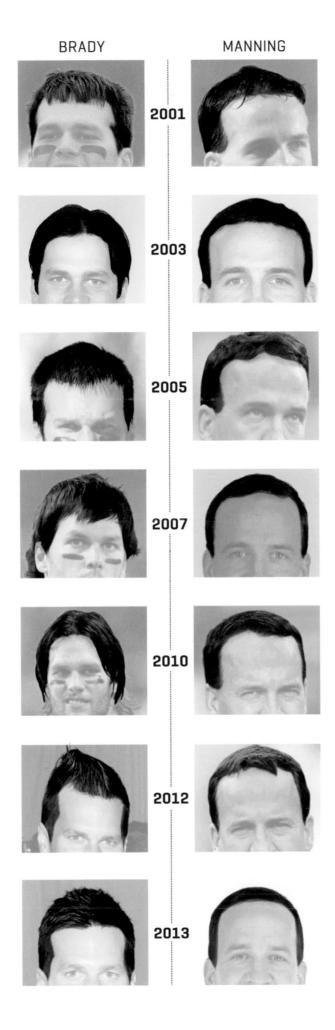

2001

2003

2005

2007

2010

2012

2013

SOURCES:

BRADY HAIR, FROM TOP:
M. DAVID LEEDS/GETTY
IMAGES, NFL PHOTOS/
AP, PETER READ MILLER/
SPORTS ILLUSTRATED,
SIMON BRUTY/
SPORTS ILLUSTRATED,
TONY DING/AP,
EVAN AGOSTINI /AP,
DIMITRIOS KAMBOURIS/
GETTY IMAGES

MANNING HAIR, FROM
TOP: WILFREDO LEE/AP,
NFL /WIREIMAGE.COM,
JOHN BIEVER/SPORTS
ILLUSTRATED, HEINZ
KLUETMEIER/SPORTS
ILLUSTRATED,
JOHN BIEVER/
SPORTS ILLUSTRATED,
ROBERT BECK/
SPORTS ILLUSTRATED,
ROBERT BECK/SPORTS
ILLUSTRATED

CHELSEA'S KALE SALAD

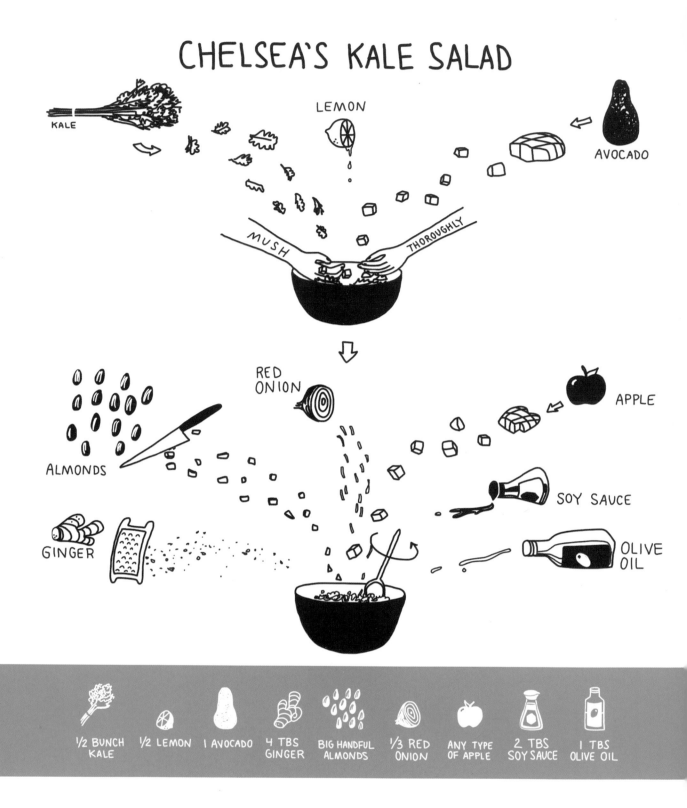

KALE

LEMON

AVOCADO

MUSH   THOROUGHLY

RED ONION

APPLE

ALMONDS

SOY SAUCE

GINGER

OLIVE OIL

½ BUNCH KALE   ½ LEMON   1 AVOCADO   4 TBS GINGER   BIG HANDFUL ALMONDS   ⅓ RED ONION   ANY TYPE OF APPLE   2 TBS SOY SAUCE   1 TBS OLIVE OIL

Visual Recipes

Cooking with few words.

ARTISTS Katie Shelly, illustrator, and Katherine Furman, editor, at Ulysses Press.

STATEMENT *Picture Cook* is a cookbook in which recipes are drawn, not written. Each step of the cooking process is represented pictographically.

I came up with the concept one day when a friend was telling me her recipe for eggplant parmesan by phone. I took notes by drawing, kind of without realizing it. The drawing was neat, but later that evening when I was cooking I was impressed by how much easier it was to cook from this visual recipe. That inspired

COMFORT POLENTA

H2O • SALT
BOIL

CORNMEAL
1 CUP AT A TIME
2 MIN

2 MIN

25 MIN

PARM

3 MIN

GARLIC
OLIVE OIL

SAUSAGE
5 MIN

COLLARDS

Ingredients

| 4½ CUPS H2O | 1½ CUPS CORNMEAL | OLIVE OIL | 3 CLOVES GARLIC | 3 LINKS SAUSAGE (ANY TYPE) | ½ BUNCH COLLARDS | ¾ CUP GRATED PARMESAN | SALT & PEPPER |

me to make more recipe drawings. I made a little PDF cookbook and sent it out to my friends via e-mail. I also submitted it to *Drawn!* (a blog) and it exploded from there.

I want to encourage people to just let go of rigid kitchen rules and be loose and free about cooking. The charm of the illustrations is great for its own sake, but it's also performing a real function in helping make cooking feel easy, lighthearted, and doable.

PUBLICATION *Picture Cook,* Ulysses Press (November 2013)

Gay and in the Closet

Where gay men live—and where they hide.

Where the Closet Is Still Common

THE TOLERANCE SPECTRUM

Here is the American landscape of acceptance and rejection of gays, based on an analysis of support for gay marriage initiatives in 2012.

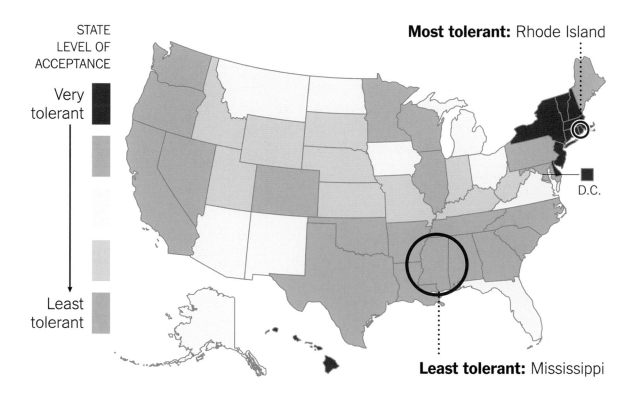

STATE LEVEL OF ACCEPTANCE

Very tolerant

Least tolerant

Most tolerant: Rhode Island

D.C.

Least tolerant: Mississippi

ARTISTS Bill Marsh, graphics editor for the *New York Times;* Seth Stephens-Davidowitz, writer.

STATEMENT Seth Stephens-Davidowitz, a quantitative analyst at Google, sought to answer the questions: How many men are gay? And are there fewer gay men living in the least tolerant states? He found that in the Internet's public sphere, on Facebook, the proportion of men identifying as gay diminished with the level of state tolerance, which was gauged by support for gay marriage initiatives in an earlier analysis done for the *Times* by Nate Silver. Alone, the figures suggest that fewer gay men live in less tolerant states. But in the private sphere of the Internet—Google porn searches for gay male imagery—his data show a larger and more consistent gay share across the country, and likely a more accurate one. This is one of a series of graphics done with Stephens-Davidowitz in which we present key parts of his analysis in a storyboard form. In this case, the last element was a simple comparison of life in the most- and least-tolerant states. We see that gay men live differently—more openly in the friendlier atmosphere of Rhode Island, more concealed in least-tolerant Mississippi.

PUBLICATION *New York Times* (December 2013)

ARE THERE FEWER GAY MEN IN THE LEAST TOLERANT STATES?

The online **public sphere** gives that impression. Percent of male Facebook profiles, of those with a gender preference, choosing men:

But in the **private sphere**, the gay share is larger and consistent. Percent of all Google porn searches seeking gay male images:

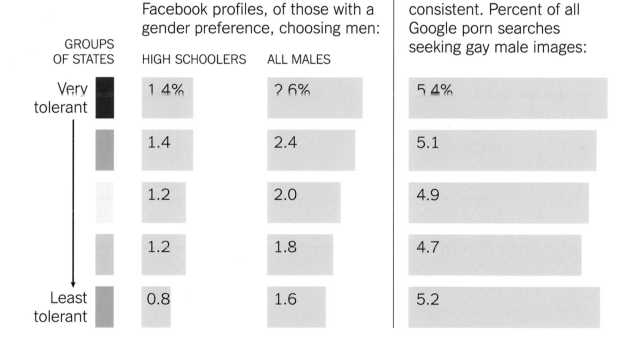

GROUPS OF STATES	HIGH SCHOOLERS	ALL MALES	
Very tolerant	1.4%	2.6%	5.4%
	1.4	2.4	5.1
	1.2	2.0	4.9
	1.2	1.8	4.7
Least tolerant	0.8	1.6	5.2

THE LEAST-ALIKE STATES: CONCEALMENT VS. OPENNESS

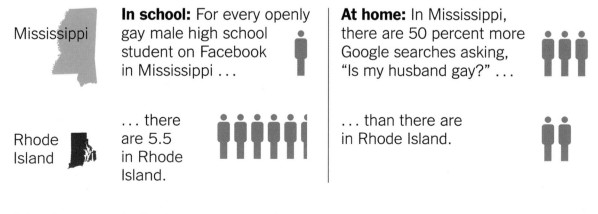

Mississippi

In school: For every openly gay male high school student on Facebook in Mississippi . . .

At home: In Mississippi, there are 50 percent more Google searches asking, "Is my husband gay?" . . .

Rhode Island

. . . there are 5.5 in Rhode Island.

. . . than there are in Rhode Island.

Calculations account for the differing populations of Mississippi and Rhode Island.

Source: Analysis by Seth Stephens-Davidowitz; 2012 marriage initiative analysis by Nate Silver for The New York Times

WHEN CONSIDERING THE WORKING CONDITIONS, YOU CATCH YOURSELF WONDERING

"This is far too much fun to be called 'work'."

HOW MUCH WILL THIS WORK IMPROVE THINGS?

"It's not like curing cancer, but it's close...(ish.)"

IS IT IN YOUR WHEELHOUSE?

"Fits like a glove!"

SO, WHAT'S THE MONEY LIKE?
(**Please answer in song.**)

[Hip-hop Lyric] *post-2001*

STEP 1▸

STEP 2▸

STEP 3▸

STEP 4▸

SHOULD I...
Take that job?

Existential Calculator

Is this creative job right for me?

ARTISTS Research, writing, design, and assembly by Kelli Anderson; proofreading and some editing by Sara Distin.

STATEMENT The existential calculator is a hand-held interactive infographic decision-making tool that helps the reader decide whether or not to take a job. It organizes the spectrum of all possible work outcomes—from pleasurable to spiritually degrading, from well-paying to debt-enhancing, from exciting to "meh"—and shows where the reader is likely to land, based on what they tell it about the potential job.

The reader answers four questions about the decision by turning the concentric wheels: "When considering the working

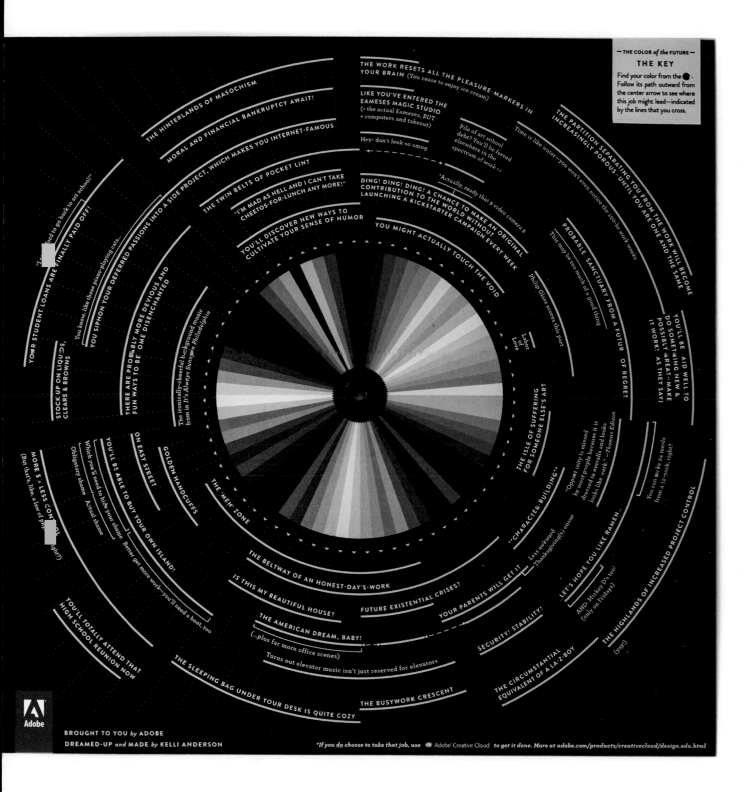

BROUGHT TO YOU *by* ADOBE

DREAMED-UP *and* MADE *by* KELLI ANDERSON

"If you do choose to take that job, use ⓐ Adobe® Creative Cloud *to get it done. More at adobe.com/products/creativecloud/design.edu.html*

conditions, you catch yourself wondering . . . " "How much will this work improve things?" "Is it in your wheelhouse?" and "So . . . what's the money like?" The calculator then yields a fortune color, landing you either in red "perfect job" territory (where "You might actually touch the void"); the green, honest day's work zone ("Your parents will totally get it!"); the pink land of sellouts and rich soulsuckers ("You'll be able to buy your own island!"/"Which you'll need to hide your shame"); or the brown zone of crappy hell jobs (at least "You'll discover new ways to cultivate your sense of humor").

One purpose of the wheel, in addition to being a legitimate voice of objectivity, is to question the limits of what we entrust programmed contraptions to decide for us. To what extent can programming convert qualitative feelings into quantitative data? Can our own social programming, as illuminated by the social sciences, be turned into tools?

PUBLICATION Custom printed (October 2013)

Us

37

WHEN HUMANS ARE
Hunted

For rural Tanzanians the threat of lion attack rises and falls with the phases of the moon (below), the nocturnal predators favoring the darkest nights. But whether the night is dark or bright, villagers living without electricity or plumbing have to walk to the outhouse or to get water and firewood. People have even been attacked inside their homes.

FEWER ATTACKS
Moon above horizon

Attacks when the moon is above the horizon are usually on cloudy nights in the rainy season—just before harvesttime, when people sleep in the fields to guard crops against bushpigs.

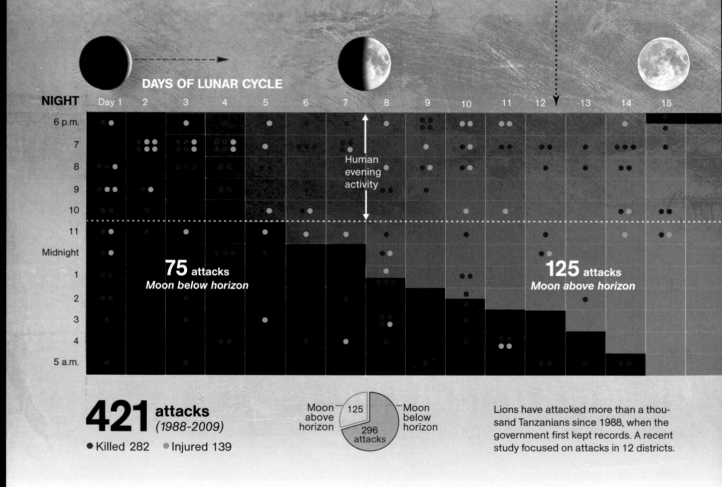

DAYS OF LUNAR CYCLE

| NIGHT | Day 1 | 2 | 3 | 4 | 5 | 6 | 7 | 8 | 9 | 10 | 11 | 12 | 13 | 14 | 15 |

Human evening activity

75 attacks
Moon below horizon

125 attacks
Moon above horizon

421 attacks (1988-2009)
● Killed 282 ● Injured 139

Moon above horizon — 125
296 attacks
Moon below horizon

Lions have attacked more than a thousand Tanzanians since 1988, when the government first kept records. A recent study focused on attacks in 12 districts.

When the Night Is Dark, the Lions Attack

Beware the days after a full moon.

ARTISTS Art by Fernando Baptista, senior graphics editor, and Daniela Santamarina, graphics specialist; text by Jane Vessels, senior text editor, at *National Geographic*. Research by Fanna Gebreyesus, freelance researcher.

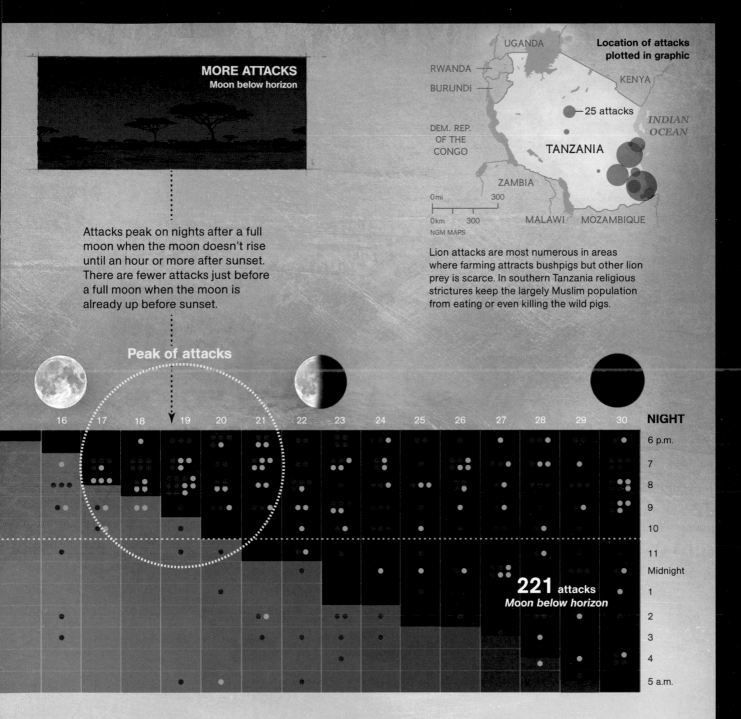

MORE ATTACKS
Moon below horizon

Location of attacks plotted in graphic

UGANDA

RWANDA

BURUNDI

DEM. REP.
OF THE
CONGO

KENYA

INDIAN
OCEAN

25 attacks

TANZANIA

ZAMBIA

0mi — 300

0km — 300

NGM MAPS

MALAWI — MOZAMBIQUE

Attacks peak on nights after a full moon when the moon doesn't rise until an hour or more after sunset. There are fewer attacks just before a full moon when the moon is already up before sunset.

Lion attacks are most numerous in areas where farming attracts bushpigs but other lion prey is scarce. In southern Tanzania religious strictures keep the largely Muslim population from eating or even killing the wild pigs.

Peak of attacks

| | | | | | | | | | | | | | | | **NIGHT** |
|16|17|18|19|20|21|22|23|24|25|26|27|28|29|30| |

6 p.m.
7
8
9
10
11
Midnight
1
2
3
4
5 a.m.

221 attacks
Moon below horizon

Near the Equator, Tanzania has close to 12 hours of day and 12 of night year-round.

FERNANDO G. BAPTISTA AND DANIELA SANTAMARINA, NGM STAFF; FANNA GEBREYESUS
SOURCES: CRAIG PACKER, ALEXANDRA SWANSON, AND HADAS KUSHNIR, UNIVERSITY
OF MINNESOTA; DENNIS IKANDA, TANZANIA WILDLIFE RESEARCH INSTITUTE

STATEMENT Lions have attacked more than 1,000 people in Tanzania since 1988. This infographic draws a correlation between the time of the night in which each attack occurred and the phases of the moon. Lions are nocturnal predators and prefer to attack in the darkest hours. Attacks peak on nights after a full moon when the moon doesn't rise until an hour or more after sunset and darkness coincides with the hours that humans are active.

PUBLICATION *National Geographic* (August 2013)

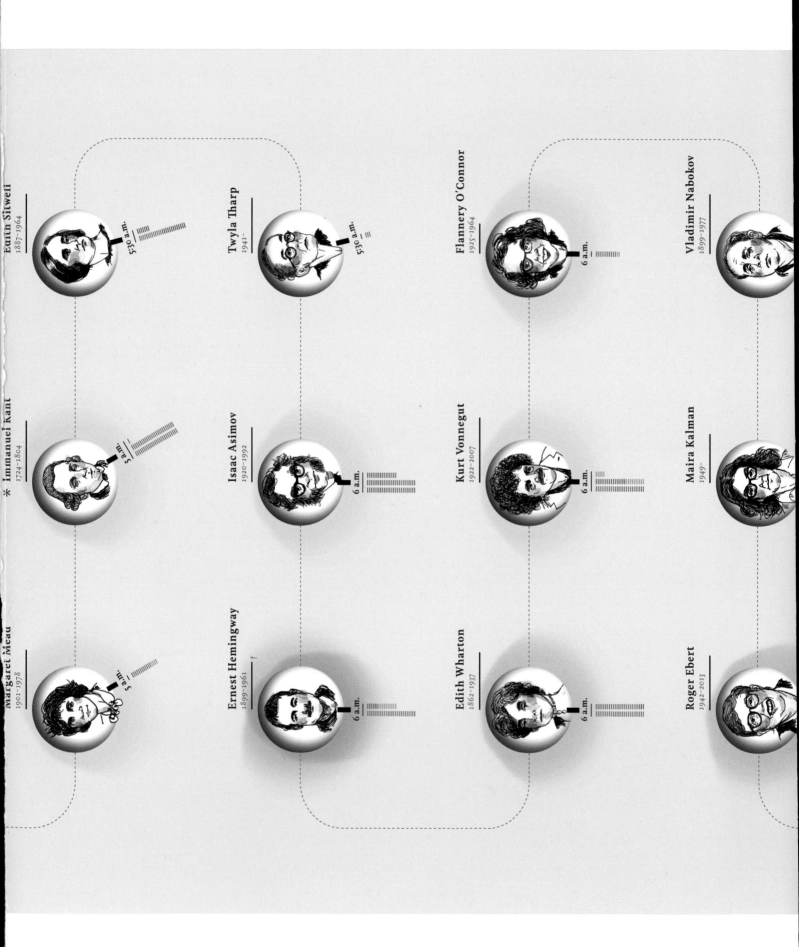

Edith Sitwell
1887–1964

5:30 a.m.

☀ Immanuel Kant
1724–1804

5 a.m.

Margaret Mead
1901–1978

5 a.m.

Twyla Tharp
1941–

5:30 a.m.

Isaac Asimov
1920–1992

6 a.m.

Ernest Hemingway
1899–1961 †

6 a.m.

Flannery O'Connor
1925–1964

6 a.m.

Kurt Vonnegut
1922–2007

6 a.m.

Edith Wharton
1862–1937

6 a.m.

Vladimir Nabokov
1899–1977

Maira Kalman
1949–

Roger Ebert
1942–2013

FAMOUS WRITERS' SLEEP HABITS AND LITERARY PRODUCTIVITY

The wakeup times of famous authors for whom the data was available, based on various interviews and biographies, are correlated with the authors' literary productivity as measured by number of works published and major awards received. Since the length of a writing career influences the volume of literary output and the historical time frame of an author's life determines the awards he or she could have received, the lifespan of each writer is also indicated for context.

How to read it

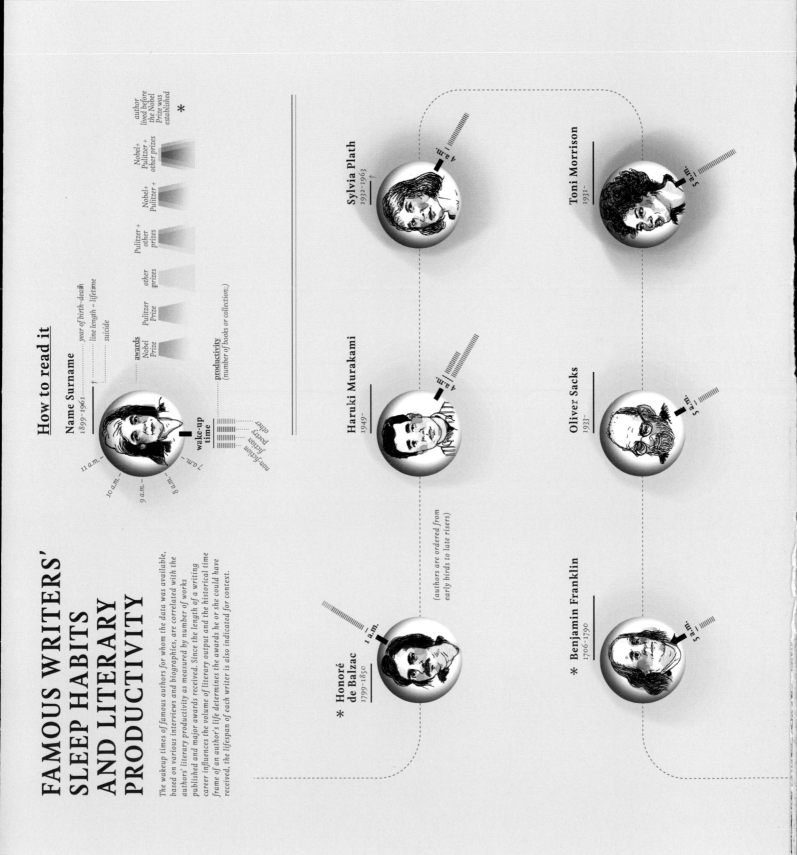

Name Surname
1899–1961
year of birth–death
† line length = lifetime
suicide

awards
Nobel Prize
Pulitzer Prize
other prizes
Pulitzer + other prizes
Nobel + Pulitzer +
Nobel + Pulitzer + other prizes
* author lived before the Nobel Prize was established

productivity
(number of books or collection)

wake-up time
non-fiction
fiction
poetry
other

11 a.m.
10 a.m.
9 a.m.
8 a.m.
7 a.m.

(authors are ordered from early birds to late risers)

* Honoré de Balzac
1799–1850
1 a.m.

Haruki Murakami
1949–
4 a.m.

Sylvia Plath
1932–1963 †
4 a.m.

* Benjamin Franklin
1706–1790
5 a.m.

Oliver Sacks
1933–
5 a.m.

Toni Morrison
1931–
5 a.m.

FAMOUS WRITERS' SLEEP HABITS AND LITERARY PRODUCTIVITY

The wakeup times of famous authors for whom the data was available, based on various interviews and biographies, are correlated with the authors' literary productivity as measured by number of works published and major awards received. Since the length of a writing career influences the volume of literary output and the historical time frame of an author's life determines the awards he or she could have received, the lifespan of each writer is also indicated for context.

How to read it

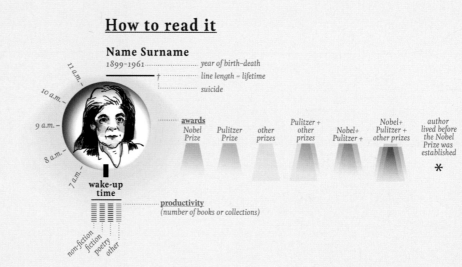

Writers, Sleep, and Productivity

When they woke, and how much they wrote.

ARTISTS Concept and direction by Maria Popova, founder of *BrainPickings.org*. Design by Accurat: Giorgia Lupi, Simone Quadri, and Gabriele Rossi with Davide Ciuffi, Federica Fragapane, and Francesco Majno. Illustrations by Wendy MacNaughton.

STATEMENT In my longtime fascination with daily routines, I found myself especially intrigued by whether successful writers' sleep habits might affect their creative output. But data is hard to find, hard to quantify, or both. To address this challenge, I turned to Giorgia Lupi and her team at Accurat, an information design agency with offices in Milan and New York. Using my notes on writers' wake-up times, culled from numerous biographies, interviews, journals, and other materials, we ended up with a data set of 37 writers for whom wake-up times were available.

There is always an enormous degree of subjectivity in assessing any creative career, and all information visualization is ostensibly an exercise in subjective editorial judgment rather than a record of objective truth, so we chose a set of nonexhaustive but quantifiable criteria to measure "productivity": the number of published works and major awards received. Since both the duration and era of an author's life affect literary output and award eligibility, those variables were also indicated.

The San Francisco–based illustrator Wendy MacNaughton drew the portraits of the writers, which served as the visual anchor for the data—surrounding each is a twelve-hour clock marking that writer's wake-up time; radiating out from that point is a "stack" of the awards he or she received. Befitting the spirit of both this particular project and of my site in general, which brings timeless treasures to new life online, I paired Accurat's sleek digital design and algorithmic visualization with MacNaughton's wonderfully analog ink-and-watercolor illustrations.

PUBLICATION *BrainPickings.org* (December 2013)

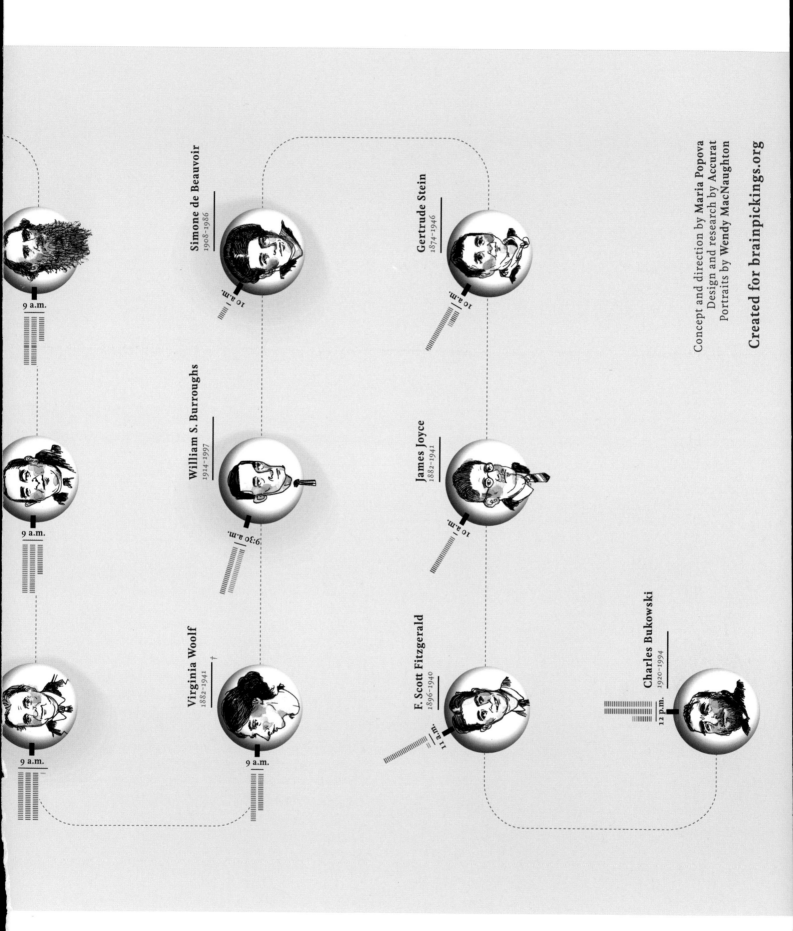

Simone de Beauvoir
1908–1986
10 a.m.

Gertrude Stein
1874–1946
10 a.m.

9 a.m.

William S. Burroughs
1914–1997
9:30 a.m.

James Joyce
1882–1941
10 a.m.

9 a.m.

Virginia Woolf
1882–1941
†
9 a.m.

F. Scott Fitzgerald
1896–1940
11 a.m.

Charles Bukowski
1920–1994
12 p.m.

9 a.m.

Concept and direction by Maria Popova
Design and research by Accurat
Portraits by Wendy MacNaughton

Created for brainpickings.org

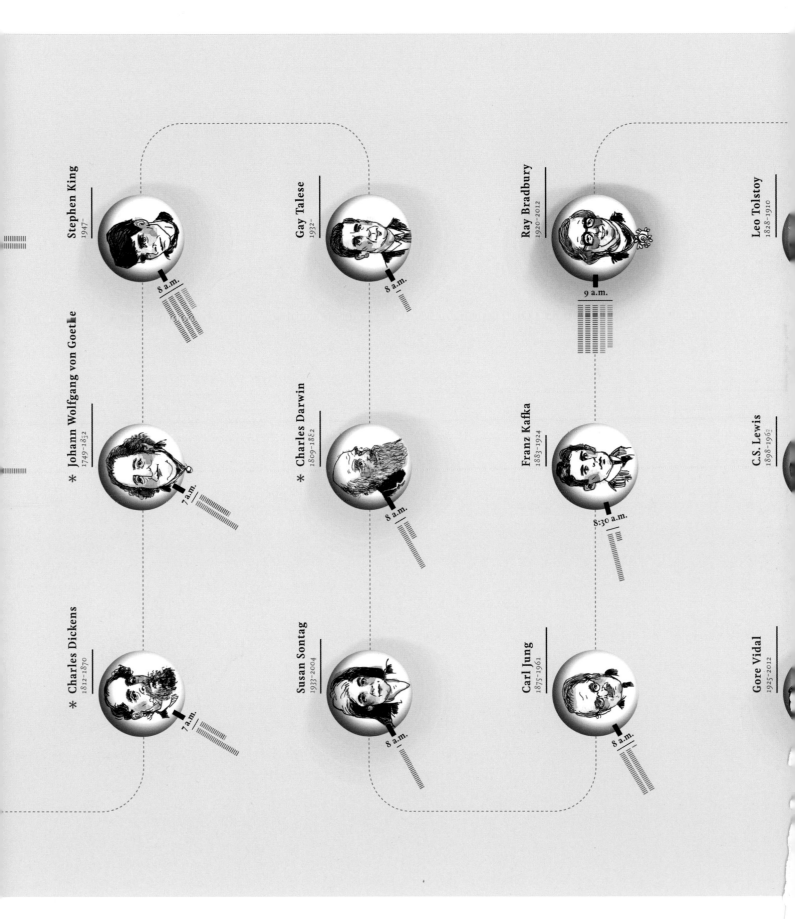

Stephen King
1947–

8 a.m.

Johann Wolfgang von Goethe
1749–1832

7 a.m.

Charles Dickens
1812–1870

7 a.m.

Gay Talese
1932–

8 a.m.

Charles Darwin
1809–1882

8 a.m.

Susan Sontag
1933–2004

8 a.m.

Ray Bradbury
1920–2012

9 a.m.

Franz Kafka
1883–1924

8:30 a.m.

Carl Jung
1875–1961

8 a.m.

Leo Tolstoy
1828–1910

C.S. Lewis
1898–1963

Gore Vidal
1925–2012

A Fire Disaster Unfolds

What went wrong.

Steps in a catastrophe

BY **BONNIE BERKOWITZ** AND **TODD LINDEMAN**

More than a year after seven volunteer firefighters were injured in an arson fire in Prince George's County, safety investigators made 46 recommendations for changes in equipment, training and procedures. Here is what happened in that fire, according to investigators.

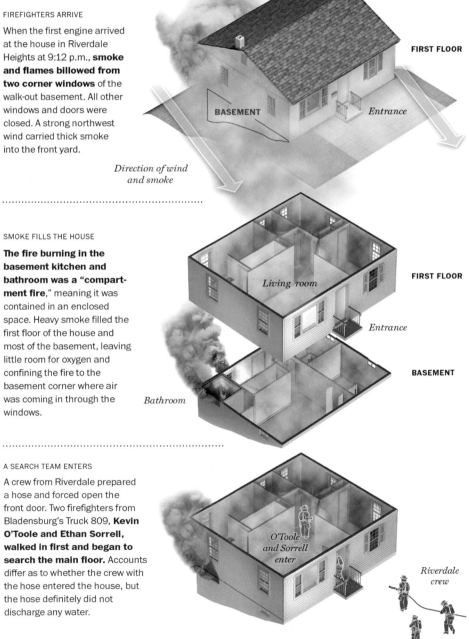

FIREFIGHTERS ARRIVE

When the first engine arrived at the house in Riverdale Heights at 9:12 p.m., **smoke and flames billowed from two corner windows** of the walk-out basement. All other windows and doors were closed. A strong northwest wind carried thick smoke into the front yard.

FIRST FLOOR

BASEMENT

Entrance

Direction of wind and smoke

SMOKE FILLS THE HOUSE

The fire burning in the basement kitchen and bathroom was a "compartment fire," meaning it was contained in an enclosed space. Heavy smoke filled the first floor of the house and most of the basement, leaving little room for oxygen and confining the fire to the basement corner where air was coming in through the windows.

Living room

FIRST FLOOR

Entrance

BASEMENT

Bathroom

A SEARCH TEAM ENTERS

A crew from Riverdale prepared a hose and forced open the front door. Two firefighters from Bladensburg's Truck 809, **Kevin O'Toole and Ethan Sorrell, walked in first and began to search the main floor.** Accounts differ as to whether the crew with the hose entered the house, but the hose definitely did not discharge any water.

O'Toole and Sorrell enter

Riverdale crew

FIRE FOLLOWS THE OXYGEN

The open front door allowed smoke to rush out. Suddenly the fire and superheated gas that had been confined to the basement had plenty of oxygen and a path to the first floor. Wind blowing from the basement windows propelled the smoke and gas through the house even faster.

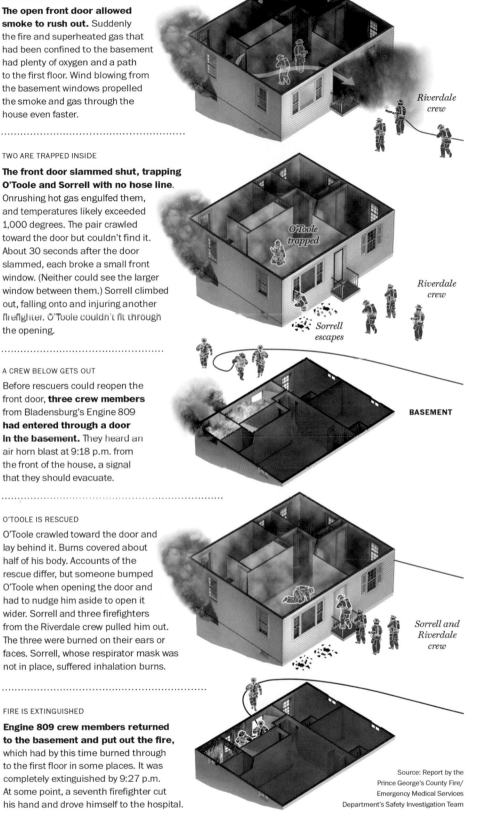

Riverdale crew

TWO ARE TRAPPED INSIDE

The front door slammed shut, trapping O'Toole and Sorrell with no hose line. Onrushing hot gas engulfed them, and temperatures likely exceeded 1,000 degrees. The pair crawled toward the door but couldn't find it. About 30 seconds after the door slammed, each broke a small front window. (Neither could see the larger window between them.) Sorrell climbed out, falling onto and injuring another firefighter. O'Toole couldn't fit through the opening.

O'Toole trapped

Riverdale crew

Sorrell escapes

A CREW BELOW GETS OUT

Before rescuers could reopen the front door, **three crew members** from Bladensburg's Engine 809 **had entered through a door in the basement.** They heard an air horn blast at 9:18 p.m. from the front of the house, a signal that they should evacuate.

BASEMENT

O'TOOLE IS RESCUED

O'Toole crawled toward the door and lay behind it. Burns covered about half of his body. Accounts of the rescue differ, but someone bumped O'Toole when opening the door and had to nudge him aside to open it wider. Sorrell and three firefighters from the Riverdale crew pulled him out. The three were burned on their ears or faces. Sorrell, whose respirator mask was not in place, suffered inhalation burns.

Sorrell and Riverdale crew

FIRE IS EXTINGUISHED

Engine 809 crew members returned to the basement and put out the fire, which had by this time burned through to the first floor in some places. It was completely extinguished by 9:27 p.m. At some point, a seventh firefighter cut his hand and drove himself to the hospital.

Source: Report by the Prince George's County Fire/ Emergency Medical Services Department's Safety Investigation Team

ARTISTS Todd Lindeman, information designer, and Bonnie Berkowitz, graphics reporter, at the *Washington Post.*

STATEMENT The article that accompanied this infographic told the story of the long recovery of two of seven volunteer firefighters who were injured fighting a fire in an abandoned house. In the graphic, we tried to show readers what went wrong that night. An internal investigation by the fire department found more than forty problems that may have contributed to injuries that day, but we didn't want to swamp readers in details. So we chose to do a step-by-step narrative that showed how one simple action—opening a door—triggered a terrifying, near-deadly chain reaction.

We went back and forth with the investigators to refine details and to try to reconcile conflicting statements from witnesses. We ended up with a stark cautionary tale that illustrated the huge consequences of seemingly mundane decisions.

PUBLICATION *Washington Post* (October 2013)

CODA

This week Billboard looks at the time it takes for songs, on average, to ascend to No. 1 on five genre airplay charts. Not only are there widely varying differences among each format, but songs at some formats, like alternative and country, take longer now (during the first six months of 2013) than in comparable periods five and 10 years ago.

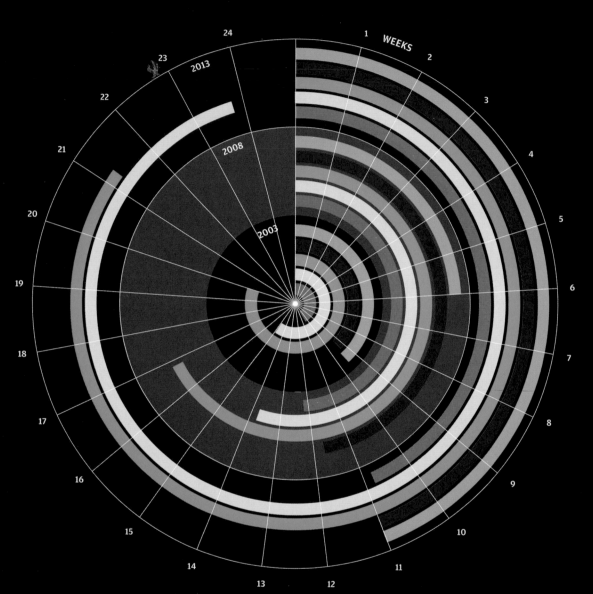

MAINSTREAM TOP 40
With the format reliant on current music for its core sound since its formation more than a half-century ago, it makes sense that songs average relatively quick rises to No. 1, and that those figures have remained steady during the last 10 years. At eight weeks, now-veteran Justin Timberlake's recent No. 1 "Mirrors" marked the fastest of his six format leaders.

ALTERNATIVE
Unlike mainstream top 40, alternative has shifted to a more gold-based presentation in recent years. Spurred in part by Arbitron's advanced Portable People Meter ratings measurement technology, which has led the niche format to favor proven hits more heavily, the six longest trips to No. 1 on the chart have all occurred in the past four years.

COUNTRY AIRPLAY
Country and alternative share a trait: Many of their hits and top artists don't cross over to other formats. Thus, with songs in each format often receiving exposure on only one station in a market, they need time to build familiarity. At 21.3 and 23.8 weeks, respectively, songs at the formats easily lead in taking the longest average trips to No. 1.

MAINSTREAM R&B/ HIP-HOP
Like mainstream top 40, mainstream R&B/hip-hop culls much of its identity from current music, with a steady flow of hip-hop acts consistently keeping the format fresh. Unsurprisingly, established stars Drake and Rihanna have reached No. 1 the fastest this year (eight weeks each), while relative newcomer Kendrick Lamar needed the longest gestation (16 weeks) with his first format No. 1, "Swimming Pools (Drank)."

LATIN AIRPLAY
Latin is akin to country and alternative in that much of its music doesn't cross over. So, why do Latin songs reach No. 1 so much faster? A likely reason: Latin Airplay is an audience-based chart and, with a handful of highly rated reporters located in major markets like New York and Los Angeles, when those stations get behind a budding hit, their weights can help propel a title up the tally quickly.

How Long It Takes to Reach #1

It's a long climb for country songs.

ARTISTS Andrew Horton, creative director, Jen Gilbert, designer, Silvio Pietroluongo, director of charts, Keith Caulfield, associate director of charts/retail, and Gary Trust, associate director of charts/radio, at *Billboard*.

STATEMENT Depending on the genre of music, songs can take different amounts of time for the public to push them to the No. 1 spot on the Billboard Hot 100 chart. It's notable that, with the exception of mainstream Top 40 artists, artists of all genres take longer to clinch the top slot than they did ten years ago.

PUBLICATION *Billboard* (June 2013)

The Hunger Strikes at Guantanamo Bay

Feeding the unwilling.

ARTISTS Richard Johnson, assistant managing editor for graphics and illustration, Andrew Barr, graphic artist, Mike Faille, graphic artist, and Michael Higgins, foreign editor, at the *National Post* in Canada.

THE HUNGER STRIKERS

Of the 106 hunger strikers 44 are in such poor condition that U.S. forces have decided to force feed them to keep them alive.

44 ARE FORCE FED DAILY

FORCE FEEDING

The Obama administration is coming under increased pressure from politicians and the medical establishment to stop force feeding hunger-striking inmates at Guantanamo Bay.

The military calls it a "lifesaving procedure." The UN has called it "torture" and a commentary in the *New England Journal of Medicine* called it "aggravated assault."

HOW MEDICAL STAFF GIVE A GUANTANAMO HUNGER STRIKER A NASOGASTRIC FEEDING

WHO IS A HUNGER STRIKER?

"A detainee may be designated a hunger striker after missing nine straight meals or weight loss to a level less than 85% ideal body weight."
-STANDARD OPERATING PROCEDURE FOR DEALING WITH DETAINEES ON HUNGER STRIKE

WHY FORCE FEED?

If, after being counselled and evaluated, a hungerstriker persists in his action, force-feeding is commenced if "continued fasting will result in a threat to life or seriously jeopardize health."
-STANDARD OPERATING PROCEDURE FOR DEALING WITH DETAINEES ON HUNGER STRIKE

THE RESTRAINT CHAIR

The U.S. military at Guantanamo Bay has been using restraint chairs for feeding hunger-striking prisoners since 2006 to prevent them from vomiting forced nutrition.

According to the 2013 Standard Operating Procedure for Dealing with Detainees on Hunger Strike, Section B, Subset 1 - Involuntary Medical Treatment (force feeding) will be considered if there is evidence of deleterious health effects reflective of end of organ involvement or damage to include, but not limited to, seizures, syncope (fainting), or pre-syncope, significant metabolic derangements, arrhythmias, muscle wasting, or weakness such that activities of daily living are significantly hampered.

The earliest known case of force feeding prisoners in Guantanamo Bay occurred in early 2002, when two hunger

1. The detainee is given an opportunity to use the restroom before restraints are applied.

2. A mask is placed over the detainee's mouth to prevent spitting or biting.

3. The detainee is escorted to the scale and weighed.

4. The detainee is escorted to the chair restraint system and is appropriately restrained by the guards.

5. When the guards advise it is safe, medical personnel obtain vital signs, and document pulse and restraint placement. The detainee is followed by medics using a "restraint checklist" every 15 minutes.

6. A topical anesthetic is applied on the detainee's nostril and the feeding tube, or a sterile surgical lubricant or olive oil is applied to the feeding tube.

7. The tube is passed through the nostril into the stomach. Placement is confirmed by using air and a 10 mL test dose of water, or X-ray.

8. The tube is secured to the nose with tape, and a nutritional fluid is poured in at a flow rate that is adjusted according to the detainee's condition. Typically a feeding takes 20-30 minutes.

9. After the feed is complete the medical staff remove the tube. The detainee is then removed from the restraint and placed in a dry-cell.

10. The guards then observe the detainee for 45-60 minutes for any indications of vomiting or attempts to induce vomiting.

11. If the detainee attempts to vomit, he is kept in the restraint chair for

Head restraints

Mouth cover

Shoulder straps

Lap belt

Wrist strap

Ankle straps

Foot plate

Wheels so that non-compliant detainees can be moved easily

THE HUNGER STRIKERS

As of June 30, 2013, of the 166 detainees who remain in Guantanamo, 106, or over 60% are now on hunger strike.

62 ARE NOT YET FORCE FED

PUBLICATION *National Post*
(June 2013)

STATEMENT This graphic was inspired by the news that a large number of Guantanamo Bay detainees had stopped eating as a protest. At the time of publication, 44 of the hunger strikers were in such poor condition that a regimen of force-feeding was implemented to keep them alive. We decided to take a look at those numbers as well as the equipment, techniques, and potential side effects of regular force-feeding. In the newspaper the naso-gastric feeding tube appeared actual size so readers could see the scale.

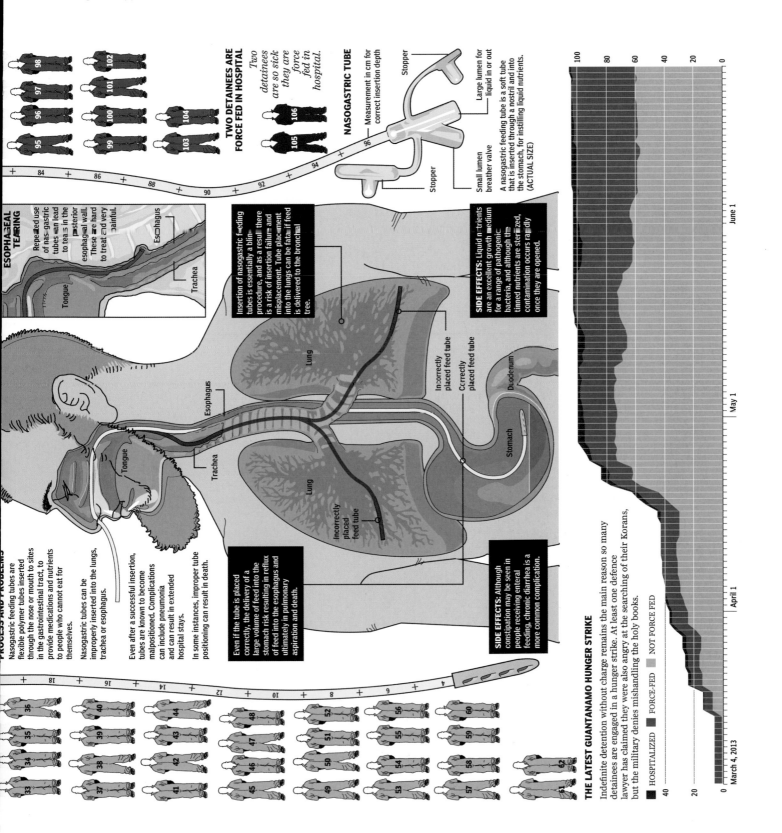

TWO DETAINEES ARE FORCE FED IN HOSPITAL

Two detainees are so sick they are force fed in hospital.

NASOGASTRIC TUBE

- Stopper
- Measurement in cm for correct insertion depth
- Large lumen for liquid in or out
- Small lumen for breather valve
- Stopper

A nasogastric feeding tube is a soft tube that is inserted through a nostril and into the stomach, for instilling liquid nutrients. (ACTUAL SIZE)

ESOPHAGEAL TEARING

Repeated use of nasogastric tubes can lead to tears in the posterior esophageal wall. These are hard to treat and very painful.

- Tongue
- Esophagus
- Trachea

Insertion of nasogastric feeding tubes is essentially a blind procedure, and as a result there is a risk of insertion failure and misplacement. Tube placement into the lungs can be fatal if feed is delivered to the bronchial tree.

SIDE EFFECTS: Liquid nutrients are an excellent growth medium for a range of pathogenic bacteria, and although the tinned nutrients are sterilized, contamination occurs rapidly once they are opened.

- Tongue
- Esophagus
- Trachea
- Lung
- Lung
- Incorrectly placed feed tube
- Correctly placed feed tube
- Incorrectly placed feed tube
- Stomach
- Duodenum

PROCESS AND PROBLEMS

Nasogastric feeding tubes are flexible polymer tubes inserted through the nose or mouth to sites in the gastrointestinal tract, to provide medications and nutrients to people who cannot eat for themselves.

Nasogastric tubes can be improperly inserted into the lungs, trachea or esophagus.

Even after a successful insertion, tubes are known to become malpositioned. Complications can include pneumonia and can result in extended hospital stays.

In some instances, improper tube positioning can result in death.

SIDE EFFECTS: Although constipation may be seen in people receiving enteral feeding, chronic diarrhea is a more common complication.

Even if the tube is placed correctly, the delivery of a large volume of feed into the stomach risk resulting in reflux of feed into the esophagus and ultimately in pulmonary aspiration and death.

THE LATEST GUANTANAMO HUNGER STRIKE

Indefinite detention without charge remains the main reason so many detainees are engaged in a hunger strike. At least one defence lawyer has claimed they were also angry at the searching of their Korans, but the military denies mishandling the holy books.

■ HOSPITALIZED ■ FORCE-FED ▨ NOT FORCE FED

March 4, 2013 — April 1 — May 1 — June 1

0 — 20 — 40 — 60 — 80 — 100

Is Your State's Highest-Paid Employee a Coach? (Probably)

State government's MVP.

ARTIST Reuben Fischer-Baum, infographics editor at *Deadspin.com*.

STATEMENT This graphic shows each state's highest-paid public employee, by total compensation, using figures drawn largely from public salary databases. In 39 states this employee was the head football or basketball coach at a major state university.

FOOTBALL COACH

FOOTBALL COACH

COLLEGE PRESIDENT

MED SCHOOL DEAN

FOOTBALL COACH

MED SCHOOL DEAN

FOOTBALL COACH

MED SCHOOL PLASTIC SURGEON

FOOTBALL COACH

FOOTBALL COACH

FOOTBALL COACH

BASKET- BALL COACH

BASKETBALL COACH

FOOTBALL COACH

FOOTBALL COACH

BASKETBALL COACH

FOOTBALL COACH

COLLEGE PRESIDENT

FOOTBALL COACH

FOOTBALL COACH

YOU   US   MATERIAL WORLD   INTERACTIVE

Credit for the inspiration goes to Ken Krayeske, a freelance journalist who, at a press conference in 2009, asked UConn men's basketball coach Jim Calhoun if he'd consider returning some of his salary, since Connecticut had a $2 billion budget deficit and Calhoun was the "highest-paid state employee." Once you think about it a bit, you realize that this isn't so surprising—what other state employee can make millions of dollars?—but I'll never forget how jarring it was to hear the point stated so plainly. Jim Calhoun, for what it's worth, practically murdered the guy.

PUBLICATION *Deadspin.com* (May 2013)

HIGHEST-PAID PUBLIC EMPLOYEES

COLLEGE PRESIDENT
COLLEGE PRESIDENT
LAW SCHOOL DEAN
MED SCHOOL CHANCELLOR
BASKETBALL COACH
BASKETBALL COACH (W)
BASKETBALL COACH
COLLEGE PRESIDENT
FOOTBALL COACH
MED SCHOOL DEPT. CHAIR
FOOTBALL COACH*

BASKETBALL COACH
BASKETBALL COACH
FOOTBALL COACH
BASKET-BALL COACH
FOOTBALL COACH
FOOTBALL COACH
FOOT-BALL COACH
FOOT-BALL COACH
FOOTBALL COACH
BASKETBALL COACH
FOOTBALL COACH
BASKETBALL COACH
FOOTBALL COACH
FOOTBALL COACH
FOOTBALL COACH
FOOTBALL COACH**
FOOTBALL COACH
FOOTBALL COACH
FOOTBALL COACH
BASKET-BALL COACH

COACHES / **NOT COACHES**

FOOTBALL

BASKETBALL

THE RECORDING SESSIONS
SOCIOGRAM

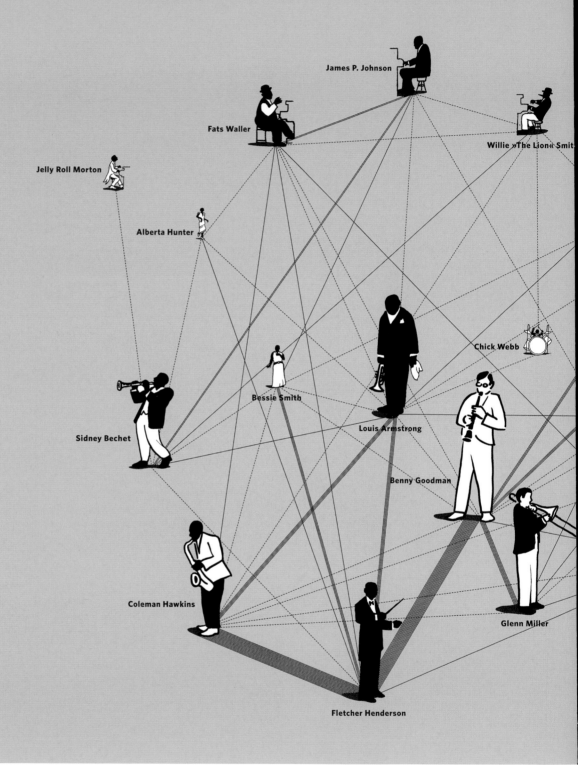

James P. Johnson

Fats Waller

Willie »The Lion« Smith

Jelly Roll Morton

Alberta Hunter

Chick Webb

Bessie Smith

Sidney Bechet

Louis Armstrong

Benny Goodman

Coleman Hawkins

Glenn Miller

Fletcher Henderson

Social Network of Jazz in 1920s
New York City

Who played with who in the Roaring Twenties.

ARTISTS Idea, research, illustration, and design by Robert Nippoldt; additional design by Christine Goppel and Tobias Glasmacher; research by the Bavarian Jazz Institute's Sylke Mehrbold.

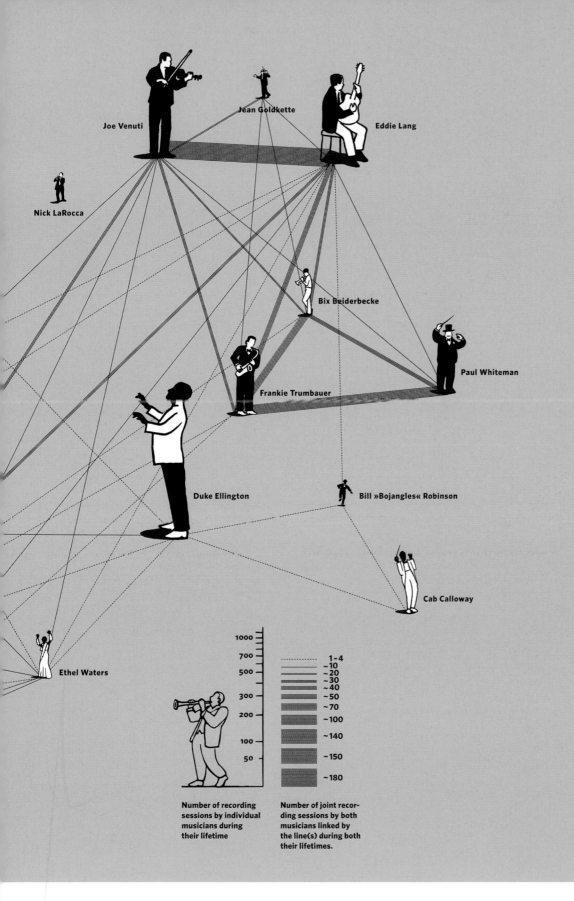

Joe Venuti

Jean Goldkette

Eddie Lang

Nick LaRocca

Bix Beiderbecke

Paul Whiteman

Frankie Trumbauer

Duke Ellington

Bill »Bojangles« Robinson

Cab Calloway

Ethel Waters

1000	
700	---- 1–4
500	~10
	~20
	~30
300	~40
	~50
200	~70
	~100
100	~140
50	~150
	~180

Number of recording sessions by individual musicians during their lifetime

Number of joint recording sessions by both musicians linked by the line(s) during both their lifetimes.

STATEMENT Twenty-four of the top jazz musicians working in New York in the Roaring Twenties are compared by numbers of recording sessions (seen in the height of icons) and connected by lines showing their joint recording sessions. Altogether, it forms a revealing sociogram of these jazz stars. During my research it was very interesting to find out more about the 24 jazz stars. For example, Louis Armstrong was not only influential and inspiring for every musician in that time, he was also very popular—everybody wanted to record with him. Nick LaRocca, the man who made the very first jazz recording in history, didn't record with any of the other great jazz stars of that time.

PUBLICATION *Jazz: New York in the Roaring Twenties,* Taschen Books (Spring 2013)

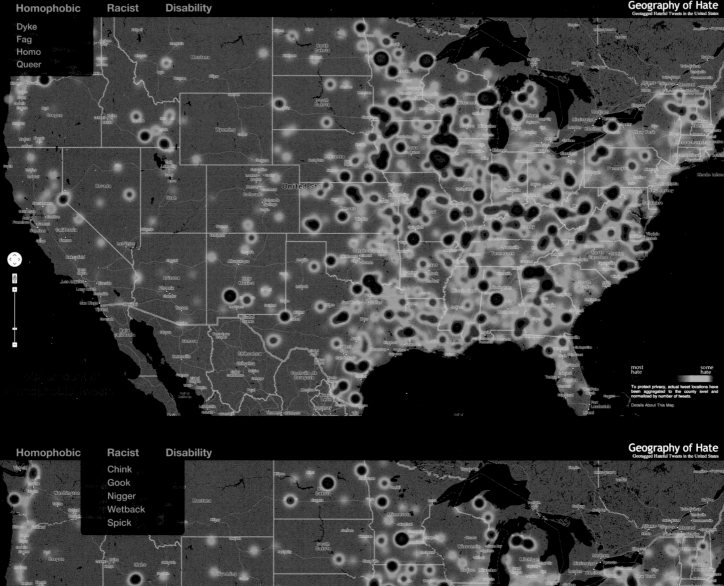

Homophobic   Racist   Disability

Dyke
Fag
Homo
Queer

Total amount of
Homophobic Tweets

most
hate   some
                                                    hate

To protect privacy, actual tweet locations have
been aggregated to the county level and
normalized by number of tweets.

Details About This Map

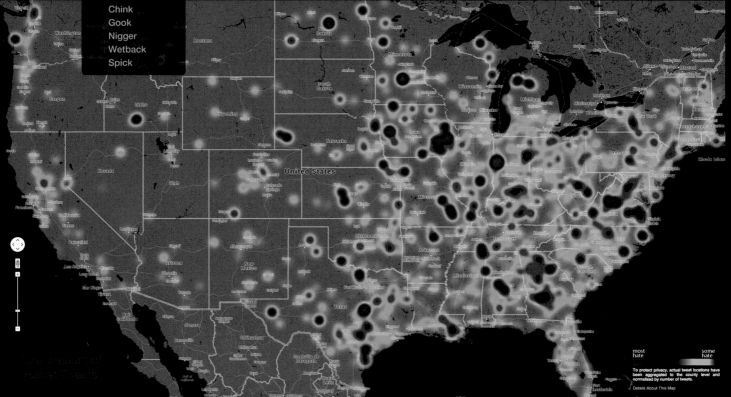

Homophobic   Racist   Disability

Chink
Gook
Nigger
Wetback
Spick

Total amount of
Racist Tweets

most
hate   some
                                                    hate

To protect privacy, actual tweet locations have
been aggregated to the county level and
normalized by number of tweets.

Details About This Map

YOU   US   MATERIAL WORLD   INTERACTIVE

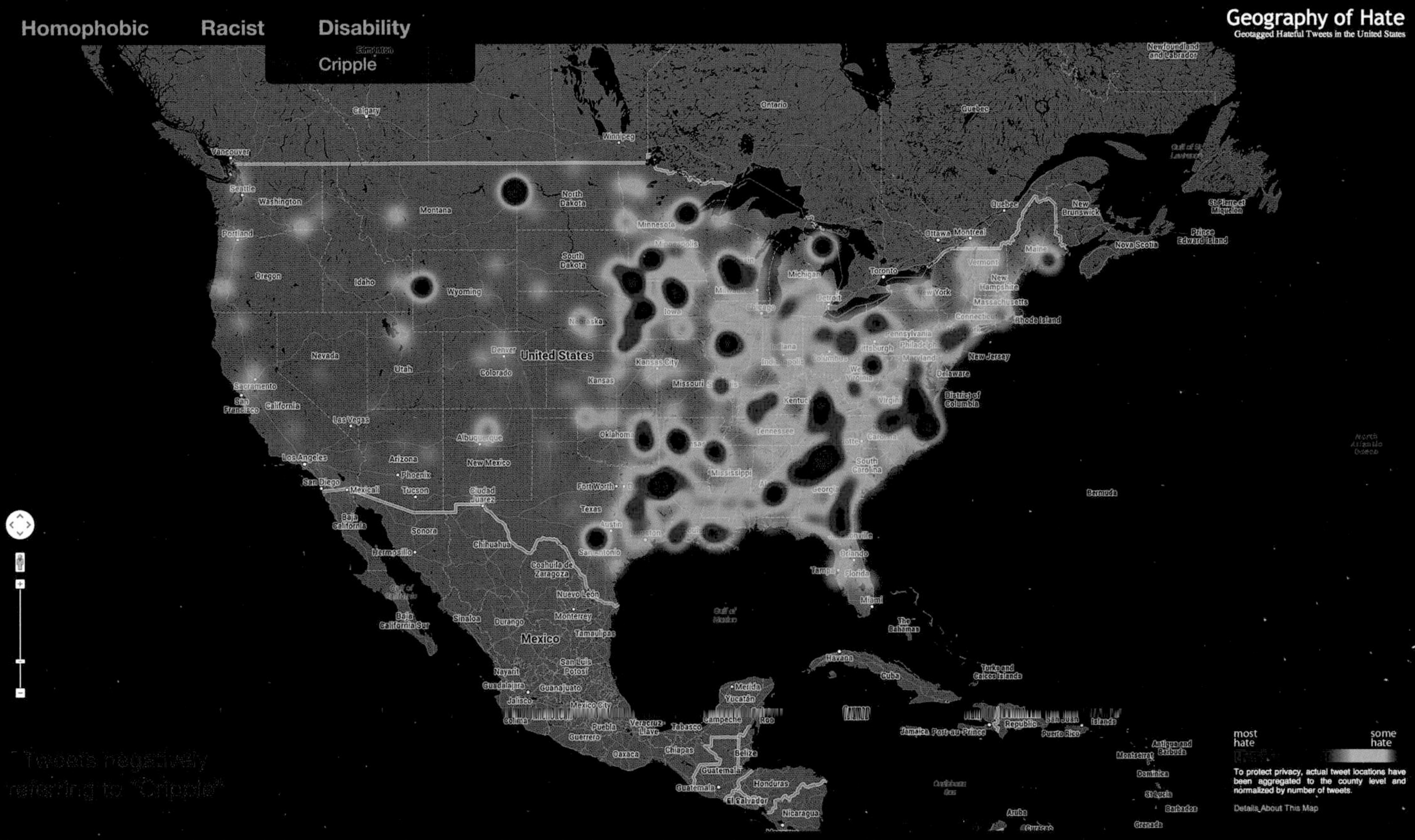

Homophobic   Racist   Disability

Cripple

most
hate

some
hate

To protect privacy, actual tweet locations have
been aggregated to the county level and
normalized by number of tweets.

Details About This Map

"Tweets negatively
relating to 'Cripple'"

ARTISTS Humboldt State University
Geography professor Monica Stephens, along
with three undergraduate students: Matthew
Eiben, Miles Ross, and Amelia Egle.

STATEMENT The prominence of debates
around online bullying and the censorship of
hate speech prompted us to examine how social media has become an important conduit
for hate speech, and how particular words
are dispersed geographically. To produce
the map, all geotagged tweets containing a
"hate word" were collected for eight months.
These tweets were aggregated to the county
level and normalized by the total Twitter
traffic in each county. This was used to
generate a heat map that demonstrates the
variability in the frequency of hateful tweets
relative to all tweets over space.

PUBLICATION *FloatingSheep.org*
(May 2013)

Hate Maps

Expressions of hate words
on Twitter, by county.

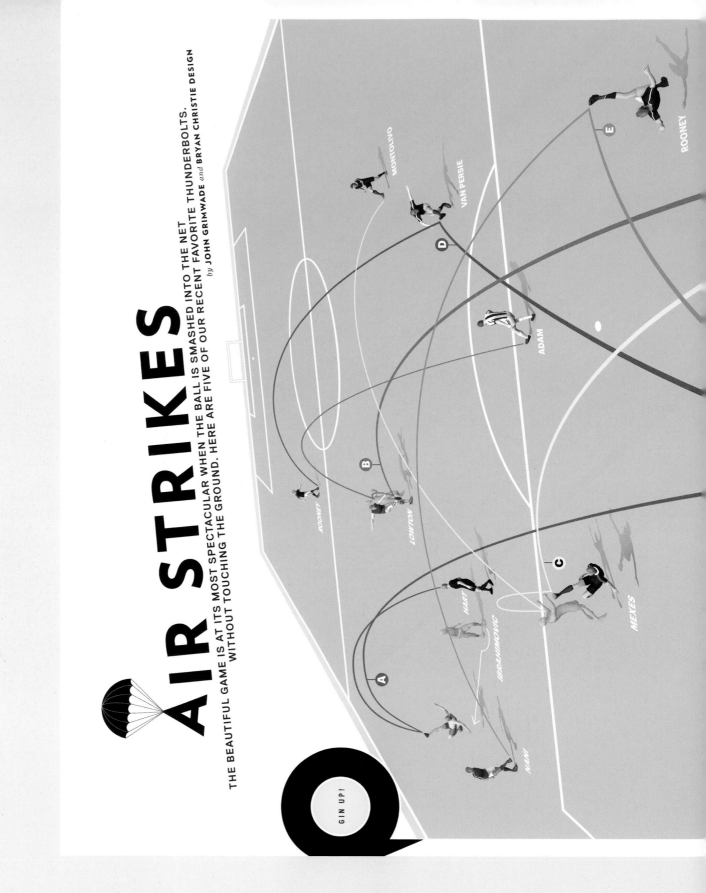

AIR STRIKES

THE BEAUTIFUL GAME IS AT ITS MOST SPECTACULAR WHEN THE BALL IS SMASHED INTO THE NET WITHOUT TOUCHING THE GROUND. HERE ARE FIVE OF OUR RECENT FAVORITE THUNDERBOLTS. *by* JOHN GRIMWADE *and* BRYAN CHRISTIE DESIGN

GIN UP!

The Most Beautiful Goals

The ball never touched the ground.

ARTISTS John Grimwade, with player renderings by Bryan Christie Design's Jeong Suh.

STATEMENT This shows five spectacular goals from the last two European soccer seasons. In each case, the ball was volleyed into the net with a startling combination of timing and accuracy. I remember describing the original idea as "Imagine you're at a game and suddenly you see several fantastic goals at once." I'd made some diagrammatic goal graphics before this,

"A strike that defied geometry let alone belief."

—THE TELEGRAPH

Ⓐ Zlatan Ibrahimović

TEAM: Sweden
AGAINST: England
WHERE: Friends Arena, Stockholm
WHEN: November 14, 2012
THE GOAL: Goalkeeper Joe Hart's headed clearance outside the penalty area led to arguably one of the greatest goals ever scored.

Ⓑ Matt Lowton

Aston Villa
Stoke City
Britannia Stadium, Stoke
April 6, 2013
Charlie Adam's lofted clearance is volleyed into the net for one of the best goals of the 2012–13 Premier League season.

Ⓒ Philippe Mexes

AC Milan
Anderlecht
Constant Vanden Stock Stadium, Brussels
November 21, 2012
Free kick from Riccardo Montolivo is chested up for a powerful bicycle kick into the opposite corner.

Ⓓ Robin van Persie

Manchester United
Aston Villa
Old Trafford, Manchester
April 22, 2013
Wayne Rooney's superb downfield pass is met on the volley by van Persie.

Ⓔ Wayne Rooney

Manchester United
Manchester City
Old Trafford, Manchester
February 12, 2011
Sensational bicycle kick from a cross by Nani wins a vital game in the Premier League title chase.

but that approach didn't seem right here. The brilliance of these goals can only be understood by seeing the trajectories in perspective. I tried a number of angles, but settled on the view from behind the goal because it seemed the most telling. The realism in the players is part of the attempt to capture the drama of being at the game. It's an infographic conceived by a soccer fan for other soccer fans.

PUBLICATION

Debut issue of *Eight by Eight* (Fall 2013)

Raising the Debt Ceiling

A recurring fight over many millions.

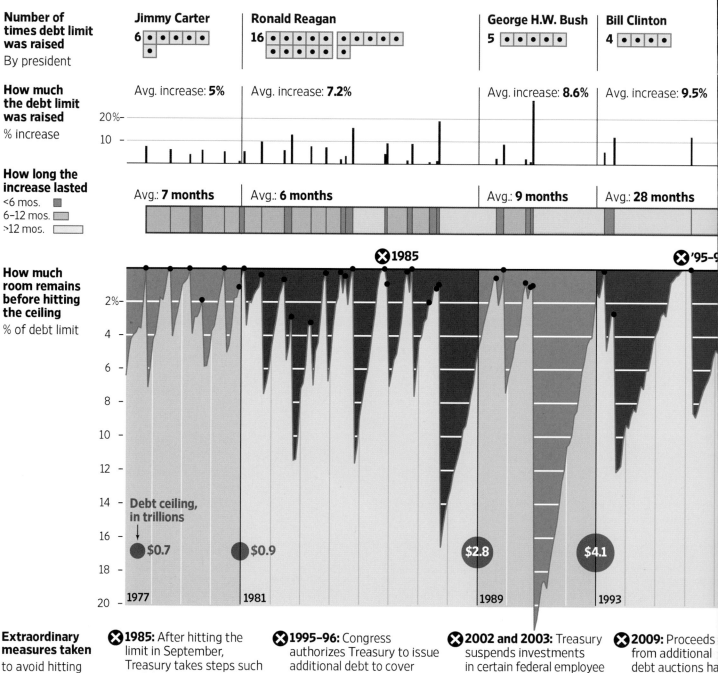

Number of times debt limit was raised
By president

Jimmy Carter	Ronald Reagan	George H.W. Bush	Bill Clinton
6	16	5	4

How much the debt limit was raised
% increase

20%–
10 –

Avg. increase: **5%** | Avg. increase: **7.2%** | Avg. increase: **8.6%** | Avg. increase: **9.5%**

How long the increase lasted
- <6 mos. ■
- 6–12 mos. ▨
- >12 mos. ☐

Avg.: **7 months** | Avg.: **6 months** | Avg.: **9 months** | Avg.: **28 months**

How much room remains before hitting the ceiling
% of debt limit

❌1985 ❌'95–9

2%–
4 –
6 –
8 –
10 –
12 –
14 – **Debt ceiling, in trillions**
16 – ●$0.7   ●$0.9   ●$2.8   ●$4.1
18 –
20 – 1977   1981   1989   1993

Extraordinary measures taken
to avoid hitting the debt limit

❌**1985:** After hitting the limit in September, Treasury takes steps such as delaying investments in various trust funds, including Social Security.

❌**1995–96:** Congress authorizes Treasury to issue additional debt to cover Social Security payments, exempting the securities from the limit.

❌**2002 and 2003:** Treasury suspends investments in certain federal employee retirement accounts to avoid reaching the debt ceiling.

❌**2009:** Proceeds from additional debt auctions ha been deposited with the Federal Reserve to fund

Note: Includes only measures to raise the debt limit amount. Those extending debt-limit expiration dates or exempting certain debt from limit aren't included

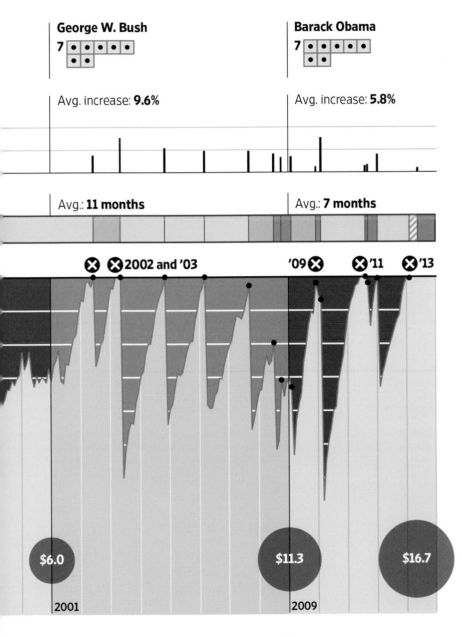

George W. Bush

7 • • • • •
  • •

Avg. increase: **9.6%**

Avg.: **11 months**

❌ ❌**2002 and '03**

$6.0

2001

Barack Obama

7 • • • • •
  • •

Avg. increase: **5.8%**

Avg.: **7 months**

'09❌   ❌'11   ❌'13

$11.3 $16.7

2009

emergency lending programs. Treasury later withdraws the funds to avoid breaching the debt limit.

❌**2011:** Debt ceiling reached in May. Treasury suspends investments in various trust funds to extend borrowing authority until August.

❌**2013:** Debt limit was briefly suspended, then raised in May to the amount outstanding at the time. Treasury has used extraordinary measures since.

Sources: White House Office of Management and Budget (debt limit); Treasury Dept. (debt); Congressional Research Service (extraordinary measures)

ARTIST Randy Yeip, graphics editor, national politics, at the *Wall Street Journal*.

STATEMENT The graphic puts the recent fight over raising the nation's borrowing limit in historical context. It summarizes how many times the ceiling has been raised, by how much, and how long it lasted before the next increase.

There was a lot of debt-limit coverage, and I thought about how we might show it using the visual metaphor of repeatedly bumping up against a ceiling. Given the partisan nature of the debate, I decided readers would want to know how the fight played out in previous administrations, how many times, and how frequently. I had been immersed in the topic for about two years at this point, and I really wanted to step outside myself and think about what an average reader would want to know. And I wanted to present that information in a way that would allow for a quick read for some, while also inviting others to linger a bit longer if they chose.

PUBLICATION *Wall Street Journal* (October 2013)

How to Pick a Pope

Behind locked doors, the selection of Francis.

ARTISTS Todd Lindeman, information designer, and Bonnie Berkowitz, graphics reporter, at the *Washington Post*.

STATEMENT Sometimes news repeats itself. The story is the same but the names and faces are different, and the reporter or artist must tackle the subject with a whole new approach and execution. Such was the case when Pope Benedict XVI announced his stunning retirement in February 2013. Colleague Laura Stanton and former colleague Brenna Maloney had done a beautiful choosing-the-pope graphic when Benedict XVI was elected in 2005, so we used that as a starting point for the election of Pope Francis. We dusted off the text and polished it with a more substantive narrative.

The art was a complete revision, both in style and technique. We wanted to bring the reader into the guarded process of the conclave, and the centerpiece 3D illustration of the Sistine Chapel was rendered in such detail that the reader could have that fly-on-the-wall experience. The hierarchy of information is structured around the lead art, from who can vote, to the process of voting, to the eventual announcement: "Habemus papam" — "We have a pope."

PUBLICATION *Washington Post* (March 2013)

Who is eligible to vote

Under a change of rules stipulated by Pope Paul VI, only cardinals who have not yet reached their 80th birthday on the day of the pope's death may enter the conclave. Those over 80 may participate in preliminary meetings.

Cardinals who are under age 80 and will be voting:

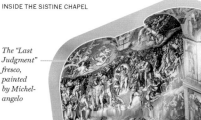

EUROPE 61	NORTH AMERICA 14	LATIN AMERICA 19	AFRICA 11	ASIA 9	OCEANIA 1

About the 115 electors

Forty-eight cardinals were appointed by Pope John Paul II. Sixty-seven were appointed by Pope Benedict XVI.

They come from 48 countries.

Italy has 28 cardinals, the most.

The average age is 72.

Note: Two additional cardinals are eligible, but have declared they will not participate in the next conclave. Ninety cardinals are age 80 or older and are ineligible to vote for a new pope.

INSIDE VATICAN CITY

Benedict's retirement home
Mater Ecclesiae monastery
The 8,600-square-foot complex on a hill, not far from the grotto where Benedict likes to take his afternoon walk, is where he plans to while away the rest of his days.

Location of conclave
Sistine Chapel
The election for a new pope happens here.

Map: Cardinals walk to and from the Sistine Chapel.

Vatican Museums

St. Peter's Basilica

Accommodations
St. Martha's House
The cardinals live in a five-story building, a Vatican residence with 105 two-room suites and 26 single rooms, during the conclave.

St. Peter's Square

Balcony where newly elected pope will appear

INSIDE THE SISTINE CHAPEL

The "Last Judgment" fresco, painted by Michelangelo

Altar

Three vote counters called scrutineers

Ballot box

Twelve panels depict the life of Christ and Moses, six on opposite facing walls.

Conclave rules

Cardinals and assistants swear an oath of absolute secrecy. Leaking information would result in excommunication.

The cardinals are not permitted any contact with the outside world: No cellphones, newspapers, television, messages, letters or signals.

The chapel is swept for listening devices before and during the conclave.

Observers can see the cardinals only when they travel between their lodging and the chapel. Vatican City workers who encounter them are not allowed to speak to them.

Each cardinal has to be present to vote and must cast his own ballot.

Other people allowed inside the conclave: two technicians, medical personnel and several assistants.

Voting begins

Ballot cards with *Eligo in summum pontificem* ("I elect as supreme pontiff") printed at the top are given to the cardinals. Each cardinal secretly fills in the name of his preferred candidate in a way that disguises his handwriting. In order of seniority, they walk to the altar, hold up the folded ballot and place it in a **silver and gilded bronze urn** (above).

Ballot card example

Eligo in summum pontificem — FOLD

When folded, the ballot is only one inch wide

Swiss Guard

Locking the chapel
Once all voting cardinals are inside the chapel and all unauthorized assistants have left, the doors are locked and then sealed with ribbons and wax.

Stoves

Ballots are threaded and tied together to form a necklace before being burned in the stove.

The central balcony at St. Peter's Basilica overlooks the square.

The pope is introduced

Once a cardinal has received the required number of votes, the dean of the College of Cardinals asks him if he accepts, and he chooses a name.

The cardinals then pledge their obedience to the new pope. The pope puts on a white cassock and skullcap; various sizes are kept on hand.

The senior deacon of the cardinals steps onto the main balcony of the Vatican and declares: "Habemus papam" — "We have a pope."

Ballots are counted

The Cardinal Camerlengo and his three assistants tally the ballots and read aloud the name of the cardinal who received each vote. The ballots and any notes are then burned. A record is kept for the Vatican archives.

How balloting takes place

Voting begins the first afternoon. If no one receives the required two-thirds of ballots cast, voting takes place twice each morning and afternoon. If after the third day no pope is elected, a one-day break for prayer can be taken. This process repeats after every seven votes.

Determining a winner

A **two-thirds majority** of the cardinals present is required to win. After 33 rounds, a runoff will occur between the top two vote-getters, according to a tweak in the rules made by Pope Benedict XVI.

A new pope is announced

Smoke signals

After each voting session, all ballots, tally sheets and notes are burned in a small stove just off the chapel. An official record of the voting is sealed and put in the Vatican archives.

White: When a candidate is elected, the papers are burned with chemicals that cause white smoke. Bells of St. Peter's Basilica also ring to clear up any confusion over smoke color.

Black: If no one has been elected, black smoke from the burning papers signals that to the waiting crowd.

TODD LINDEMAN AND BONNIE BERKOWITZ/THE WASHINGTON POST

Sources: "When a Pope Dies," by Christopher M Bellitto; "Papal Transition" by the Rev. Thomas J. Reese; Woodstock Theological Center at Georgetown University; www.AmericanMagazine.org; www.catholic-pages.com; Vatican; BBC; National Catholic Reporter; Google Earth Pro; staff reports

TOBACCO TRADE

THE U.S. IMPORTS FAR MORE TOBACCO THAN IT EXPORTS AND LEADS THE WORLD IN THE MANUFACTURE AND DISTRIBUTION OF CIGARETTES. WHERE DOES THE LEAF GO?
by NICOLAS RAPP AND RYAN BRADLEY

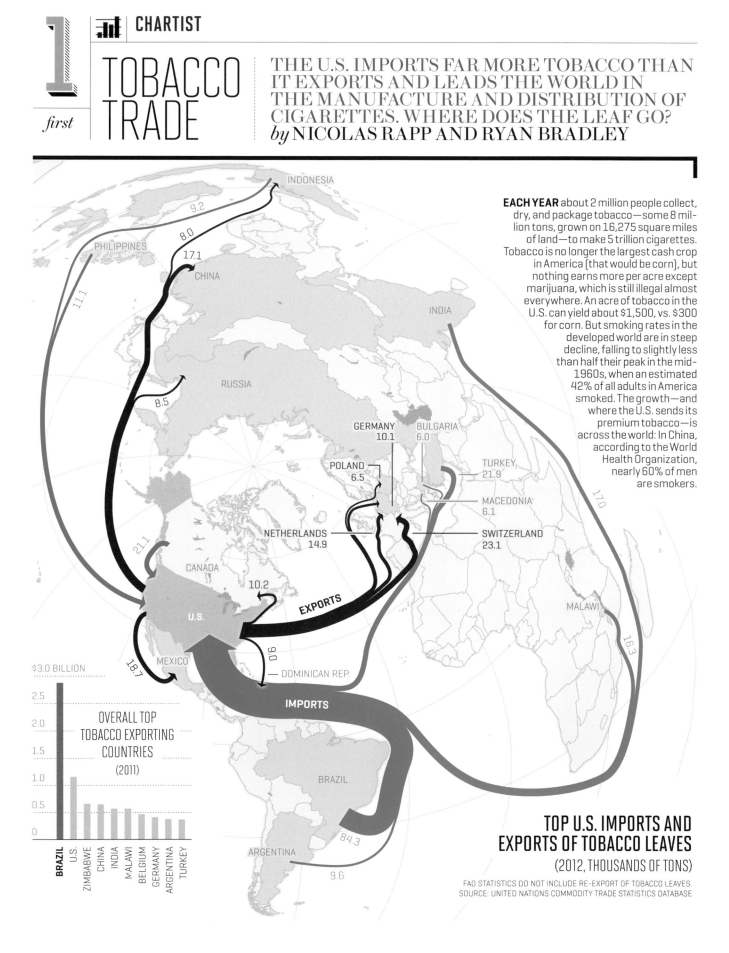

EACH YEAR about 2 million people collect, dry, and package tobacco—some 8 million tons, grown on 16,275 square miles of land—to make 5 trillion cigarettes. Tobacco is no longer the largest cash crop in America (that would be corn), but nothing earns more per acre except marijuana, which is still illegal almost everywhere. An acre of tobacco in the U.S. can yield about $1,500, vs. $300 for corn. But smoking rates in the developed world are in steep decline, falling to slightly less than half their peak in the mid-1960s, when an estimated 42% of all adults in America smoked. The growth—and where the U.S. sends its premium tobacco—is across the world: In China, according to the World Health Organization, nearly 60% of men are smokers.

OVERALL TOP TOBACCO EXPORTING COUNTRIES (2011)

$3.0 BILLION
2.5
2.0
1.5
1.0
0.5
0

BRAZIL · U.S. · ZIMBABWE · CHINA · INDIA · MALAWI · BELGIUM · GERMANY · ARGENTINA · TURKEY

TOP U.S. IMPORTS AND EXPORTS OF TOBACCO LEAVES
(2012, THOUSANDS OF TONS)

FAO STATISTICS DO NOT INCLUDE RE-EXPORT OF TOBACCO LEAVES.
SOURCE: UNITED NATIONS COMMODITY TRADE STATISTICS DATABASE

The Global Flow of Tobacco

The United States is a global hub.

ARTISTS   Nicolas Rapp, information graphics director, and Ryan Bradley, editor, at *Fortune*.

STATEMENT   This map shows the import and export of tobacco leaves to and from the United States. Tobacco trade is a huge business, for both the raw tobacco leaves and the finished product. Brazil is the largest exporter of tobacco leaf, and Russia and the USA are the largest importers. American tobacco is popular around the world and tends to be more expensive than tobacco from other countries. This graphic is also a tribute to the old maps that *Fortune* magazine used to print in the '50s.

PUBLICATION   *Fortune* (December 2013)

Bieber, Then and Now

How a pop sensation grew up, in meticulous detail.

BIEBER vs. BIEBER

When Justin Bieber burst onto the scene in 2009, he was an uncontroversial, shaggy-haired, prepubescent 15-year-old. He'd been discovered on YouTube by some big music stars, and with his debut single 'One Time,' he was, for a brief moment, a shining example of young Canadian talent. The Stratford, Ont., -raised singer quickly became the most famous person on the planet. Since his humble beginnings, Bieber sold out a Madison Square Garden concert in 22 minutes, amassed nearly three billion YouTube views, sold more than 15 million albums worldwide, and became the focus of intense public scrutiny. From 'Baby' to 'Boyfriend,' mop-hair to gel-hair, purple hoodie to leather, dog tag to gas mask, the evolution of Bieber from 'cuddly' to 'gnarly' in these short four years has gripped the world.
Which Bieber do you prefer?

CUDDLY 2009 BIEBER

JUSTIN'S BEGINNINGS

Cuddly Biebs used to busk, before he made it big, pocketing US$150-$200 a day during Stratford's summer tourist season, a princely sum for a 12-year-old kid but peanuts compared to the US$100-a -minute (asleep or awake) he makes now.

Bieber's big splurge, as a wee lad, was saving up his busker-nickels to take his mom to Disneyworld to meet Mickey and the gang. Now it's Los Cabos, Mexico, and wild nights with Selena Gomez in Vegas.

Baby Biebs' childhood neighbour was a kindly senior named Agnes. The pretty people on the far side of his backyard hedge in Calabasas, Calif., include Jennifer Lopez and the Kardashians.

Justin took his first ever date to King's Buffet, where it's all you can eat for $6.99. At the Mint Leaf, in London in 2013, the Biebs filled his belly, if not his heart, with Indian cuisine, at $60 a plate.

Cuddly Biebs' first album release party was at Stratford's City Hall, a nice enough spot, but garishly public compared to the Sons of Essex, in NYC. Where he rented out the whole place last summer, partying with 75 of his 'closest friends,' eating "truffle" grilled cheese, toasting the success of his titanic hit 'Believe.'

It used to be just a boy, and a yappy lapdog dog named Sammy. In recent years, Bieber's animal menagerie has almost grown with the addition of a Russian dwarf hamster (since deceased) and white-headed Capuchin monkey (since seized by German authorities).

Height: 158cm
Weight: 50kg
Inseam: 61cm

Hair: The shaggy swoop, always with a head flick to reposition the bangs, is the 'Rachel' of popstar haircuts—the quintessential Bieber 'do. Legions of 13-year-old boys unwillingly became lookalikes in 2009, enduring nicknames and catcalls like 'Justin' and 'Bieber.' Look #1 will be etched on the star's tombstone, despite his many failed efforts to erase it from the public conscience.

Piercings: Justin got his left ear pierced at age nine, but a few million more paid attention when he showed off matching left and right diamond studs in 2011.

Dog tag: He's quoted as saying, "A fan actually gave it to me. It was someone very special to them that had passed away in the war and this was his dog tag. I wear it for the fans."

Tattoos: What started slowly as a seeming profession of familial love and religious faith has accelerated in the last 12 months when the Biebz added nine new tattoos in rapid concession. The early days of adorable father-son matching tattoos and Christian symbolism turned to crowns and tigers as the singer grew up and began spiralling deep into a public meltdown of monkeys and gas masks.

Jackets: Bieber's recent proclivity for leather jackets surfaced most notably at the 2013 Billboard Music Awards, where he was also booed by the audience. Donning the single-sleeve bomber jacket with a 'Bieber Air' logo, the faux pilot made everyone wish for the days when he just wore the regular clothes his mom chose.

Jewellery: The bling around Bieber's neck usually outshines the bling around his wrists. But the star's diamond-cut bracelets and gold Daytona watches at least outshine Cuddly Bieber's tamer selection.

This bit: Cummerbund? Apron? We at the Post clearly have no idea what this bit is. Justin?

Hands in pockets: Either an expression of disinterest, brattiness, or a PR fashion tip taken too far, Bieber's hands-in-pockets look has a long history.

The glove: Maybe Justin really is channelling his inner 'King of Pop' with this odd fashion choice. There is something reminiscent of Michael Jackson's 'Bad' with this look. Also, it is clearly bad. One glove? So impractical.

Pants: As his voice lowered, so did the crotch of his 'droopy-pooper' pants. 2009's straightforward denim jeans became 2013's leather homage to b-boys and '70s rock. And his rear end must be getting cold.

Dog: Despite rumours to the contrary Justin's dog Sam is alive and well.

Monkey: German authorities confiscated Bieber's pet monkey Mally at the airport when it was found to be without the required paperwork.

Shoes: High-top sneakers have always been a part of the Biebs' wardrobe. They signify a youthfulness and athleticism that he has displayed in the past (Bieber isn't a bad little basketball player!). The sneakers could also come in handy if he needs to run from the cops.

Dance: Justin has never been confused with Michael Jackson when it comes to dance moves (though he does do a great impression of Jackson's famous crotch-grab), but the kid is getting better - it helps that his choreography budget is approaching Broadway levels.

GNARLY 2013 BIEBER

JUSTIN'S TATTOOS

1. Stratford Culliton - Jan. 2012. Left shoulder blade. Ice hockey logo from his days watching with his grandfather.

2. Roman numerals - Jan. 2013. Right collarbone

3. Crown - Sept. 2012. Left side of chest.

4. Yeshua - April 2011. Left ribcage. Got matching tattoo with Dad.

5. Tiger - April 2013. Left bicep.

6. Music - July 2012. Inside right forearm. Japanese symbol for 'music.'

7. Believe - June 2012. Inside left forearm. His latest album is called 'Believe.'

8. Owl - Oct. 2012. Left arm.

9. Seagull - March 2010. Left stomach near hip. Dad and uncle have same tattoo.

10. Chi - Feb 2013. Left arm. Greek alphabet character is abbreviation for 'Christ.'

11. Carp - April 2013. Left arm. Known to symbolize good luck.

12. Angel - April 2013. Left forearm. It was rumoured it represents his old flame Selena Gomez.

13. Jesus Christ - 2012 Left calf. Bieber is a faithful Christian lad.

14. Praying hands - March 2012. Left calf. Bieber has a song called 'Pray.' Roses added in Dec. 2012

Height: 170cm
Weight: 60kg
Inseam: 43cm

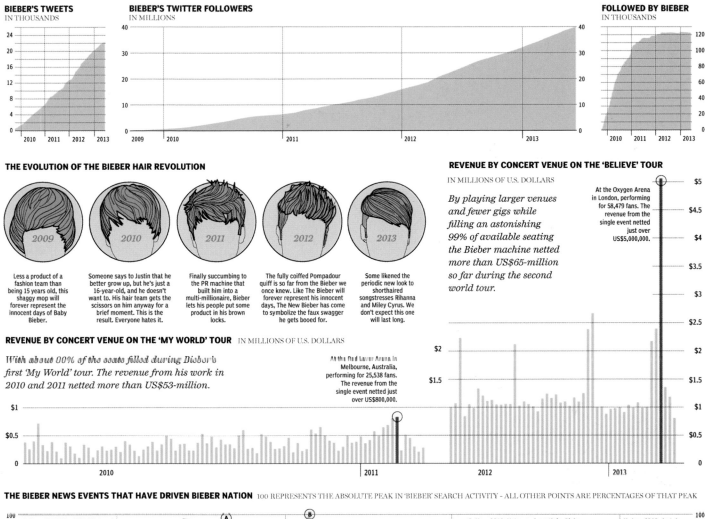

BIEBER'S TWEETS
IN THOUSANDS

24
20
16
12
8
4
0
2010 2011 2012 2013

BIEBER'S TWITTER FOLLOWERS
IN MILLIONS

40
30
20
10
0
2009 2010 2011 2012 2013

FOLLOWED BY BIEBER
IN THOUSANDS

120
100
80
60
40
20
0
2010 2011 2012 2013

THE EVOLUTION OF THE BIEBER HAIR REVOLUTION

2009 — Less a product of a fashion team than being 15 years old, this shaggy mop will forever represent the innocent days of Baby Bieber.

2010 — Someone says to Justin that he better grow up, but he's just a 16-year-old, and he doesn't want to. His hair team gets the scissors on him anyway for a brief moment. This is the result. Everyone hates it.

2011 — Finally succumbing to the PR machine that built him into a multi-millionaire, Bieber lets his people put some product in his brown locks.

2012 — The fully coiffed Pompadour quiff is so far from the Bieber we once knew. Like The Bieber will forever represent his innocent days, The New Bieber has come to symbolize the faux swagger he gets booed for.

2013 — Some likened the periodic new look to shorthaired songstresses Rihanna and Miley Cyrus. We don't expect this one will last long.

REVENUE BY CONCERT VENUE ON THE 'BELIEVE' TOUR
IN MILLIONS OF U.S. DOLLARS

By playing larger venues and fewer gigs while filling an astonishing 99% of available seating the Bieber machine netted more than US$65-million so far during the second world tour.

At the Oxygen Arena in London, performing for 58,479 fans. The revenue from the single event netted just over US$5,000,000.

$5
$4.5
$4
$3.5
$3
$2.5
$2
$1.5
$1
$0.5
0

REVENUE BY CONCERT VENUE ON THE 'MY WORLD' TOUR IN MILLIONS OF U.S. DOLLARS

With about 90% of the seats filled during Bieber's first 'My World' tour. The revenue from his work in 2010 and 2011 netted more than US$53-million.

At the Rod Laver Arena in Melbourne, Australia, performing for 25,538 fans. The revenue from the single event netted just over US$800,000.

$1
$0.5
0
2010   2011   2012   2013

THE BIEBER NEWS EVENTS THAT HAVE DRIVEN BIEBER NATION 100 REPRESENTS THE ABSOLUTE PEAK IN 'BIEBER' SEARCH ACTIVITY – ALL OTHER POINTS ARE PERCENTAGES OF THAT PEAK

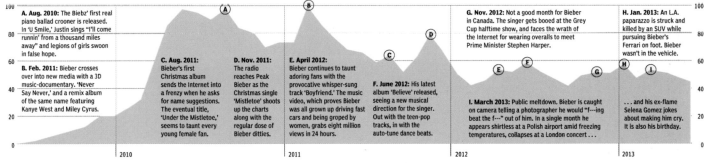

A. Aug. 2010: The Biebz' first real piano ballad crooner is released. In 'U Smile,' Justin sings "I'll come runnin' from a thousand miles away" and legions of girls swoon in false hope.

B. Feb. 2011: Bieber crosses over into new media with a 3D music-documentary. 'Never Say Never,' and a remix album of the same name featuring Kanye West and Miley Cyrus.

C. Aug. 2011: Bieber's first Christmas album sends the Internet into a frenzy when he asks for name suggestions. The eventual title, 'Under the Mistletoe,' seems to taunt every young female fan.

D. Nov. 2011: The radio reaches Peak Bieber as the Christmas single 'Mistletoe' shoots up the charts along with the regular dose of Bieber ditties.

E. April 2012: Bieber continues to taunt adoring fans with the provocative whisper-sung track 'Boyfriend.' The music video, which proves Bieber was all grown up driving fast cars and being groped by women, grabs eight million views in 24 hours.

F. June 2012: His latest album 'Believe' released, seeing a new musical direction for the singer. Out with the teen-pop tracks, in with the auto-tune dance beats.

G. Nov. 2012: Not a good month for Bieber in Canada. The singer gets booed at the Grey Cup halftime show, and faces the wrath of the Internet for wearing overalls to meet Prime Minister Stephen Harper.

H. Jan. 2013: An L.A. paparazzo is struck and killed by an SUV while pursuing Bieber's Ferrari on foot. Bieber wasn't in the vehicle.

I. March 2013: Public meltdown. Bieber is caught on camera telling a photographer he would "f---ing beat the f---" out of him. In a single month he appears shirtless at a Polish airport amid freezing temperatures, collapses at a London concert . . .

. . . and his ex-flame Selena Gomez jokes about making him cry. It is also his birthday.

100
80
60
40
20
0
2010   2011   2012   2013

TRACKING ONLINE BIEBER GOOGLE SEARCHES BY COUNTRY SHADES ARE PROPORTIONAL TO THE REGION WITH THE PEAK PER-CAPITA SEARCHES SET BY THE PHILIPPINES IN 2009

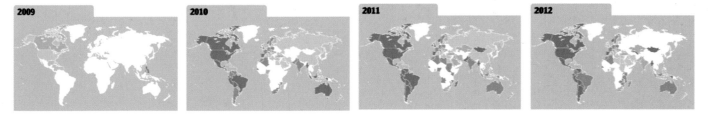

2009   2010   2011   2012

ARTISTS Richard Johnson, assistant managing editor for graphics and illustration, Andrew Barr, graphic artist, Jonathan Forani, intern, David Corrigan, intern, and Rob Roberts, national editor, at the *National Post.*

STATEMENT This graphic came out of an editorial conversation based around the perception that Canadians were becoming somewhat embarrassed by the antics of Justin Bieber, after he was accused of spitting on fans from a hotel room window. Bieber had been arguably Canada's biggest entertainment export of the last decade. A decision was made to poll readers who they preferred, the 2009 Bieber or the 2013 Bieber? In order that readers might make this important decision based on all available facts, an information graphic was prepared.

PUBLICATION *National Post* (July 2013)

The NSA's Vast Net

The agency that wants to know everything.

ARTISTS Graphic by Heather Jones, infographics designer; writing and reporting by Emily Maltby, at *Time*.

STATEMENT Along with a major feature in *Time*'s annual Person of the Year issue on Edward Snowden, we were tasked with decoding how much of your personal data is captured by the National Security Agency. At first we wanted to annotate a citizen, showing all the ways the NSA could tap into his or her information, but after much research it became impossibly complicated. So we decided to focus in on the types of devices, which simplified things but also showed the depth and reach of the US intelligence system. After drawing the orbs and weblike vortex, I wanted to put some human life with the tiny users into it at the bottom, to hint at how big this thing really is.

PUBLICATION *Time* (December 2013)

LISTENING IN

THE NSA GATHERS INFORMATION FROM ALL CORNERS
OF THE WORLD'S COMMUNICATION SYSTEMS

The NSA can access
huge amounts of
data (inner rings)

Specific devices,
including emerging
technologies, are
also vulnerable
(outer ring)

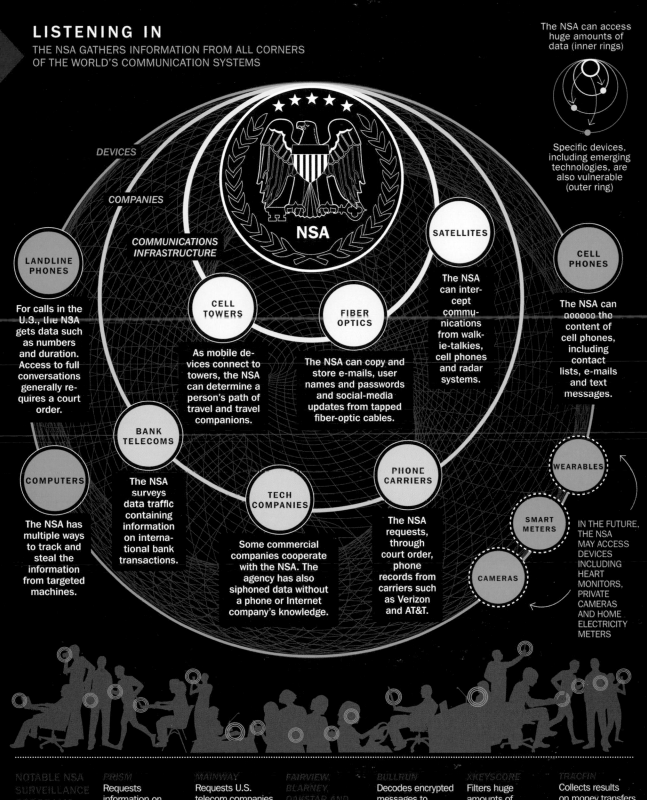

DEVICES

COMPANIES

COMMUNICATIONS
INFRASTRUCTURE

NSA

LANDLINE PHONES
For calls in the U.S., the NSA gets data such as numbers and duration. Access to full conversations generally requires a court order.

CELL TOWERS
As mobile devices connect to towers, the NSA can determine a person's path of travel and travel companions.

FIBER OPTICS
The NSA can copy and store e-mails, user names and passwords and social-media updates from tapped fiber-optic cables.

SATELLITES
The NSA can intercept communications from walkie-talkies, cell phones and radar systems.

CELL PHONES
The NSA can access the content of cell phones, including contact lists, e-mails and text messages.

BANK TELECOMS
The NSA surveys data traffic containing information on international bank transactions.

COMPUTERS
The NSA has multiple ways to track and steal the information from targeted machines.

TECH COMPANIES
Some commercial companies cooperate with the NSA. The agency has also siphoned data without a phone or Internet company's knowledge.

PHONE CARRIERS
The NSA requests, through court order, phone records from carriers such as Verizon and AT&T.

WEARABLES

SMART METERS

CAMERAS

IN THE FUTURE, THE NSA MAY ACCESS DEVICES INCLUDING HEART MONITORS, PRIVATE CAMERAS AND HOME ELECTRICITY METERS

NOTABLE NSA SURVEILLANCE PROGRAMS

PRISM
Requests information on foreign intelligence targets from American technology companies

MAINWAY
Requests U.S. telecom companies to hand over call records, which are then stored in databases

FAIRVIEW, BLARNEY, OAKSTAR AND STORMBREW
Gather communications that move along fiber-optic cables

BULLRUN
Decodes encrypted messages to defeat network security

XKEYSCORE
Filters huge amounts of captured data by specific search terms

TRACFIN
Collects results on money transfers and credit-card transactions

Sources: Washington *Post*; *Guardian*; *Der Spiegel*; *Wired*; Electronic Frontier Foundation; James Bamford

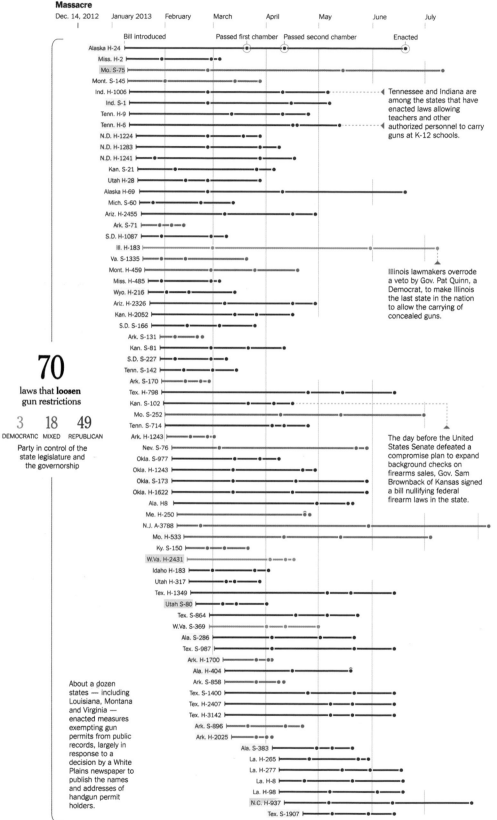

January 2013   February   March   April   May   June   July

Bill introduced   Passed first chamber   Passed second chamber   Enacted

Alaska H-24
Miss. H-2
Mo. S-75
Mont. S-145
Ind. H-1006
Ind. S-1
Tenn. H-9
Tenn. H-6
N.D. H-1224
N.D. H-1283
N.D. H-1241
Kan. S-21
Utah H-28
Alaska H-69
Mich. S-60
Ariz. H-2455
Ark. S-71
S.D. H-1087
Ill. H-183
Va. S-1335
Mont. H-459
Miss. H-485
Wyo. H-216
Ariz. H-2326
Kan. H-2052
S.D. S-166
Ark. S-131
Kan. S-81
S.D. S-227
Tenn. S-142
Ark. S-170
Tex. H-798
Kan. S-102
Mo. S-252
Tenn. S-714
Ark. H-1243
Nev. S-76
Okla. S-977
Okla. H-1243
Okla. S-173
Okla. H-1622
Ala. H8
Me. H-250
N.J. A-3788
Mo. H-533
Ky. S-150
W.Va. H-2431
Idaho H-183
Utah H-317
Tex. H-1349
Utah S-80
Tex. S-864
W.Va. S-369
Ala. S-286
Tex. S-987
Ark. H-1700
Ala. H-404
Ark. S-858
Tex. S-1400
Tex. H-2407
Tex. H-3142
Ark. S-896
Ark. H-2025
Ala. S-383
La. H-265
La. H-277
La. H-8
La. H-98
N.C. H-937
Tex. S-1907

Tennessee and Indiana are among the states that have enacted laws allowing teachers and other authorized personnel to carry guns at K-12 schools.

Illinois lawmakers overrode a veto by Gov. Pat Quinn, a Democrat, to make Illinois the last state in the nation to allow the carrying of concealed guns.

The day before the United States Senate defeated a compromise plan to expand background checks on firearms sales, Gov. Sam Brownback of Kansas signed a bill nullifying federal firearm laws in the state.

70

laws that **loosen** gun restrictions

3   **18**   **49**
DEMOCRATIC   MIXED   REPUBLICAN

Party in control of the state legislature and the governorship

About a dozen states — including Louisiana, Montana and Virginia — enacted measures exempting gun permits from public records, largely in response to a decision by a White Plains newspaper to publish the names and addresses of handgun permit holders.

State Gun Laws Enacted in Year Since Newtown

About 1,500 state gun bills have been introduced since the Newtown massacre. 109 have become law.

By KAREN YOURISH and LARRY BUCHANAN

In the 12 months since the mass shooting at Sandy Hook Elementary School in Newtown, Conn., almost every state has enacted at least one new gun law. Nearly two-thirds of the new laws ease restrictions and expand the rights of gun owners. Most of those bills were approved in states controlled by Republicans. Those who support stricter regulations won some victories — mostly in states where the legislature and governorship are controlled by Democrats — to increase restrictions on gun use and ownership.

Party in control of state legislature and the governorship

— Republican
— Democratic
— Mixed

Laws that contain provisions about

Carrying concealed weapons in public and in schools

Background checks and mental health reporting

Issues addressed by the new gun laws	Loosen gun restrictions	Tighten gun restrictions
Carrying concealed weapons in public and in schools	31	0
Background checks and mental health reporting	4	27
Gun permits (including requirements and confidentiality)	28	1
Keeping guns away from people prohibited from having them	2	9
Assault weapons and high-capacity magazines	1	6
Nullifying federal gun laws	4	0
Other	6	7

Some laws addressed multiple issues, so figures do not add up to 109.

Source: The analysis includes laws based on lists from the Law Center to Prevent Gun Violence and the National Conference of State Legislatures, as well as data from Open States and the National Rifle Association. The timelines show the dates that the bills first passed each chamber of the state legislature.

Gun Laws Since Newtown

The sea change that wasn't.

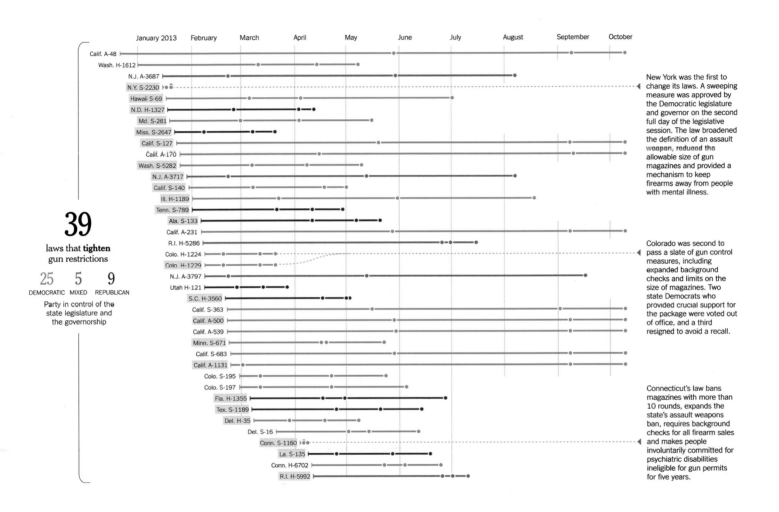

39

laws that **tighten** gun restrictions

25	5	9
DEMOCRATIC	MIXED	REPUBLICAN

Party in control of the state legislature and the governorship

New York was the first to change its laws. A sweeping measure was approved by the Democratic legislature and governor on the second full day of the legislative session. The law broadened the definition of an assault weapon, reduced the allowable size of gun magazines and provided a mechanism to keep firearms away from people with mental illness.

Colorado was second to pass a slate of gun control measures, including expanded background checks and limits on the size of magazines. Two state Democrats who provided crucial support for the package were voted out of office, and a third resigned to avoid a recall.

Connecticut's law bans magazines with more than 10 rounds, expands the state's assault weapons ban, requires background checks for all firearm sales and makes people involuntarily committed for psychiatric disabilities ineligible for gun permits for five years.

ARTISTS Karen Yourish, graphics editor, and Larry Buchanan, graphics editor, at the *New York Times.*

STATEMENT The mass shooting at Sandy Hook Elementary School in Newtown, CT, killed twenty first graders as well as six teachers and arguably focused the public's attention on gun laws more than any other massacre in recent history. We wanted to give readers a sense of the impact the shooting had on state legislative activity in the year following the tragedy, so we crunched a number of datasets to provide a comprehensive analysis. The final graphic shows all of the gun-related bills that were enacted into state law, how long it took each bill to wend its way through the states, whether the new laws tighten or loosen gun restrictions, and the party composition of the state legislatures and the sitting governor.

PUBLICATION *New York Times* (December 2013)

French Kisses

Twice on the cheek, or three or more?

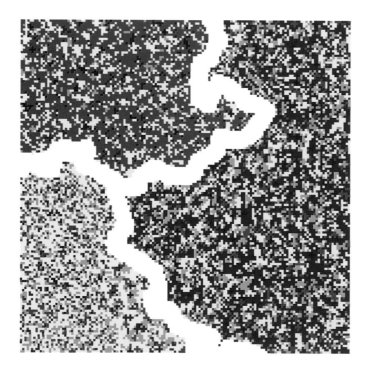

ARTIST Bill Rankin, Yale University.

STATEMENT This map shows the regional geography of cheek kissing in France. The data is from a web-based survey begun in 2007 that now has over 100,000 responses. There are strong regional patterns. Although most people greet with two kisses (including more than 75 percent of Parisians), outside the capital there are significant minority cultures: one kiss in Brittany, three in the south, and four in most of the north. (Five kisses is not common anywhere, and these responses are probably noise.) This regionalism reminds me of the "soda," "pop," and "Coke" controversy in the US: subtle and seemingly meaningless differences that nevertheless show strong—and deeply held—cultural divisions.

This same data has appeared before, but the published maps—like many other statistical maps—enforce the tyranny of the majority. They shade each administrative département with one of five colors according to the most common local response. But this all-or-nothing approach has serious drawbacks. It produces fragmentation in the four-kiss area in northern France; it also makes it impossible to distinguish the diversity of the north from the strong homogeneity of the south. Using a pointillist approach, where the color of each département results from the aggregation of thousands of small dots, preserves the nuance of the original data.

PUBLICATION *RadicalCartography.net* (March 2013)

When you greet a friend, how many times do you kiss?

Legend:
- Once
- Twice
- Three times
- Four times
- Five times (18% of Corsica)

Lille
Paris
Strasbourg
Nantes
Bordeaux
Lyon
Montpellier
Toulouse
Marseilles
Nice

Color mixes show relative proportion of answers at combiendebises.free.fr, by *département*.
Total votes: 102,406. Minimum in one *département*: 214. Map by Bill Rankin, 2013.

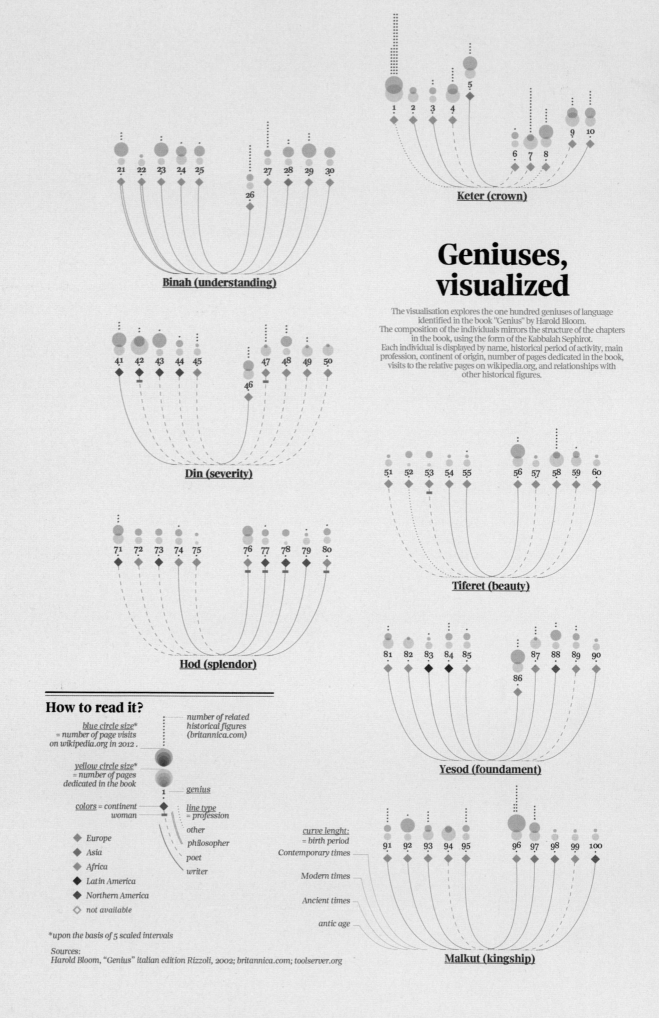

Geniuses, visualized

The visualisation explores the one hundred geniuses of language identified in the book "Genius" by Harold Bloom. The composition of the individuals mirrors the structure of the chapters in the book, using the form of the Kabbalah Sephirot. Each individual is displayed by name, historical period of activity, main profession, continent of origin, number of pages dedicated in the book, visits to the relative pages on wikipedia.org, and relationships with other historical figures.

Keter (crown)

Binah (understanding)

Din (severity)

Tiferet (beauty)

Hod (splendor)

Yesod (foundament)

How to read it?

blue circle size*
= number of page visits
on wikipedia.org in 2012 .

number of related
historical figures
(britannica.com)

yellow circle size*
= number of pages
dedicated in the book

1 — *genius*

colors = continent
woman

line type
= profession

other

philosopher

◆ Europe

poet

◆ Asia

writer

◆ Africa

◆ Latin America

◆ Northern America

◇ not available

curve lenght:
= birth period

Contemporary times

Modern times

Ancient times

antic age

Malkut (kingship)

*upon the basis of 5 scaled intervals

Sources:
Harold Bloom, "Genius" italian edition Rizzoli, 2002; britannica.com; toolserver.org

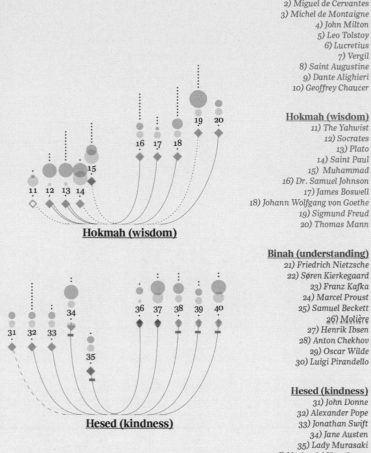

Keter (crown)
1) William Shakespeare
2) Miguel de Cervantes
3) Michel de Montaigne
4) John Milton
5) Leo Tolstoy
6) Lucretius
7) Vergil
8) Saint Augustine
9) Dante Alighieri
10) Geoffrey Chaucer

Hokmah (wisdom)
11) The Yahwist
12) Socrates
13) Plato
14) Saint Paul
15) Muhammad
16) Dr. Samuel Johnson
17) James Boswell
18) Johann Wolfgang von Goethe
19) Sigmund Freud
20) Thomas Mann

Hokmah (wisdom)

The Varieties of Genius

Great minds from Harold Bloom's *Genius*, visualized according to Jewish esoteric thought.

Binah (understanding)
21) Friedrich Nietzsche
22) Søren Kierkegaard
23) Franz Kafka
24) Marcel Proust
25) Samuel Beckett
26) Molière
27) Henrik Ibsen
28) Anton Chekhov
29) Oscar Wilde
30) Luigi Pirandello

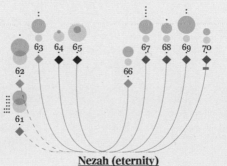

Hesed (kindness)

Hesed (kindness)
31) John Donne
32) Alexander Pope
33) Jonathan Swift
34) Jane Austen
35) Lady Murasaki
36) Nathaniel Hawthorne
37) Herman Melville
38) Charlotte Brontë
39) Emily Jane Brontë
40) Virginia Woolf

ARTISTS Davide Ciuffi, Federica Fragapane, Francesco Majno, Giorgia Lupi, Simone Quadri, and Gabriele Rossi of Accurat.

STATEMENT This visualization explores the 100 geniuses of language identified in the book *Genius* by Harold Bloom. The composition of the individuals mirrors the structure of the chapters in the book, using the form of the Kabbalah Sephirot from Jewish esoteric thought. Each individual is displayed by name, historical period of activity, main profession, continent of origin, number of pages dedicated in Bloom's book, visits to the relative pages on wikipedia.org, and relationships with other historical figures. We were very inspired by this book and we tried to literally represent geniuses as the author might have imagined them.

The analysis was made by combining data from three sources: The Italian edition of the book (Rizzoli, 2002) by Harold Bloom, the biographical pages of britannica.com, and wikipedia.org pages of the 100 people identified through toolserver.org.

PUBLICATION *BrainPickings.org, La Lettura* (March 2013)

Din (severity)
41) Ralph Waldo Emerson
42) Emily Dickinson
43) Robert Frost
44) Wallace Stevens
45) T.S. Eliot
46) William Wordsworth
47) Percy Bysshe Shelley
48) John Keats
49) Giacomo Leopardi
50) Alfred, Lord Tennyson

Nezah (eternity)

Tiferet (beauty)
51) Algernon Charles Swinburne
52) Dante Gabriel Rossetti
53) Christina Rossetti
54) Walter Pater
55) Hugo von Hofmannsthal
56) Victor Hugo
57) Gérard de Nerval
58) Charles Baudelaire
59) Arthur Rimbaud
60) Paul Valéry

Nezah (eternity)
61) Homer
62) Luis Vaz de Camões
63) James Joyce
64) Alejo Carpentier
65) Octavio Paz
66) Stendhal
67) Mark Twain
68) William Faulkner
69) Ernest Hemingway
70) Flannery O'Connor

Hod (splendor)
71) Walt Whitman
72) Fernando Pessoa
73) Hart Crane
74) Federico García Lorca
75) Luis Cernuda
76) George Eliot
77) Willa Cather
78) Edith Wharton
79) F. Scott Fitzgerald
80) Iris Murdoch

Yesod (foundation)
81) Gustave Flaubert
82) José Maria Eça de Queiroz
83) Joaquim Maria Machado de Assis
84) Jorge Luis Borges
85) Italo Calvino
86) William Blake
87) D.H. Lawrence
88) Tennessee Williams
89) Rainer Maria Rilke
90) Eugenio Montale

Malkut (kingship)
91) Honoré de Balzac
92) Lewis Carroll
93) Henry James
94) Robert Browning
95) William Butler Yeats
96) Charles Dickens
97) Fyodor Dostoevsky
98) Isaac Babel
99) Paul Celan
100) Ralph Ellison

In the Labor Force

47%
Employed Full-Time

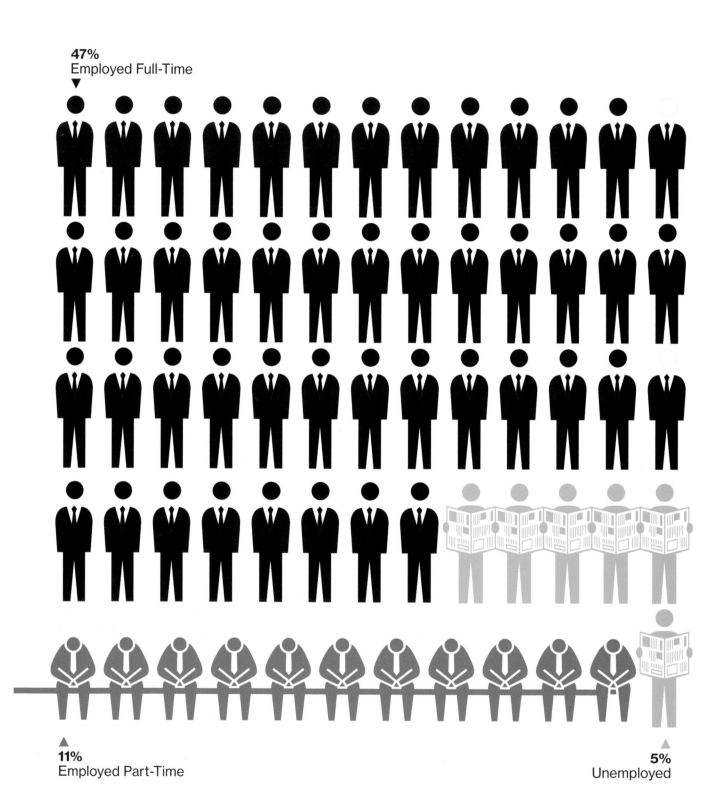

11%
Employed Part-Time

5%
Unemployed

Not the Labor Force

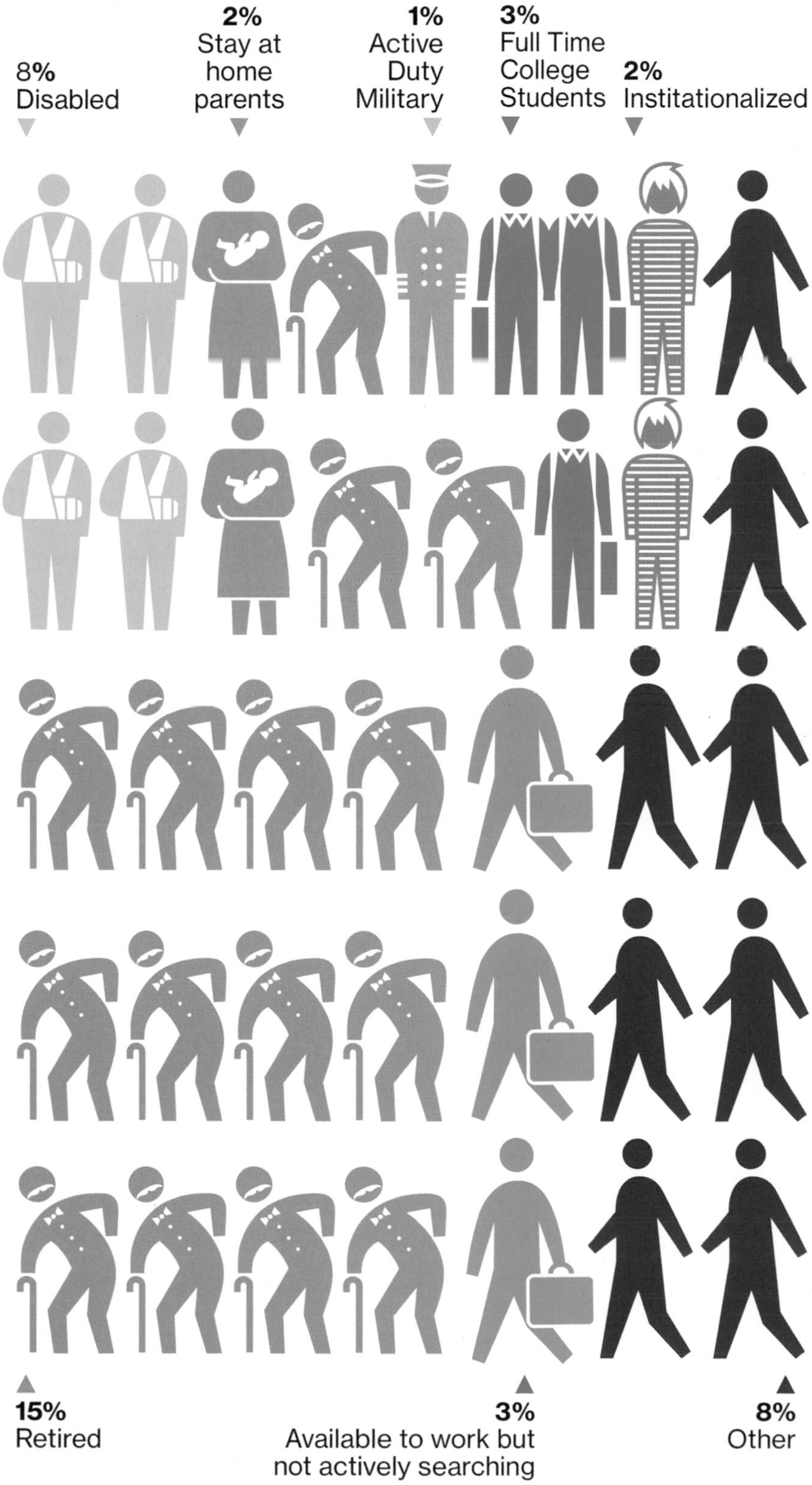

8%
Disabled

2%
Stay at
home
parents

1%
Active
Duty
Military

3%
Full Time
College
Students

2%
Institationalized

15%
Retired

3%
Available to work but
not actively searching

8%
Other

ARTISTS Jennifer Daniel and Dorothy
Gambrell of *Bloomberg Businessweek.*

STATEMENT News stories often cite the
unemployment rate, but when you look
at Americans of working age, the "unemployed" include a much larger population—the retired, the full-time students,
and, yes, people who don't have jobs.

PUBLICATION *Bloomberg Businessweek*
(April 2013)

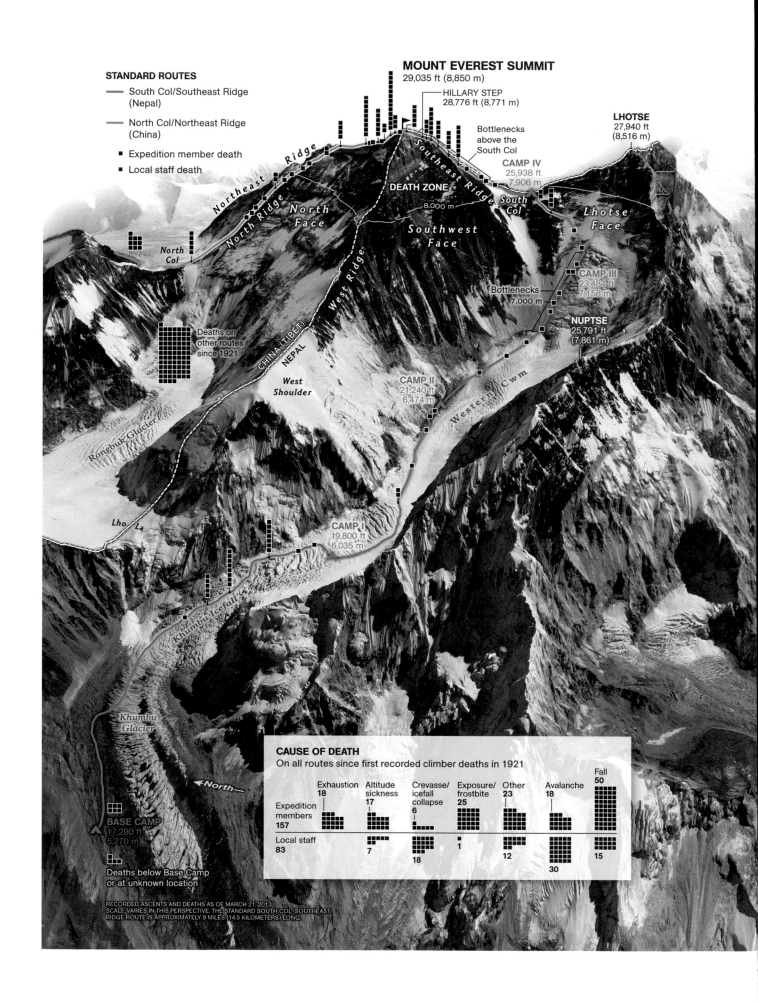

STANDARD ROUTES

— South Col/Southeast Ridge (Nepal)

— North Col/Northeast Ridge (China)

■ Expedition member death

■ Local staff death

MOUNT EVEREST SUMMIT
29,035 ft (8,850 m)

HILLARY STEP
28,776 ft (8,771 m)

Bottlenecks above the South Col

LHOTSE
27,940 ft (8,516 m)

Northeast Ridge

North Ridge

North Face

DEATH ZONE

8,000 m

Southeast Ridge

CAMP IV
25,938 ft
7,906 m

South Col

Lhotse Face

North Col

Southwest Face

West Ridge

CAMP III
23,484 ft
7,158 m

Bottlenecks 7,000 m

NUPTSE
25,791 ft
(7,861 m)

Deaths on other routes since 1921

CHINA (TIBET)
NEPAL

West Shoulder

CAMP II
21,240 ft
6,474 m

Western Cwm

Rongbuk Glacier

Lho La

CAMP I
19,800 ft
6,035 m

Khumbu Icefall

Khumbu Glacier

← North—

BASE CAMP
17,290 ft
5,270 m

Deaths below Base Camp or at unknown location

RECORDED ASCENTS AND DEATHS AS OF MARCH 21, 2013
SCALE VARIES IN THIS PERSPECTIVE. THE STANDARD SOUTH COL–SOUTHEAST
RIDGE ROUTE IS APPROXIMATELY 9 MILES (14.5 KILOMETERS) LONG.

CAUSE OF DEATH
On all routes since first recorded climber deaths in 1921

	Exhaustion 18	Altitude sickness 17	Crevasse/ icefall collapse 6	Exposure/ frostbite 25	Other 23	Avalanche 18	Fall 50
Expedition members 157							
Local staff 83	7	18	1		12	30	15

EVEREST OVERRUN

More than half of all climbers now reach the top, despite the hazards of overcrowding.

TAMING THE MOUNTAIN

The success rate of climbers has more than tripled since 1990, largely due to more guides and better gear.

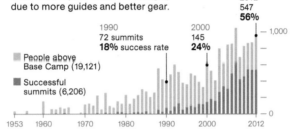

1990
72 summits
18% success rate

2000
145
24%

2012
547
56%

People above Base Camp (19,121)

Successful summits (6,206)

1953   1960   1970   1980   1990   2000   2012

MORE BOTTLENECKS

Improved weather forecasts have led climbers to time their attempts on the same few days each year.

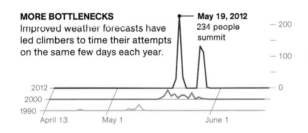

May 19, 2012
234 people summit

2012
2000
1990

April 13   May 1   June 1

FEWER ROUTES

With the rise of guided climbing, most ascents are made on only two routes: one in Nepal, the other in China.

Summits by Routes
▲ South Col (Nepal)
▲ North Col (China)
▲ Other

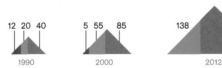

12 20 40   5 55 85   138   409

1990   2000   2012

NO RISE IN MORTALITY

Despite the recent boom in the number of climbers, the death rate has not increased.

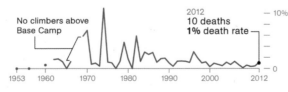

No climbers above Base Camp

2012
10 deaths
1% death rate

1953   1960   1970   1980   1990   2000   2012

MARTIN GAMACHE AND MATTHEW TWOMBLY, NGM STAFF; MESA SCHUMACHER
SOURCES: GERMAN AEROSPACE CENTER; RAYMOND B. HUEY, UNIVERSITY OF WASHINGTON; RICHARD SALISBURY, HIMALAYAN DATABASE

Deadly Everest

The climb is safer than ever, but the mountain is overcrowded and still dangerous.

ARTISTS Map by Martin Gamache, senior editor, cartography; charts by Matt Twombly, graphic design specialist, at *National Geographic*.

STATEMENT Mount Everest is overcrowded with climbers, with as many as 234 people reaching the summit in a single day, as happened in May 2012. More guides, better gear, and fewer, safer routes make the climb a less dangerous journey than it once was. Still, the mountain has claimed 240 lives since 1921. The high-resolution 3D image of Everest, provided by the German Aerospace Center, is used to show the main routes as well as the locations of fatalities and their cause.

PUBLICATION *National Geographic* (June 2013)

THE MIDWEST
according to 100 maps published by the following organizations

Alpha Chi Omega
American Association for Nude Recreation
American Chemical Society
American Eurocopter
American Orthopaedic Society for Sports Medicine
Apartment Therapy
Approach Systems, Inc.
Arts Midwest
Asian Pacific American Medical Student Association
Blaupunkt
Cat Fanciers Association
Cause Matters Corporation
Charles Schwab Investment Management
Chinese American Librarians Association
City-data.com
DudeRanch.com
FAICO Information Solutions
FilmInAmerica.com
Financial Industry Regulatory Authority
FMC Agricultural Products
Freemasonry
Gillaspy Associates
Guardian Water and Power
Haiku Society of America
Heartland Express
Home Depot
I-Con Systems, Inc.
Interior Design Educators Council
International Association of Voice Stress Analysts
Invesco
Kindermorgan Terminals
La Bloga
Learner.org

LifeDuringPregnancy.com
Lowrance
Maps.com (twice)
Marlen Textiles
Marten Transport
Megatrux Transportation
Midwest Dairy Association
Midwest Forensic Resource Center
Midwest Outdoors Television
Midwest Regional Rail System
Midwestern Magical Authority
MK Diamond Products
Moostash Joe Tours
Munich Re
National Association of Engineering Student Councils
National Coalition of Blacks for Reparations in America
National Council of Corvette Clubs
National Equity Fund
National Farm to School Network
National Model Railroad Association
National Precision Bearing
Northeast Biomanufacturing Center and Collaborative
Northwest Designs of Illinois
Northwood University
On Site Energy
Perkett PR
Phannenberg Signaling
Phi Delta Theta
Plunkett's Pest Control
Professional Trailbuilders Association
Project Lead The Way
Rails-to-Trails Conservancy
Rand McNally

Reliable Sprinkler
Siemer Enterprises
Single Action Shooting Club
Society for Photographic Education
Society of Quality Assurance
South African Consulate
Southern Fulfillment Services
Sportscar Club of America
Square 9
SVF Flow Controls, Inc.
Ulano Corporation
University of Michigan
University of Minnesota Duluth
U.S. Army Corps of Engineers
U.S. Bureau of Labor Statistics
U.S. Census Bureau
U.S. Centers for Disease Control
U.S. Department of Energy
U.S. Department of Labor
U.S. Environmental Protection Agency
U.S. Federal Energy Regulatory Commission
U.S. Geological Survey
U.S. Fish and Wildlife Service
U.S. Library of Congress
U.S. National Institute of Science and Technology
U.S. National Park Service
U.S. National Weather Service
U.S. Tennis Association
Verizon
Western Interstate Commission for Higher Education
Wikipedia
Wisconsin Milk Marketing Board
Women of Reform Judaism

The Midwest by Consensus

Mapping fuzzy boundaries.

ARTIST Bill Rankin, Yale University.

STATEMENT This map overlays 100 different defini-tions of the American Midwest. There is little agreement, and the shape that emerges is remarkably fuzzy—and quite vast.

The Midwest has no obvious boundaries. It is, at best, a collection of ill-defined ideals about landscape, labor, and culture that vaguely invoke the westward march of US expansion in the nineteenth century. What is its geography? Rather than trying to legislate one true defi-nition, this map takes a much messier approach. After using Google to find 100 different maps of the Midwest (with a preference for those with some official organiza-tional status), I simply overlaid them all.

One important thing to note is that even though Illinois emerges as the most Midwestern state, there is no area that was included on every single map. The sum of all possible Midwests, however, is incredibly vast, stretch-ing from Newfoundland to New Mexico and Idaho to Georgia. It is everywhere and nowhere at once. The great majority of the maps I found identified the Midwest us-ing state boundaries, but there were also maps that used counties, area codes, ecosystems, and even freehand shapes.

PUBLICATION *RadicalCartography.net* (April 2013)

INTERFERENCE

The surfer who has inside position for a wave has unconditional right of way for the duration of that ride. Interference will be called if during that ride a majority of judges feel that a fellow competitor has hindered the scoring potential of that surfer with the right of way. Interference can happen in many ways. Here are two examples:

Inside position | Offending surfer

Inside position | Offending surfer

Snaking: When an offending surfer interferes with the original surfer's right of way, causing them to out or lose the wave.

Paddling: If the offending surfer makes contact with or forces the inside surfer to change their line while paddling to catch the wave.

Open

As the 2013 Vans U.S. Open of Surfing competition enters its third day, judges continue the daunting task of culling the field of 300 athletes down to its winners. By the end of the competition Sunday, the panel of judges will have observed more than 9,000 maneuvers and scored more than 3,000 waves over nine days. Here's a look at the various components of the U.S. Open of Surfing and how it is judged:

MANEUVERS

The competition is all about maneuvers, all of which fall into one of two categories: major or minor. The major maneuvers are the most likely to influence the judges' scores. But all maneuvers are categorized by degree of difficulty. The quantity of maneuvers performed doesn't make a high-scoring wave as much as the quality of the overall performance.

1 TAKE OFF: The beginning of a ride when the hands leave the rails and the surfer has made an attempt to stand.
■ No score

WAVES

Although a good wave enhances a surfer's performance, the quality of the wave is not judged, but rather what the surfer does with the wave he or she rides.

Major maneuvers
Difficult
Tube ride
Aerial
Re-entry
Cutback
Power slide
Moderate
Floater
Bottom turn
Top turn

Minor maneuvers
Moderate
Minor examples of major maneuvers
Foam floater
Foam turns
Fade
Mid-face turns
Pump turns
Trim
Foam trim
Easy
Stalling

2 TUBE RIDE: When the surfer disappears behind the curtain of the breaking wave. A clean entry and exit, how deep and length of time in the tube will measure the degree of difficulty.
■ Difficult

SCORING

Each surfer can surf up to 15 waves. Only the top two scores are counted. Each wave is awarded points according to classification. The points are totaled and the two top scores advance.

Poor 0.1 to 1.9   **Fair** 2.0-3.9   **Average** 4.0 to 5.9   **Good** 6.0 to 7.9   **Excellent** 8.0 to 10.0

Wave #	1	2	3	4	5	6	7	8	9	10	11	12	13	14	15	Total	Place
Surfer 1	(6.5)	3.5	4.0	(8.0)	2.0	1.5	6.0									14.5	2nd
Surfer 2	7.0	5.5	(7.5)	(8.5)	1.0	1.3										16.0	1st
Surfer 3	(5.5)	4.5	(5.0)	2.5	2.0	1.2										10.5	4th
Surfer 4	3.0	(4.3)	(6.8)	2.0	0.5											11.1	3rd

SURFERS TO WATCH

KELLY SLATER
The 11-time ASP World Champion is always a crowd pleaser at the U.S. Open. He is currently ranked second.

KOLOHE ANDINO
The San Clemente surfer made it to the semifinals here in 2011. He's strong in aerials, which may work in his favor if surf gets dumpy.

COURTNEY CONLOGUE
The Santa Ana surfer is O.C.'s most outstanding surfer. She won the U.S. Open of Surfing a few years ago and comes in strong with two World Championship Tour victories.

Sources: International Surfing Association; Richard Porta, ASP International head judge; ASP; Artie Castro and U.S. Open of Surfing

Competitive Surfing

What makes a winner.

ARTIST Jeff Goertzen, art director at the *Orange County Register*.

STATEMENT This explains how the judging works at the US Open Surf competition, the biggest surf competition in Southern California. It is held every year in Huntington Beach, lasts nine days, and draws hundreds of thousands of people.

I am fascinated with surfing and, living in the surf capital of the world, I wanted to do a series of surf

judging

RULE OF JUDGING

...ompetitors must perform to the ASP judging key ...ements to maximize their scores. Judges analyze ...e following major elements when scoring waves: ...ommitment and degree of difficulty; innovative ...d progressive maneuvers; combination of major ...aneuvers; variety of maneuvers; speed, power ...d flow. The emphasis of some elements depend ...the location and the conditions on the day, as ...ell as how conditions change during the day.

CRITICAL SECTION

...his is the pocket closest to the curl and is the ...ost difficult area to perform maneuvers. This ...ea has a high scoring potential.

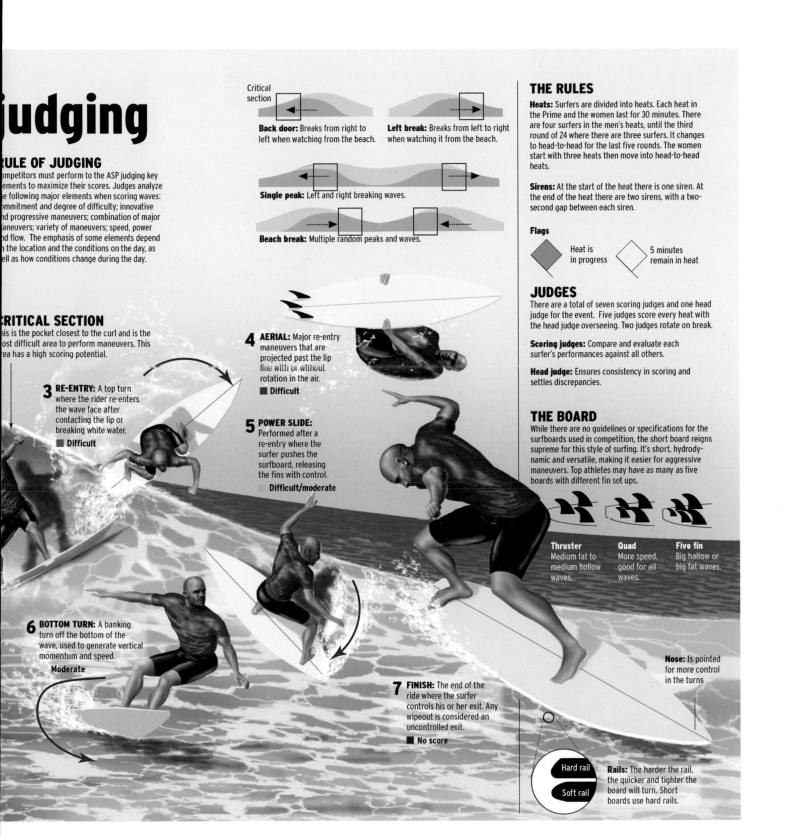

Critical section

Back door: Breaks from right to left when watching from the beach.

Left break: Breaks from left to right when watching it from the beach.

Single peak: Left and right breaking waves.

Beach break: Multiple random peaks and waves.

3 RE-ENTRY: A top turn where the rider re-enters the wave face after contacting the lip or breaking white water.
■ Difficult

4 AERIAL: Major re-entry maneuvers that are projected past the lip line with or without rotation in the air.
■ Difficult

5 POWER SLIDE: Performed after a re-entry where the surfer pushes the surfboard, releasing the fins with control.
■ Difficult/moderate

6 BOTTOM TURN: A banking turn off the bottom of the wave, used to generate vertical momentum and speed.
■ Moderate

7 FINISH: The end of the ride where the surfer controls his or her exit. Any wipeout is considered an uncontrolled exit.
■ No score

THE RULES

Heats: Surfers are divided into heats. Each heat in the Prime and the women last for 30 minutes. There are four surfers in the men's heats, until the third round of 24 where there are three surfers. It changes to head-to-head for the last five rounds. The women start with three heats then move into head-to-head heats.

Sirens: At the start of the heat there is one siren. At the end of the heat there are two sirens, with a two-second gap between each siren.

Flags

Heat is in progress

5 minutes remain in heat

JUDGES

There are a total of seven scoring judges and one head judge for the event. Five judges score every heat with the head judge overseeing. Two judges rotate on break.

Scoring judges: Compare and evaluate each surfer's performances against all others.

Head judge: Ensures consistency in scoring and settles discrepancies.

THE BOARD

While there are no guidelines or specifications for the surfboards used in competition, the short board reigns supreme for this style of surfing. It's short, hydrodynamic and versatile, making it easier for aggressive maneuvers. Top athletes may have as many as five boards with different fin set ups.

Thruster
Medium fat to medium hollow waves.

Quad
More speed, good for all waves.

Five fin
Big hallow or big fat waves.

Nose: Is pointed for more control in the turns

Hard rail

Soft rail

Rails: The harder the rail, the quicker and tighter the board will turn. Short boards use hard rails.

graphics to be published in the *Register*. This was part of the series. One of the skills I learned in illustrating this graphic was how to paint waves. I spent quite a bit of time studying waves at the beach to really understand wave dynamics. It's amazing how the flow of foam textures, the water ripples on the surface, and the translucency of the wave can tell you so much about

hydrodynamics. And you have to really understand that to be able to illustrate the wave and make it feel like it's moving on the page. It's like studying anatomy.

PUBLICATION
Orange County Register (July 2013)

The Shape of the Income Ladder Depends on Where You Live

In the United States, opportunities vary.

The chance a child raised in the bottom quintile rose to the top quintile.

The top quintile is equal to family income of more than **$70,000** for the child by age 30, or more than **$100,000** by age 45.

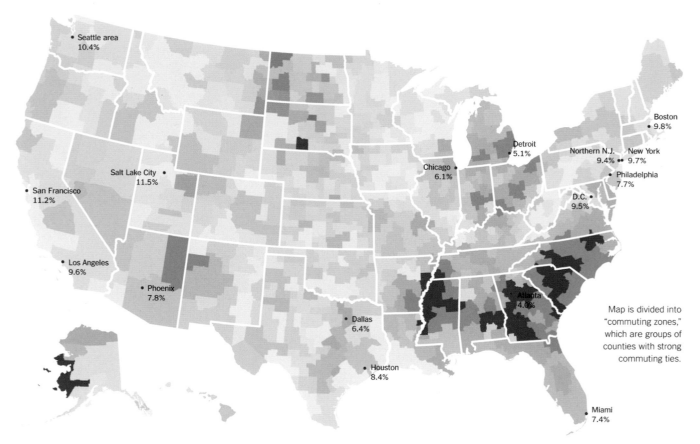

Map is divided into "commuting zones," which are groups of counties with strong commuting ties.

Seattle area
10.4%

Salt Lake City
11.5%

San Francisco
11.2%

Los Angeles
9.6%

Phoenix
7.8%

Dallas
6.4%

Houston
8.4%

Chicago
6.1%

Detroit
5.1%

Atlanta
4.0%

Boston
9.8%

Northern N.J.   New York
9.4%   9.7%

Philadelphia
7.7%

D.C.
9.5%

Miami
7.4%

ARTISTS Shan Carter, Amanda Cox, and Alicia Parlapiano, graphics editors at the *New York Times*.

STATEMENT Based on millions of anonymous earnings records, researchers at Harvard and Berkeley were able to connect the incomes of adults in their thirties to their parents' income when they were children. Their research showed, for the first time, how economic mobility varies across the United States. Among the poor children raised in the oil fields of North Dakota, 1 in 3 had risen to the top 20 percent as adults. For poor children raised in the Memphis area, that figure was 1 in 40.

The geographic disparity is striking, but we also wanted to reveal patterns across income. For example, growing up poor in Salt Lake City is about the same as growing up middle class in Atlanta, at least in terms of your chances of reaching the top. And while the Los Angeles area is one of the best for poor children, rich children raised there are less likely to stay in that quintile than the rich children raised in Chicago or New York.

PUBLICATION *New York Times* (July 2013)

The Best and Worst Major Areas for Poor, Middle-Class and Rich Children

The chance of ending up in the **top quintile** for a child raised in the . . .

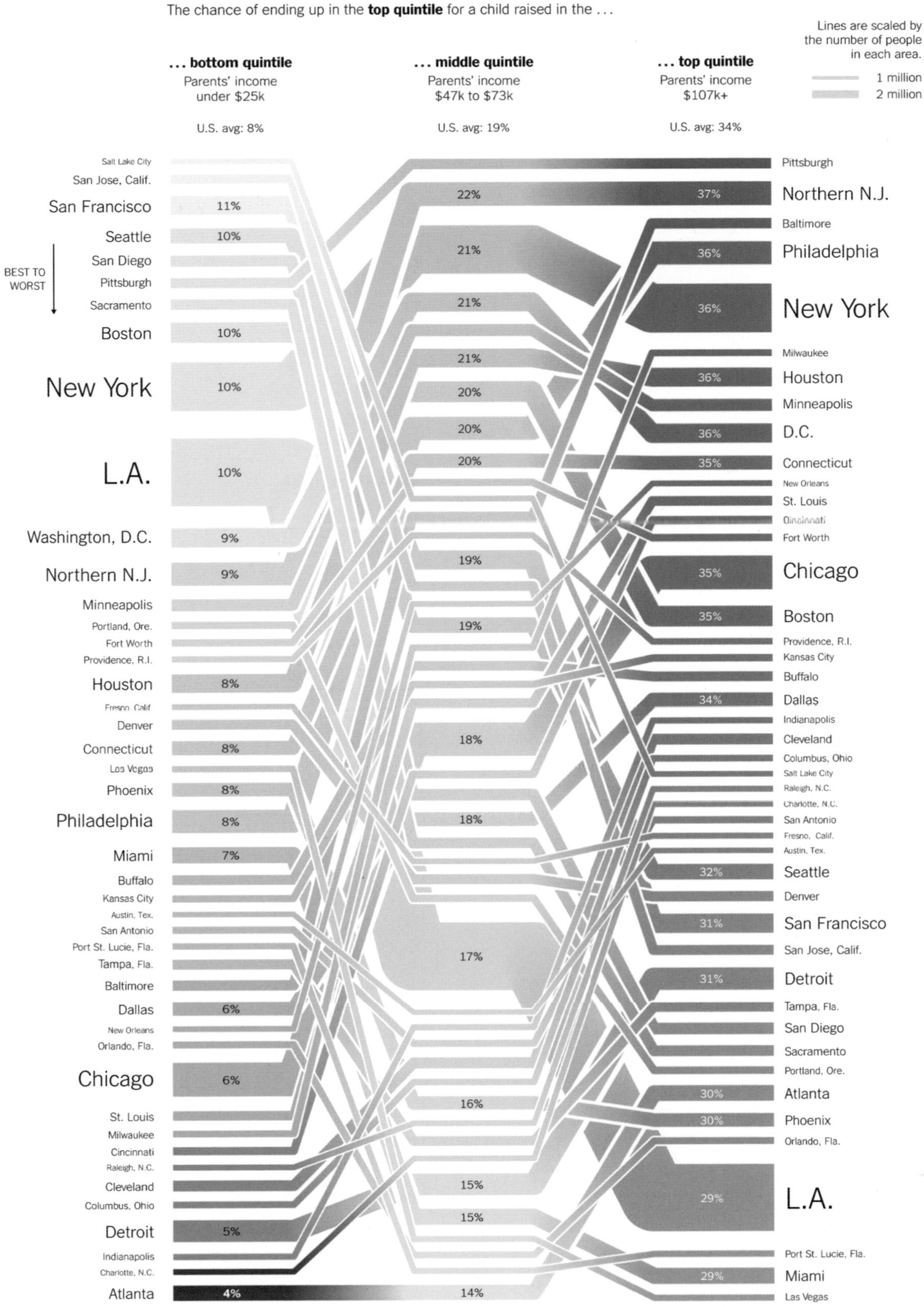

Lines are scaled by the number of people in each area.
1 million
2 million
. . . bottom quintile
Parents' income under $25k
U.S. avg: 8%
. . . middle quintile
Parents' income $47k to $73k
U.S. avg: 19%
. . . top quintile
Parents' income $107k+
U.S. avg: 34%
BEST TO WORST
Salt Lake City
San Jose, Calif.
San Francisco 11%
Seattle 10%
San Diego
Pittsburgh
Sacramento
Boston 10%
New York 10%
L.A. 10%
Washington, D.C. 9%
Northern N.J. 9%
Minneapolis
Portland, Ore.
Fort Worth
Providence, R.I.
Houston 8%
Fresno, Calif.
Denver
Connecticut 8%
Las Vegas
Phoenix 8%
Philadelphia 8%
Miami 7%
Buffalo
Kansas City
Austin, Tex.
San Antonio
Port St. Lucie, Fla.
Tampa, Fla.
Baltimore
Dallas 6%
New Orleans
Orlando, Fla.
Chicago 6%
St. Louis
Milwaukee
Cincinnati
Raleigh, N.C.
Cleveland
Columbus, Ohio
Detroit 5%
Indianapolis
Charlotte, N.C.
Atlanta 4%
22%
21%
21%
21%
20%
20%
20%
19%
19%
18%
18%
17%
16%
15%
15%
14%
Pittsburgh
Northern N.J. 37%
Baltimore
Philadelphia 36%
New York 36%
Milwaukee
Houston 36%
Minneapolis
D.C. 36%
Connecticut 35%
New Orleans
St. Louis
Cincinnati
Fort Worth
Chicago 35%
Boston 35%
Providence, R.I.
Kansas City
Buffalo
Dallas 34%
Indianapolis
Cleveland
Columbus, Ohio
Salt Lake City
Raleigh, N.C.
Charlotte, N.C.
San Antonio
Fresno, Calif.
Austin, Tex.
Seattle 32%
Denver
San Francisco 31%
San Jose, Calif.
Detroit 31%
Tampa, Fla.
San Diego
Sacramento
Portland, Ore.
Atlanta 30%
Phoenix 30%
Orlando, Fla.
L.A. 29%
Port St. Lucie, Fla.
Miami 29%
Las Vegas

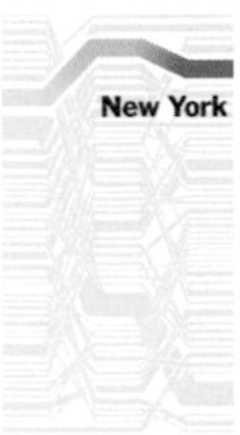

New York

Children raised at any income level in the New York City area were more likely to end up in the top quintile than children raised at the same income level in most major cities.

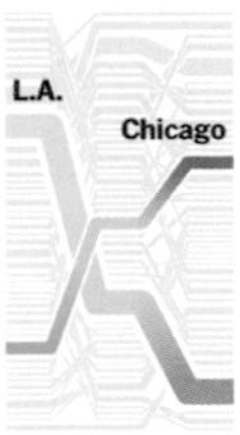

L.A.
Chicago

Lower-class children raised in Los Angeles did better than the average for such children, while upper-class children did worse. The opposite was true in Chicago.

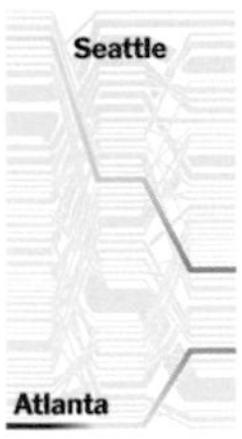

Seattle
Atlanta

Seattle and Atlanta had similar average incomes, but children raised in Seattle were more likely to reach the top. The biggest difference was for poor children.

Source: Raj Chetty and Nathaniel Hendren, Harvard, and Patrick Kline and Emmanuel Saez, U.C. Berkeley, "The Economic Impacts of Tax Expenditures: Evidence from Spatial Variation Across the U.S."

ARTIST Valentina D'Efilippo, a multidisciplinary designer, art director, and author based in London.

STATEMENT "Field of Commemoration" is part of *The Infographic History of the World,* a book that narrates history through data visualization. This particular infographic visualizes nearly 95 million casualties of war from the twentieth century. Data made available by the Polynational War Memorial make clear that war was a near-constant characteristic in the last century, allowing for just two years of peace. The remembrance poppy commemorates soldiers who have died in war. Each poppy in the diagram depicts a war of the last century. The stem grows from the year when the war started. The poppy flowers in the year the war ended. Its size reflects the number of deaths.

The sadness of the subject is represented here in a poetic light: the composition suggests movement, calm, and life, projecting a serious yet gentle light onto the subject of war and death. Given the magnitude of war's toll, this visualization only considers conflicts exceeding 10,000 deaths — unfortunately, in the static form, it is still not feasible to label every conflict. The aim was to provide a snapshot of the last century, revealing patterns in the timing, duration, involvement, and human toll of war.

PUBLICATION *The Infographic History of the World,* Harper Collins, London (June 2013)

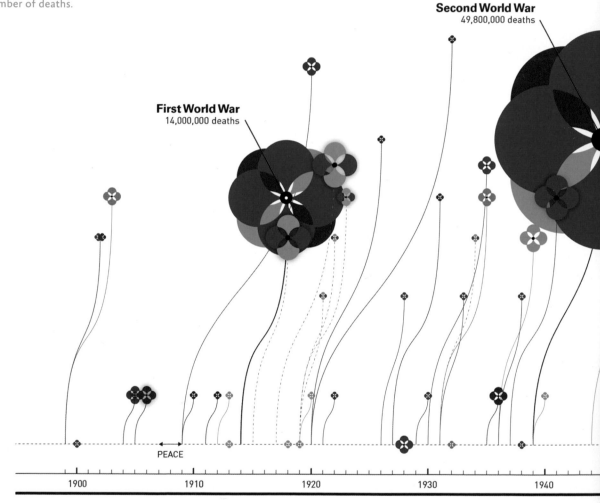

Second World War
49,800,000 deaths

First World War
14,000,000 deaths

PEACE

1900   1910   1920   1930   1940

POPPY DIAGRAM

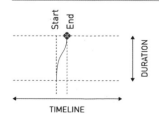

Start
End
DURATION
TIMELINE

The remembrance poppy commemorates soldiers who have died in war. Each poppy in the diagram depicts a war of the last century (with more than 10,000 deaths). The stem grows from the year when the war started. The poppy flowers in the year the war ended. Its size shows the number of deaths.

Fields of Commemoration

The casualties of twentieth-century war.

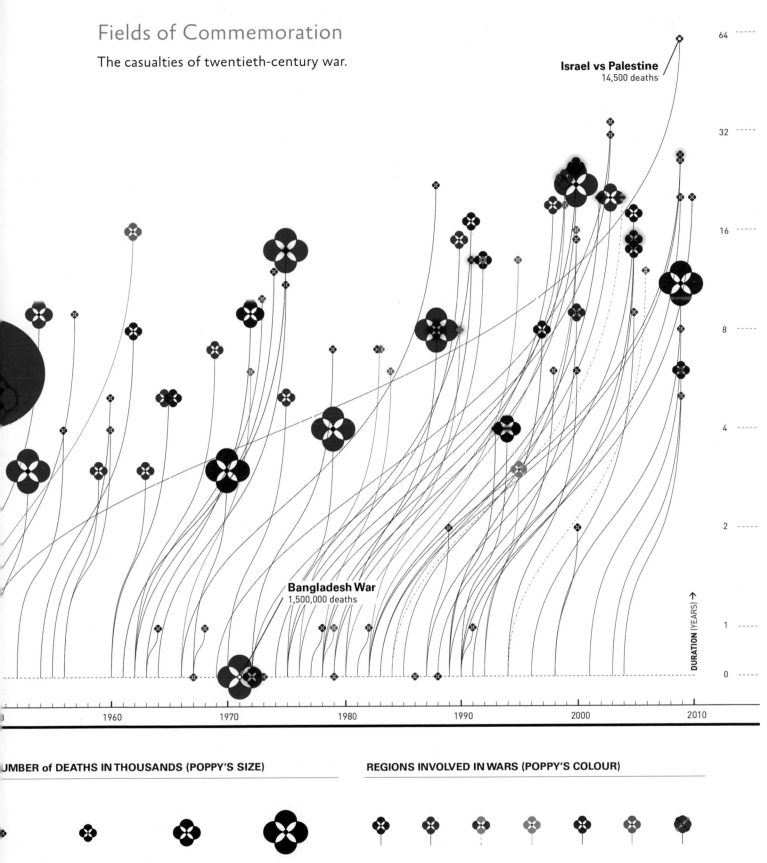

Israel vs Palestine
14,500 deaths

64
32
16
8
4
2
1
0

DURATION (YEARS) →

Bangladesh War
1,500,000 deaths

1960   1970   1980   1990   2000   2010

UMBER of DEATHS IN THOUSANDS (POPPY'S SIZE)

–99   100–499   500–999   1,000–3,000

REGIONS INVOLVED IN WARS (POPPY'S COLOUR)

Africa   Asia   Asia/Europe   Europe   N. America   S. America   Global

87

The Material World

A Wheel of 65 Cheeses

Categorized and delicious.

ARTIST Pop Chart Lab

STATEMENT A charting of 65 delightful cheeses from
around the world, assembled into one wondrous wheel.
The cheeses are broken down by the animal that produced
the luscious milk, and then by the texture of the resultant
cheese, forming a cornucopia of cheese that ranges from
the mild to the stinky and from the rock hard to the silky
smooth.

PUBLICATION *PopChartLab.com* (June 2013)

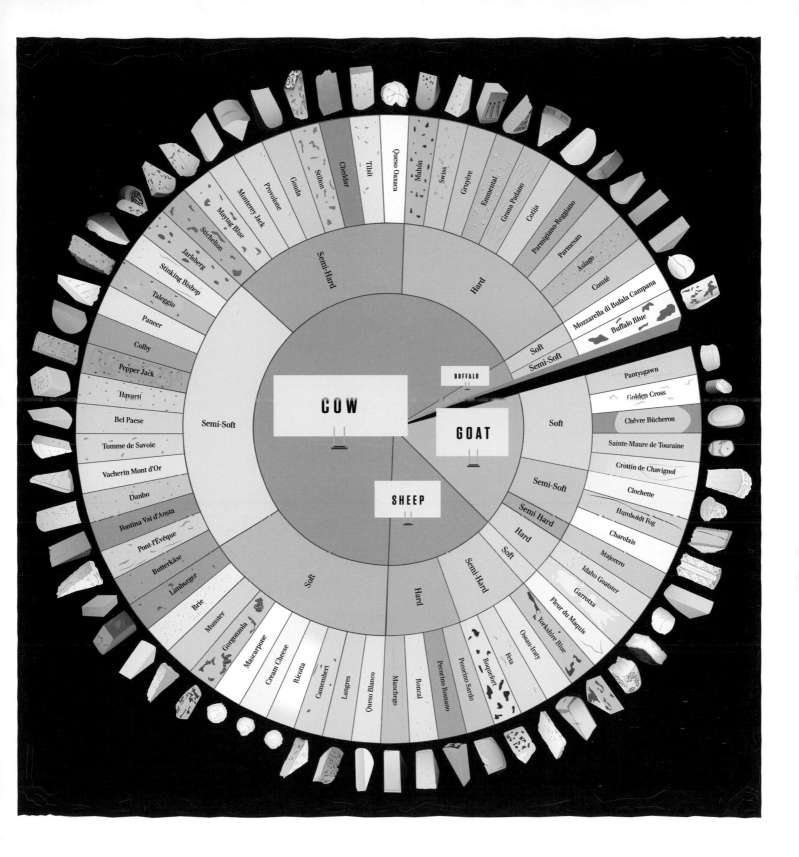

The CHARTED CHEESE WHEEL

COSMIC JOURNEYS

Humans have traveled to the far shores of the solar system through the eyes of robotic explorers—spacecraft, probes, and rovers that have sent back progressively more astonishing data and images. The colored lines illustrate nearly 200 unmanned missions since 1958: flybys, orbits, soft landings, and intentional crashes, as well as some of the failures. No human has left low Earth orbit since 1972, when Apollo 17 made the last of NASA's nine manned missions to the moon. But odds are we will. A privately funded mission aims to have a man and woman circle Mars in 2018.

SUN
8 missions

MO
72 missi

20
20
19
19

19

19

MERCURY
2 missions

Messenger

Heading to Mercury,
Mariner 10 flew near
Venus in 1974, taking
images and getting
a gravity assist to
speed its trip

VENUS
40 missions

2010
2000
1980
1970

Earth
flyby
(twice)

Earth
gravity
assist

Venus
flybys

Venus gravity assist
(twice)

SUN
MERCURY
EARTH
MARS
JUPITER
SATURN
URANUS
NEPTUNE
P
VENUS
ASTEROID
BELT
NEW
HORIZONS
KUIPER E

BILLIONS
OF MILES ▶ 0

1
2
3

YOU
US
MATERIAL WORLD
INTERACTIVE

To the Moon and Beyond

All unmanned space missions since 1958.

ARTISTS Graphic by Sean McNaughton, senior graphics editor; production by Matthew Twombly, graphics design specialist; text by Jane Vessels, senior text editor/graphics, at *National Geographic.* Art by Samuel Velasco, 5W Infographics. Research by Amanda Hobbs, freelance researcher.

STATEMENT No human has left low Earth orbit since 1972, when Apollo 17 made the last trip to the moon. This graphic shows all unmanned space missions since 1958 by country of origin, from the moon to the Voyager missions out of the solar system and into interstellar space. The graphic includes failed missions and flybys.

PUBLICATION *National Geographic* (updated June 2013)

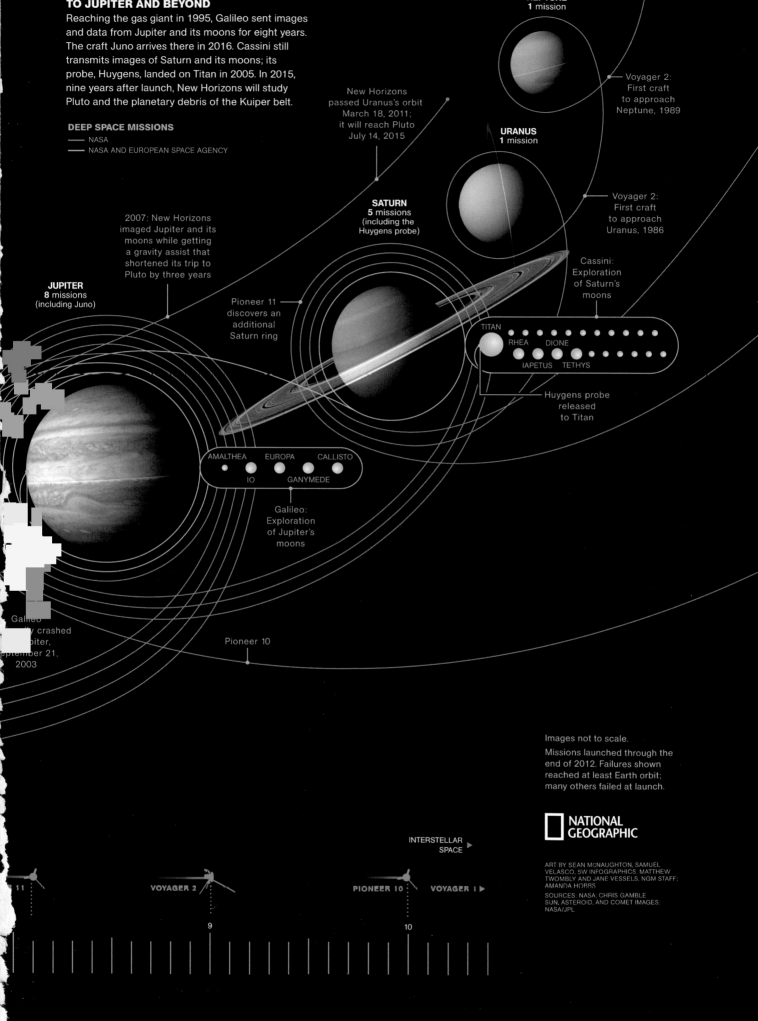

THE INNER SOLAR SYSTEM

Soviets reached the moon first, deliberately crashing Luna 2 into the surface in 1959. NASA made the first successful trip to Venus with the Mariner 2 flyby in 1962; Mariner 4 sent images from Mars in 1965. NASA's current Messenger mission is the first to orbit and map Mercury. A fleet of solar missions monitors the sun's activity—and its impact on Earth.

MISSIONS TO INNER SOLAR SYSTEM

SUCCESS FAILURE
——	——	NASA
		U.S.S.R./RUSSIA
——	——	EUROPEAN SPACE AGENCY
		JAPAN
——	——	CHINA
——		INDIA

ASTEROIDS AND COMETS

On its way to Jupiter, in 1991, Galileo took the first close-up images of an asteroid (Gaspra) and found the first asteroid satellite (Dactyl, which orbits Ida). NASA's Dawn will reach the asteroid/dwarf planet Ceres in 2015. The European Space Agency's Rosetta probe will try to land on a comet in 2014.

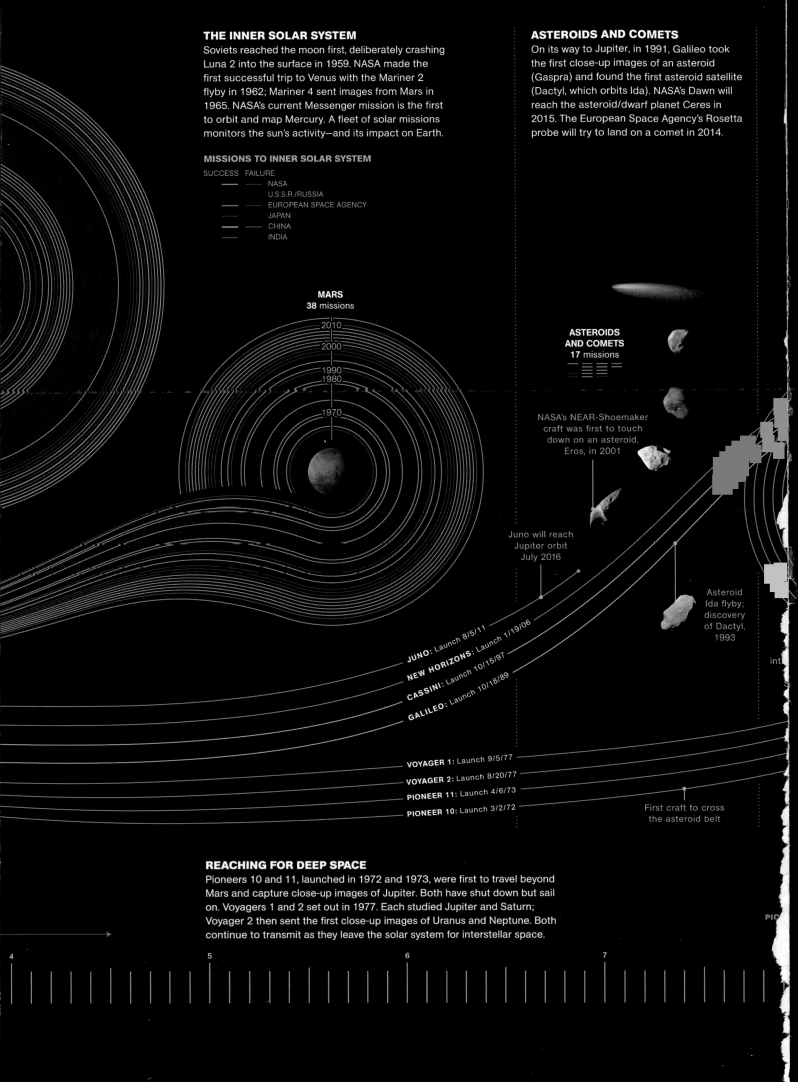

MARS
38 missions

2010
2000
1990
1980

1970

**ASTEROIDS
AND COMETS
17** missions

NASA's NEAR-Shoemaker craft was first to touch down on an asteroid, Eros, in 2001

Juno will reach Jupiter orbit July 2016

Asteroid Ida flyby; discovery of Dactyl, 1993

int

JUNO: Launch 8/5/11
NEW HORIZONS: Launch 1/19/06
CASSINI: Launch 10/15/97
GALILEO: Launch 10/18/89

VOYAGER 1: Launch 9/5/77
VOYAGER 2: Launch 8/20/77
PIONEER 11: Launch 4/6/73
PIONEER 10: Launch 3/2/72

First craft to cross the asteroid belt

REACHING FOR DEEP SPACE

Pioneers 10 and 11, launched in 1972 and 1973, were first to travel beyond Mars and capture close-up images of Jupiter. Both have shut down but sail on. Voyagers 1 and 2 set out in 1977. Each studied Jupiter and Saturn; Voyager 2 then sent the first close-up images of Uranus and Neptune. Both continue to transmit as they leave the solar system for interstellar space.

PIO

4   5   6   7

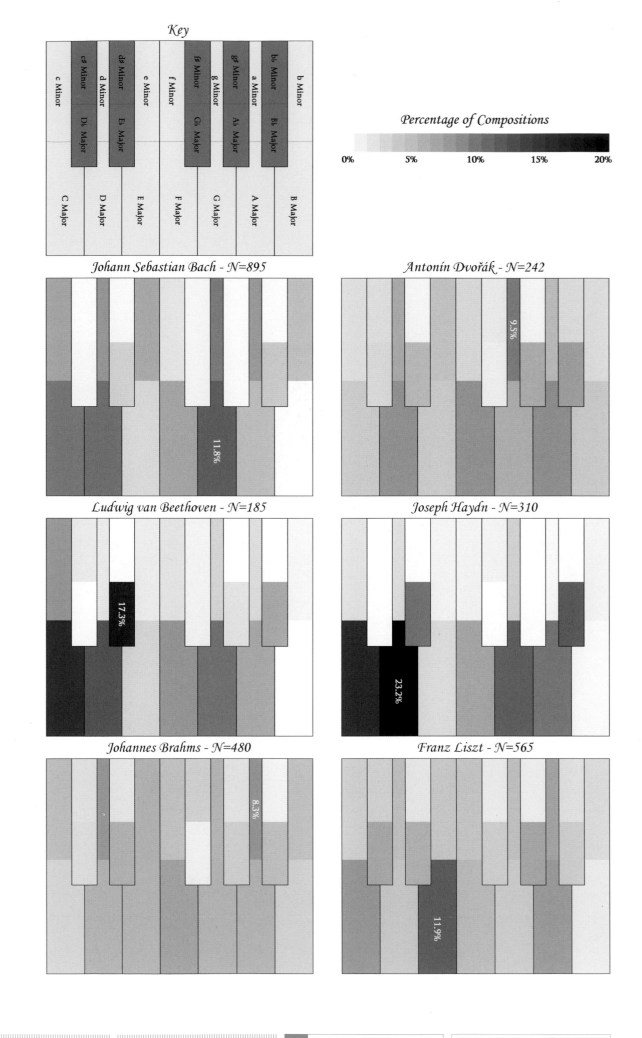

Key

Percentage of Compositions

0%   5%   10%   15%   20%

Johann Sebastian Bach - N=895

Antonín Dvořák - N=242

Ludwig van Beethoven - N=185

Joseph Haydn - N=310

Johannes Brahms - N=480

Franz Liszt - N=565

Felix Mendelssohn - N=555

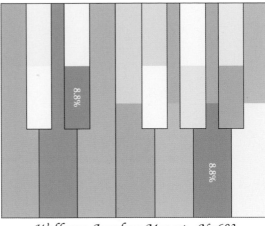

8.8%

8.8%

Wolfgang Amadeus Mozart - N=683

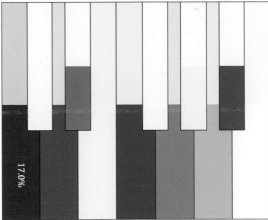

17.0%

Sergei Rachmaninoff - N=236

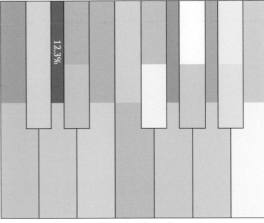

12.3%

Pyotr Ilyich Tchaikovsky - N=380

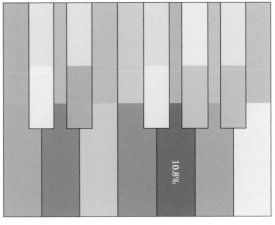

10.8%

Composers

Favorite keys of classical music.

ARTIST Seth Kadish, data scientist, Portland, OR

STATEMENT The infographic is a series of heat maps—one for each classical composer—that highlights trends in the preferred keys in which they wrote their scores. The heat maps are shaped like pianos, with minor keys represented on the top halves of notes, and major keys on the bottom halves. Darker shades correspond to higher percentages of pieces composed in that key. The values were derived from a database of thousands of scores; the number of pieces used for each composer is shown by the N-value next to the name.

I thought composers would prefer key signatures with fewer accidentals, which turned out to be true. I was also curious as to whether the musical period would affect the distribution of keys used. Beethoven, Haydn, and Mozart all show strong preferences for a specific key. Other composers, particularly Dvorak, Brahms, and Mendelssohn, show less favoritism; these three had no keys associated with more than 10 percent of their compositions. All three composers whose most-used key was minor were from the Romantic era. The least-used key across the board was G-sharp minor, with Brahms using it most (in only 1.5 percent of his compositions). Rachmaninoff was the only composer to produce more pieces in minor keys than major keys; Haydn and Mozart most frequently wrote in major keys.

I took piano lessons for twelve years. My mom worked very hard getting me to practice, and I really appreciate her efforts, so this was designed as a tribute to her.

PUBLICATION *Vizual-Statistix. tumblr.com* (March 2013)

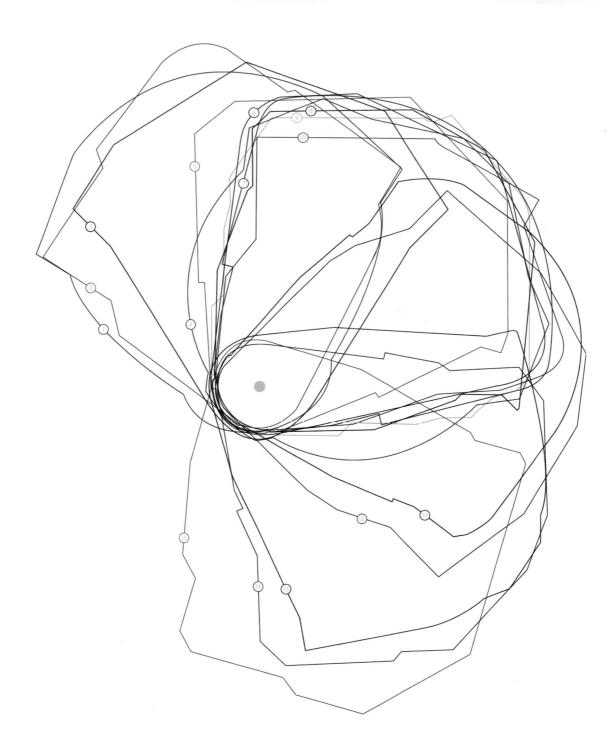

AMERICAN LEAGUE BASEBALL PARKS

TO SCALE AND COMPASS ORIENTATION

1 BLUE JAYS/ROGERS CENTRE   2 ASTROS/MINUTE MAID PARK   3 INDIANS/PROGRESSIVE FIELD   4 ATHLETICS/OAKLAND COLISEUM   5 ORIOLES/CAMDEN YARDS
6 ANGELS/ANGEL STADIUM   7 ROYALS/KAUFFMAN STADIUM   8 MARINERS/SAFECO FIELD   9 RAYS/TROPICANA FIELD   10 REDSOX/FENWAY PARK
11 YANKEES/YANKEE STADIUM   12 TWINS/TARGET FIELD   13 WHITE SOX/U S CELLULAR FIELD   14 RANGERS/BALLPARK IN ARLINGTON   15 TIGERS/COMERICA PARK

Baseball Parks

Major League parks, to scale
and by compass orientation.

ARTIST Jeremy Huggins, graphic
designer, Chicago, IL

STATEMENT The posters show all
Major League Baseball fields, to scale and
by compass orientation Baseball fields
come in all different shapes and sizes,
unlike the fields, courts, and rinks of the
other major sports. And they all face
east, generally, to prevent the setting

sun interfering with the hitter's vision.
When you place all the fields on top of
one another, hinged on home plate, the
similarities and the differences all become strikingly clear. It transforms into
abstract art, a spirograph-like explosion
of lines that is both chaotic and ordered.

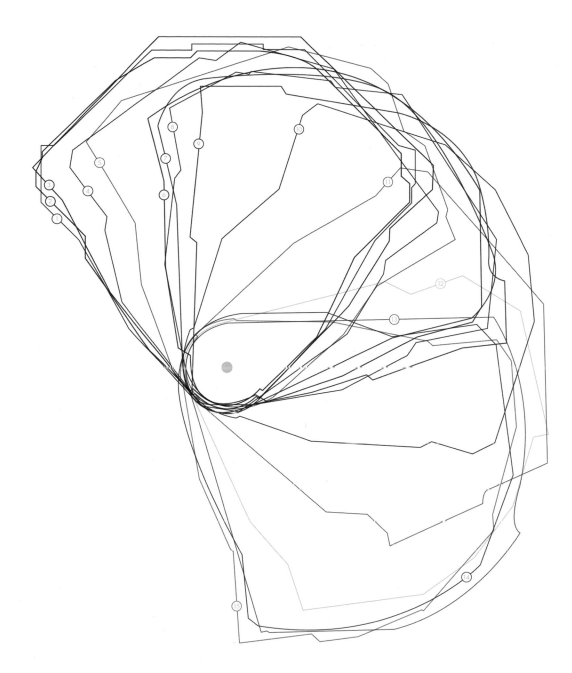

NATIONAL LEAGUE BASEBALL PARKS

TO SCALE AND COMPASS ORIENTATION

1 DIAMONDBACKS/CHASE FIELD   2 PADRES/PETCO PARK   3 ROCKIES/COORS FIELD   4 PHILLIES/CITIZENS BANK PARK   5 METS/CITI FIELD
6 BRAVES/TURNER FIELD   7 DODGERS/DODGER STADIUM   8 NATIONALS/NATIONALS PARK   9 CUBS/WRIGLEY FIELD   10 CARDINALS/BUSCH STADIUM
11 GIANTS/AT&T PARK   12 PIRATES/PNC PARK   13 MARLINS/MARLINS PARK   14 REDS/GREAT AMERICAN BALL PARK   15 BREWERS/MILLER PARK

This poster set falls into a series of personal projects I've worked on that, in hindsight, seem to be pushing back against many trends in recent infographics work. It's easy to recognize those long-scrolling images, sometimes a bit skeevy-seeming in a factual sense, all in the service of getting page views on the web. I made a conscious effort to take the parts of infographics that I loved—the mash-up of information—but tear away some of the tropes and visual clutter. I wanted to force people who roll their eyes at any mention of "infographics" to stop and look, to see the possibilities in using graphic design as the reason instead of page clicks.

PUBLICATION *JeremyHuggins.com* (February 2013)

Preserving Mount Rushmore in Cyberspace

Recorded by high-speed laser scanners for safekeeping.

Generating a point cloud
Bouncing light off rock, 3-D scanners measured points less than a quarter inch apart to create a data set, or point cloud. Colors represent the intensity of reflection from the surface.
Meshing
The point cloud contains about 1.3 billion data points. A triangulated surface mesh is made by connecting them.
Re-creating Rushmore
Sculptors took 14 years to carve the presidential heads on Mount Rushmore in South Dakota, finishing in 1941. In 2010 imaging specialists with high-speed laser scanners covered nearly every inch of the surface in 16 days—the first step in making an identical 3-D digital model, a new tool in the conservation of cultural treasures.
JOHN BAXTER, TODD JAMES, JOHN TOMANIO, AND MATTHEW TWOMBLY, NGM STAFF; AMANDA HOBBS
SOURCES: CENTRE FOR DIGITAL DOCUMENTATION AND VISUALISATION; CYARK; DIGITAL DESIGN STUDIO, GLASGOW SCHOOL OF ART; FOURFRONT DESIGN; HISTORIC SCOTLAND; NATIONAL PARK SERVICE; RESPEC; WYSS ASSOCIATES

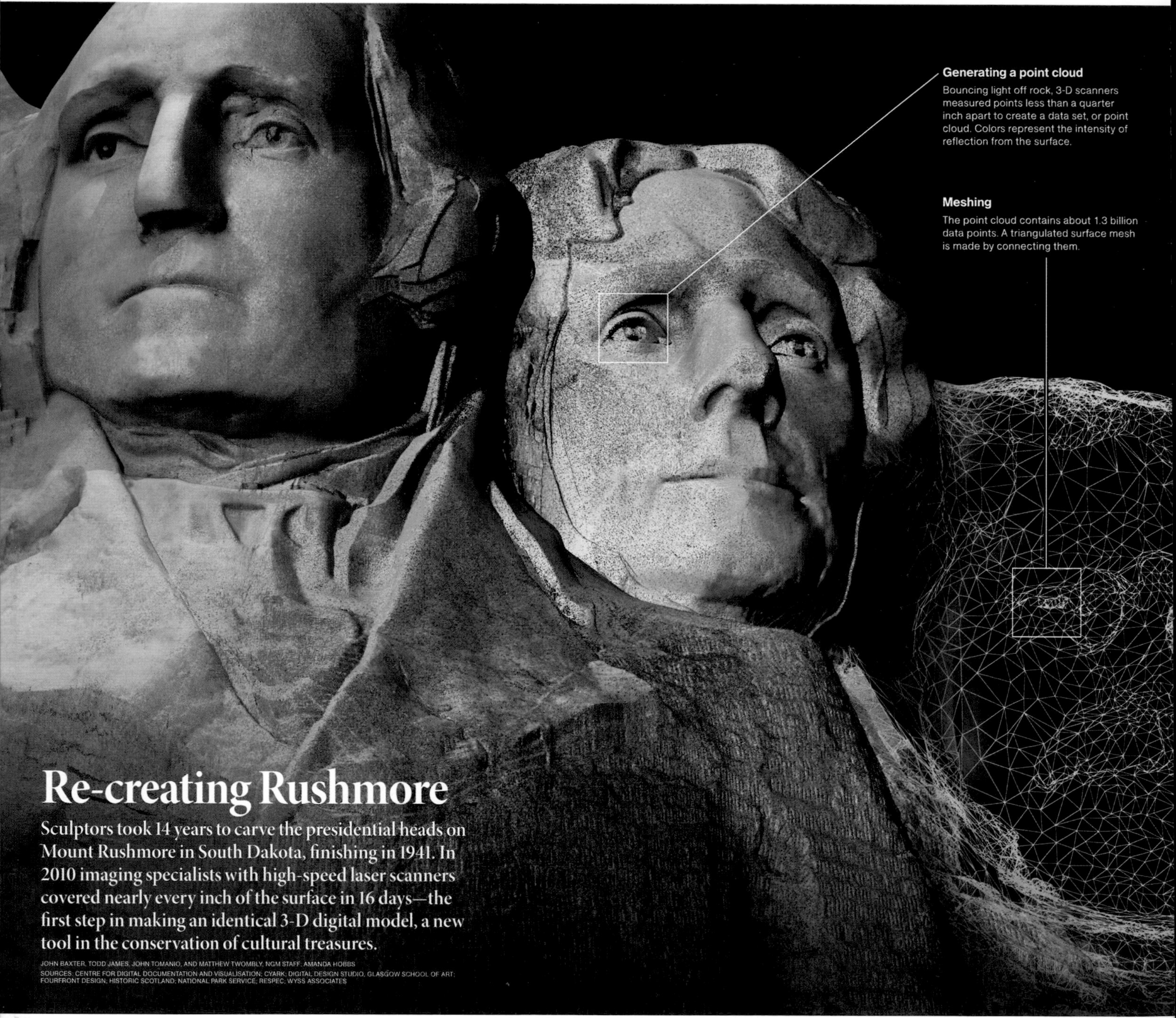

ARTISTS Design by John Baxter, senior design editor; photo editing by Todd James, senior photo editor; graphics by John Tomanio, senior graphics editor, and Matt Twombly, graphic design specialist, at *National Geographic.*

3-D modeling

Software aligns points in the mesh with the same points in digital photographs, then applies the photos like a skin over the mesh. On the CyArk website visitors can navigate the 3-D simulation to gaze into Abraham Lincoln's eye.

Scanner locations shown on a 3-D digital model

Suspended by ropes
● Tripod mounted
○ Tripod mounted; placement hidden from view

Taking the measure of a monument

Taking laser scans of giant sculpted heads on a rubble-strewn mountainside posed challenges. Besides dealing with fog, rain, snow, and hail, specialists had to rope equipment into position to scan hard-to-reach places like chins and eye sockets. Circles show scanner locations, from tricky places on the faces to the easiest ones, on top of the heads.

TWO TYPES OF SCANNERS DO THE JOB

For part of the data gathering, specialists used two tripod-mounted scanners made for long-distance, large-scale measurements. The scanners were positioned above the monument and on the talus slope.

To record features like eyes, the imaging team lowered a short-range scanner by ropes and aimed it at their targets. The remotely operated scanner captured data up to ten times faster than the stationary ones.

TRIPOD-MOUNTED SCANNER

ROPE-RIGGED SCANNER

STATEMENT High-speed laser scanners are being used by preservationists in a global effort to document threatened historical treasures and monuments. The graphic describes the steps used to create a 3D model of Mount Rushmore, in South Dakota, using an array of tripod-mounted and short-range rope-rigged scanners. The scanners capture a high-resolution point cloud model that is then converted into mesh polygons with 3D software and finally skinned with photographs to provide realistic texture and light.

PUBLICATION *National Geographic*
(December 2013)

Earthquake Concrete

Strength by design.

ARTISTS Art by Raoul Rañoa; writing and research by Rong-Gong Lin II, Rosanna Xia, and Doug Smith; and direction by Len DeGroot at the *Los Angeles Times*.

STATEMENT It's difficult to tell how strong or brittle a concrete column may be—or how well it could withstand an earthquake—from its appearance. This graphic looks inside two types of concrete columns, visualizes key differences between the two, and explains how those differences could impact a building's structural integrity.

Reporters Rong-Gong Lin II, Rosanna Xia, and Doug Smith, along with artist Raoul Rañoa, did extensive research and interviewed structural engineers from UCLA, Caltech, and elsewhere. Our goal was to present the complicated engineering in a simply drawn fashion that could be quickly understood. Our analysis found that about 1,000 older concrete buildings could be at risk of collapse and that many building owners simply did not know if their structures could withstand an earthquake.

PUBLICATION *Los Angeles Times* (October 2013)

Weak versus strong concrete columns

Steel support is a key factor in the strength of a concrete building.

Brittle concrete column	**Stronger concrete column**
Too little steel allows concrete to break apart from the column.	A flexible column has more steel reinforcing bars to keep the concrete in place during shaking.

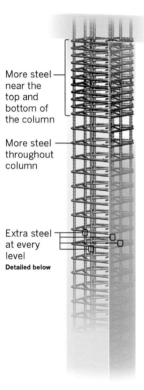

No extra steel at the top and bottom of columns.

Less internal steel
Detailed below

More steel near the top and bottom of the column

More steel throughout column

Extra steel at every level
Detailed below

Poor steel design
This steel reinforcement configuration can easily bend apart during shaking.

Stronger steel design
A second square steel bar is added, and the ends are curved at about 135 degrees to keep the steel in place.

Extra vertical steel   *Second steel bar*

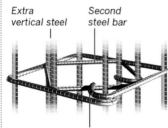

Curved steel loops

During an earthquake

Cracks form in both concrete columns. In the poorly reinforced column at left, concrete chunks begin to fall. The well-reinforced column remains intact.

The brittle column begins to collapse as more chunks of concrete fall. Interlaced steel reinforcing bars hold the concrete in place in the strong column.

The weight of the building deforms the steel bars of the weak column, allowing the remaining concrete to explode out. The well-reinforced column bends sideways but retains its strength.

Source: UCLA engineering professor John Wallace

ARTISTS   Graphic by Moritz Stefaner, bee illustrations
by Jillian Walters, and art direction by *Scientific American*'s
Jen Christiansen.

STATEMENT   The graphic is based on a study by Laura Burkle
and colleagues on the change in bee-plant interactions over
the course of 120 years. By reproducing a study from the late
nineteenth century, the researchers were able to compare
not only the bee populations, but also changes in the plants
they interact with. The results are staggering. Half of the bee
species could not be observed anymore, and almost 2/3 of bee-
plant interactions were lost. But life proves resilient as well:
in 121 instances, Burkle observed bees attending flowers they
had not pollinated in the past.

The graphic represents this dynamic network in a series of
small multiples. Read on a macro level, the graphic illustrates
the drastic demise in wild bee population. Yet, on a micro level,
the fate and individual "plant profile" of each bee species can
be read with ease. In this case, moving away from traditional
network representations, with lines or matrix arrangements,
was key to untangling the complexity of the dataset.

PUBLICATION   *Scientific American* (December 2013)

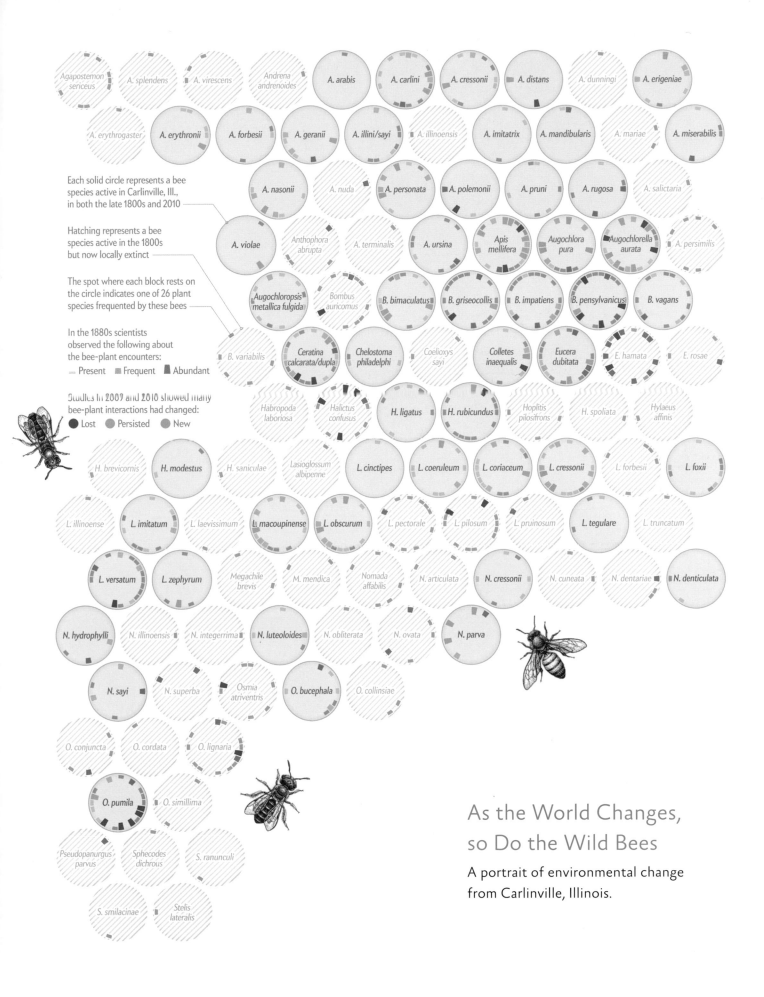

Each solid circle represents a bee species active in Carlinville, Ill., in both the late 1800s and 2010

Hatching represents a bee species active in the 1800s but now locally extinct

The spot where each block rests on the circle indicates one of 26 plant species frequented by these bees

In the 1880s scientists observed the following about the bee-plant encounters:
— Present   ▪ Frequent   ▮ Abundant

Studies in 2009 and 2010 showed many bee-plant interactions had changed:
● Lost   ● Persisted   ● New

As the World Changes, so Do the Wild Bees

A portrait of environmental change from Carlinville, Illinois.

In Harm's Way

Tornadoes have touched down in every state. But big ones happen most regularly each spring in Tornado Alley, from Texas to the northern Great Plains. Here warm, moist air from the Gulf of Mexico collides with fast-moving cold, dry air from the Rockies, generating strong wind shear and atmospheric instability—key elements of tornadic thunderstorms.

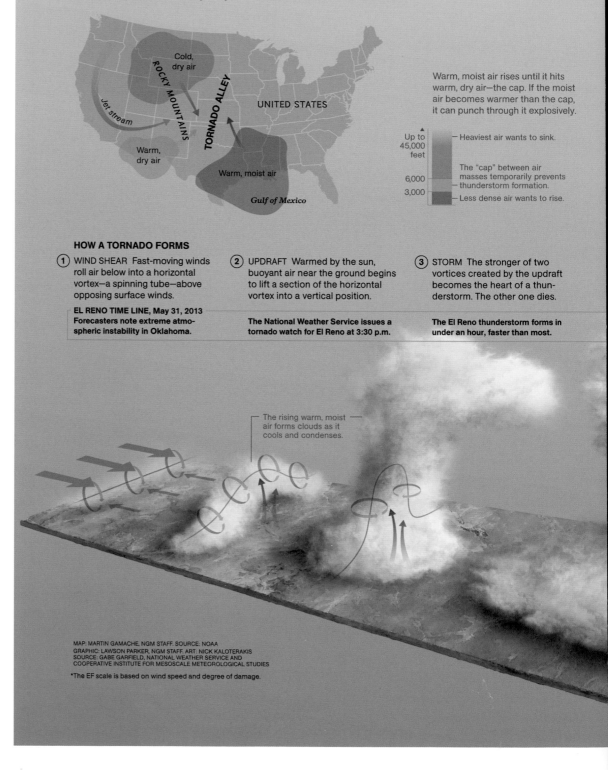

Cold, dry air

ROCKY MOUNTAINS

Jet stream

Warm, dry air

TORNADO ALLEY

UNITED STATES

Warm, moist air

Gulf of Mexico

Warm, moist air rises until it hits warm, dry air—the cap. If the moist air becomes warmer than the cap, it can punch through it explosively.

Up to 45,000 feet — Heaviest air wants to sink.

The "cap" between air masses temporarily prevents thunderstorm formation.

6,000

3,000 — Less dense air wants to rise.

HOW A TORNADO FORMS

1 WIND SHEAR Fast-moving winds roll air below into a horizontal vortex—a spinning tube—above opposing surface winds.

EL RENO TIME LINE, May 31, 2013 Forecasters note extreme atmospheric instability in Oklahoma.

2 UPDRAFT Warmed by the sun, buoyant air near the ground begins to lift a section of the horizontal vortex into a vertical position.

The National Weather Service issues a tornado watch for El Reno at 3:30 p.m.

3 STORM The stronger of two vortices created by the updraft becomes the heart of a thunderstorm. The other one dies.

The El Reno thunderstorm forms in under an hour, faster than most.

The rising warm, moist air forms clouds as it cools and condenses.

MAP: MARTIN GAMACHE, NGM STAFF. SOURCE: NOAA
GRAPHIC: LAWSON PARKER, NGM STAFF. ART: NICK KALOTERAKIS
SOURCE: GABE GARFIELD, NATIONAL WEATHER SERVICE AND
COOPERATIVE INSTITUTE FOR MESOSCALE METEOROLOGICAL STUDIES

*The EF scale is based on wind speed and degree of damage.

The Biggest Storm

A deadly tornado.

ARTISTS Graphic by Lawson Parker, graphics editor; map by Martin Gamache, senior editor, cartography; and art by Nick Kaloterakis at *National Geographic*.

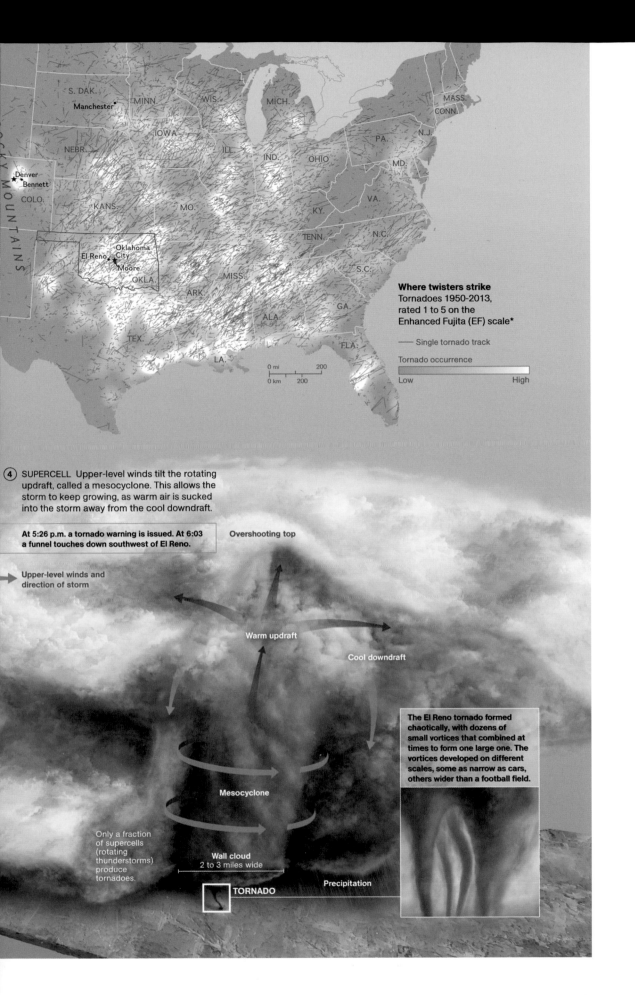

Where twisters strike
Tornadoes 1950-2013, rated 1 to 5 on the Enhanced Fujita (EF) scale*

—— Single tornado track

Tornado occurrence

Low   High

0 mi   200
0 km   200

(4) SUPERCELL Upper-level winds tilt the rotating updraft, called a mesocyclone. This allows the storm to keep growing, as warm air is sucked into the storm away from the cool downdraft.

At 5:26 p.m. a tornado warning is issued. At 6:03 a funnel touches down southwest of El Reno.

Overshooting top

Upper-level winds and direction of storm

Warm updraft

Cool downdraft

Mesocyclone

Only a fraction of supercells (rotating thunderstorms) produce tornadoes.

Wall cloud
2 to 3 miles wide

TORNADO

Precipitation

The El Reno tornado formed chaotically, with dozens of small vortices that combined at times to form one large one. The vortices developed on different scales, some as narrow as cars, others wider than a football field.

CONTINUED

THE TORNADO

6:03:49 P.M.
The twister is unusually wide from the second it touches down—a half mile across. Multiple vortices appear and disappear, confusing chasers as the tornado moves south-southeast.

6:09
Rain wraps around the tornado, hiding it. Accelerating to 40 to 50 miles an hour, the storm turns east, forming subvortices around the main funnel; some last only seconds.

6:15
Just missing El Reno's airport, the tornado pauses, possibly looping in its track, then reorganizes into a single large vortex that rapidly expands and surges eastward.

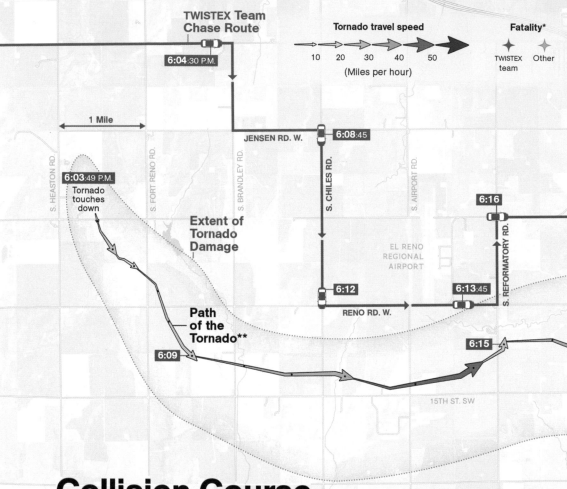

TWISTEX Team Chase Route

6:04:30 P.M.

Tornado travel speed

10   20   30   40   50

(Miles per hour)

Fatality*

TWISTEX team   Other

1 Mile

JENSEN RD. W.   6:08:45

S. HEASTON RD.

S. FORT RENO RD.

S. BRANDLEY RD.

S. CHILES RD.

S. AIRPORT RD.

6:16

S. REFORMATORY RD.

S. COUNTRY CLUB RD.

6:03:49 P.M.
Tornado touches down

Extent of Tornado Damage

EL RENO REGIONAL AIRPORT

6:12   6:13:45

RENO RD. W.

Path of the Tornado**

6:09

6:15

15TH ST. SW

Collision Course

On May 31 Tim Samaras and team drove into the path of a powerful, erratic storm near El Reno, Oklahoma. It rapidly doubled in size.

TIM SAMARAS

6:04:30 P.M.
From the shoulder of a farm road southwest of El Reno, Tim Samaras and his TWISTEX team watch the tornado forming. "This is gonna be a monster wedge," he says.

6:12
Racing to catch up with the fast-moving twister, the team navigates around the airport. But rain obscures their view. "Turn to the north," Samaras tells Carl Young.

6:16
Once on Reuter Road, the team races east, looking for a chance to deploy instrument probes. But they have trouble getting ahead of the tornado on the slippery road.

*The parent storm was responsible for 22 deaths; 8 are shown on this map.

**Generalized tornado track: From start to 6:18 p.m. and 6:26 to end, data collected by the Advanced Radar Research Center of the University of Oklahoma's RaXpol instrument. From 6:18 to 6:26, data provided by the Center for Severe Weather Research's Doppler on Wheels.

STATEMENT The El Reno tornado hit Oklahoma in the spring of 2013 with massive force. The diagram shows how tornadoes form when warm, moist air from the Gulf of Mexico encounters dry, cold air from the Rockies and originates the large supercell storms that produce tornadoes. The El Reno tornado became massive in size and unpredictable, with dozens of vortices. It killed several people,

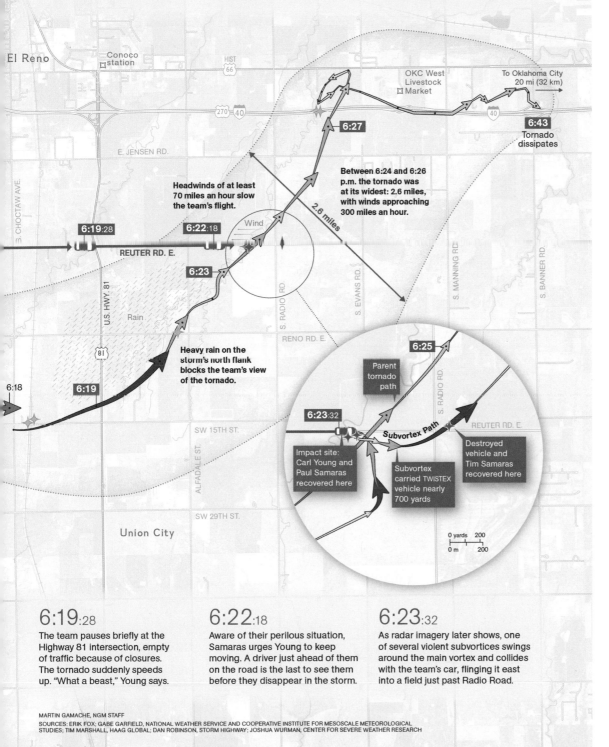

6:19
As it crosses Highway 81, the twister veers to the northeast, still expanding. Surface winds feeding the storm uproot trees well beyond the base of the funnel.

6:23
The rain parts, revealing the main vortex. A few minutes later, wind speeds approach 300 miles an hour as the tornado's diameter maxes out.

6:27
Steered by the rotating parent storm, the twister makes a loop north of I-40 and heads east. Having spent 40 minutes on the ground, it finally dissipates at 6:43 p.m.

El Reno
Conoco station
HIST 66
270 40
OKC West Livestock Market
To Oklahoma City 20 mi (32 km)
6:27
6:43 Tornado dissipates

E. JENSEN RD.

Headwinds of at least 70 miles an hour slow the team's flight.

Between 6:24 and 6:26 p.m. the tornado was at its widest: 2.6 miles, with winds approaching 300 miles an hour.

2.6 miles

Wind

6:19:28   6:22:18
REUTER RD. E.
6:23

S. CHOCTAW AVE.
U.S. HWY. 81
S. RADIO RD.
S. EVANS RD.
S. MANNING RD.
S. BANNER RD.

Rain

Heavy rain on the storm's north flank blocks the team's view of the tornado.

6:18
6:19

RENO RD. E.
81

SW 15TH ST.
ALFADALE ST.
SW 29TH ST.

Union City

Parent tornado path
6:25
S. RADIO RD.

6:23:32
Subvortex Path
REUTER RD. E.

Impact site: Carl Young and Paul Samaras recovered here

Subvortex carried TWISTEX vehicle nearly 700 yards

Destroyed vehicle and Tim Samaras recovered here

0 yards 200
0 m 200

6:19:28
The team pauses briefly at the Highway 81 intersection, empty of traffic because of closures. The tornado suddenly speeds up. "What a beast," Young says.

6:22:18
Aware of their perilous situation, Samaras urges Young to keep moving. A driver just ahead of them on the road is the last to see them before they disappear in the storm.

6:23:32
As radar imagery later shows, one of several violent subvortices swings around the main vortex and collides with the team's car, flinging it east into a field just past Radio Road.

MARTIN GAMACHE, NGM STAFF
SOURCES: ERIK FOX; GABE GARFIELD, NATIONAL WEATHER SERVICE AND COOPERATIVE INSTITUTE FOR MESOSCALE METEOROLOGICAL STUDIES; TIM MARSHALL, HAAG GLOBAL; DAN ROBINSON, STORM HIGHWAY; JOSHUA WURMAN, CENTER FOR SEVERE WEATHER RESEARCH

including storm chaser and long-time *National Geographic* photographer Tim Samaras.

PUBLICATION *National Geographic* (November 2013)

Clock of the Present

Measure life by the seasons, not the hours.

ARTIST Scott Thrift, designer, Brooklyn, NY

STATEMENT In this clock, a single hand takes 365 days to complete a single revolution, gradually introducing its owner to a larger, more natural understanding of time. It follows the rhythm of the seasons. The "twelve o'clock" position is December 21st, the Winter Solstice. At "three o'clock" we have March 21st, the Spring Equinox, and at "six o'clock" June 21st, the Summer Solstice. The Autumn Equinox, September 22nd, falls at the "nine o'clock" position.

Life seemed to be getting bigger every year and I could not figure out how to live in the present. I found myself only being able to enjoy my life six to eight months after the fact. I would think back and remember that "I loved that!" but I could not figure out how to simply live in the moment. Then it occurred to me, "How can I live in the moment if the moment changes every second?" The twenty-first century demands a new scale of time to be fully appreciated. I believe that life is a gift, and helping others to feel the same by being more present is the best use of my time.

PUBLICATION Unpublished (Spring 2013)

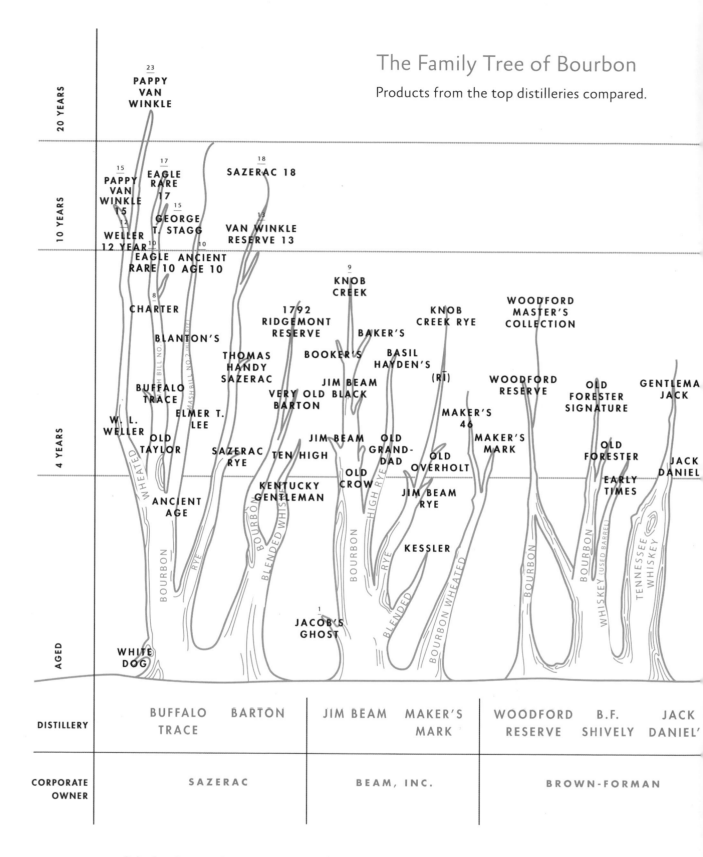

The Family Tree of Bourbon
Products from the top distilleries compared.

ARTISTS Colin Spoelman, author, and Sebit Min, designer.

STATEMENT I first got interested in whiskey partly because it is mysterious. It's a substance heavy on myth, which can be frustrating at times, though more often that's part of the fun. Still, when David Haskell and I set out to write a book about whiskey, there seemed an opportunity to demystify some of the marketing and to try to be very rigorous about exploring the world of commercial whiskey, a daunting task considering there are hundreds of labels of bourbon, rye, and Tennessee whiskies.

But nearly all of them are made at a handful of distilleries, and each of those distilleries produces only a few recipes (or mash bills), and those whiskies are aged

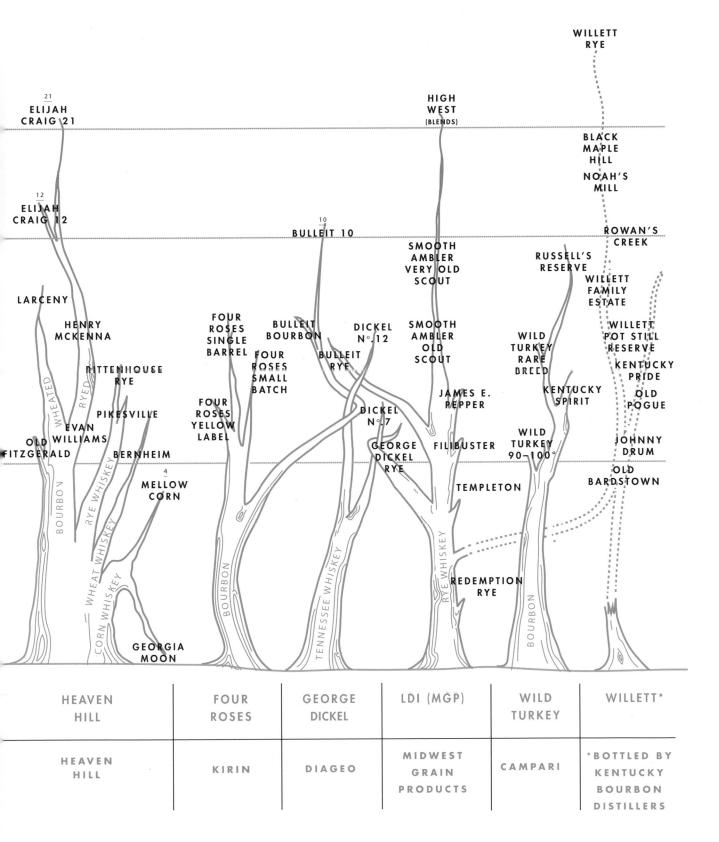

more or less to make the variety of whiskies from top shelf to bottom shelf. So a kind of order emerged: a series of trees with trunks representing the distillery, branches representing the mash bills, and height on the tree representing age.

I drew the drawing in pencil and one of the book's illustrators, Sebit Min, drew it in Illustrator. Our designer, Deb Wood, worked to plot each of the brands as pre-cisely as I had located them, which was not an easy job. When *GQ* ran the chart as an excerpt from the book, it really took on a life of its own.

PUBLICATION *The Kings County Distillery Guide to Urban Moonshining: How to Make and Drink Whiskey,* Abrams Books (October 2013)

The Literal Meaning of the States

North America from the Atlantic to the "Peaceful World Stream."

ARTISTS Stephan Hormes and Silke Peust of Kalimedia.

STATEMENT *The Atlas of True Names,* the parent project to this map, reveals the etymological roots, or original meanings, of the familiar terms on today's maps of the world. The "true names" of countless cities, countries, rivers, oceans, and mountain ranges are displayed through this series of fascinating maps, each of which includes a comprehensive index of derivations. This map of the United States is atypical; rather than communicate how to drive cross-country, it tells you what you'll see on the way there and what mattered to the people who named it so. *The Atlas of True Names* restores an element of enchantment to the world we all think we know so well. It takes the reader on a journey into the unknown—a unique exploration of uncharted territory in that familiar place we all know as "home."

PUBLICATION *Kalimedia.de* (June 2013)

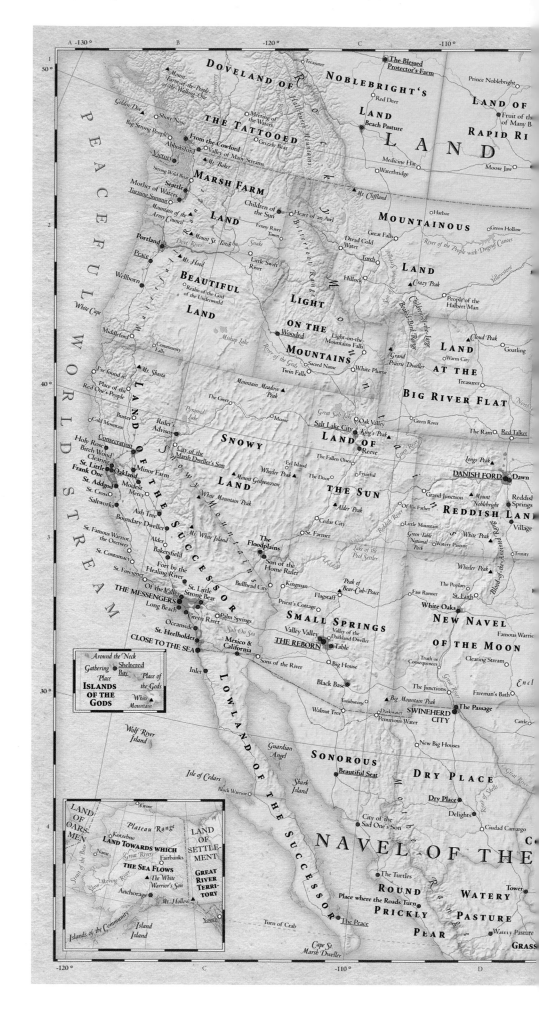

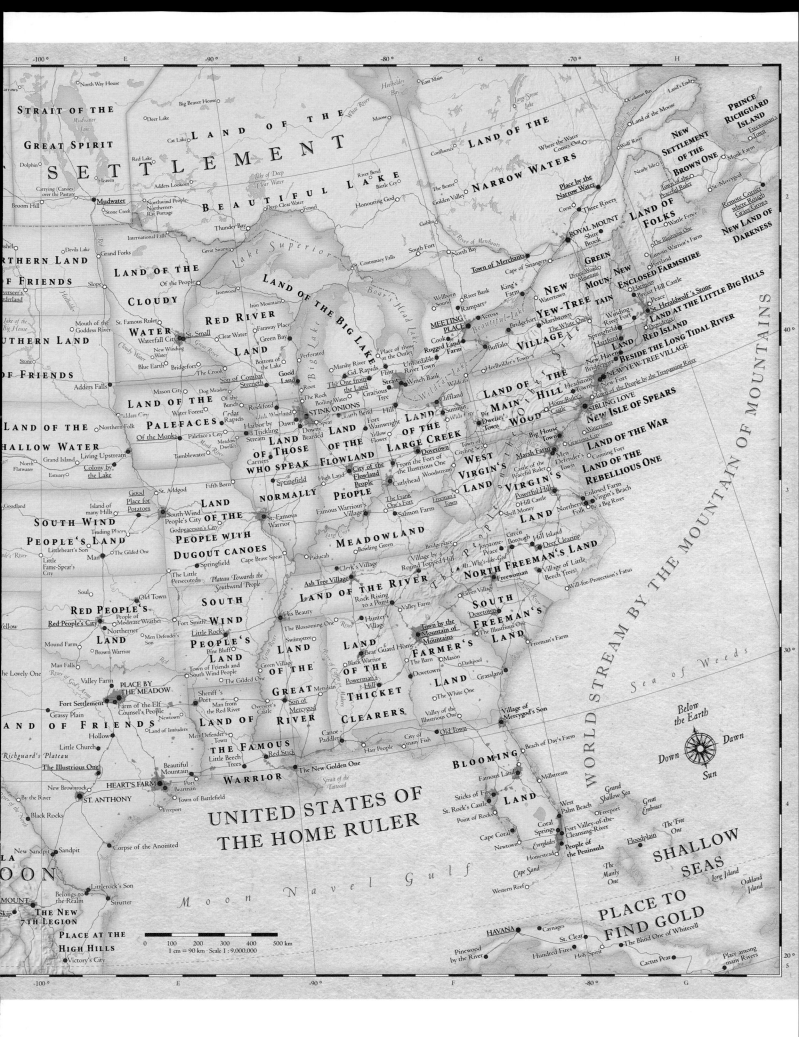

THE BEST AMERICAN INFOGRAPHICS 2014

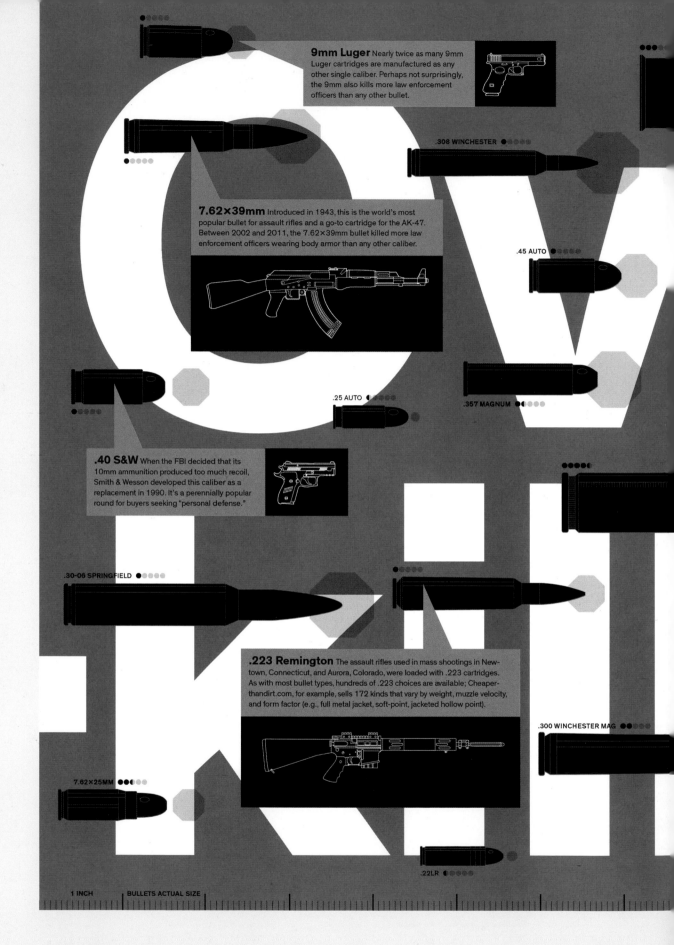

9mm Luger Nearly twice as many 9mm Luger cartridges are manufactured as any other single caliber. Perhaps not surprisingly, the 9mm also kills more law enforcement officers than any other bullet.

.308 WINCHESTER ●●●●●

7.62×39mm Introduced in 1943, this is the world's most popular bullet for assault rifles and a go-to cartridge for the AK-47. Between 2002 and 2011, the 7.62×39mm bullet killed more law enforcement officers wearing body armor than any other caliber.

.45 AUTO ●●●●●●

.25 AUTO ●●●●●

.357 MAGNUM ●●●●●

.40 S&W When the FBI decided that its 10mm ammunition produced too much recoil, Smith & Wesson developed this caliber as a replacement in 1990. It's a perennially popular round for buyers seeking "personal defense."

.30-06 SPRINGFIELD ●●●●●

.223 Remington The assault rifles used in mass shootings in Newtown, Connecticut, and Aurora, Colorado, were loaded with .223 cartridges. As with most bullet types, hundreds of .223 choices are available; Cheaperthandirt.com, for example, sells 172 kinds that vary by weight, muzzle velocity, and form factor (e.g., full metal jacket, soft-point, jacketed hollow point).

.300 WINCHESTER MAG ●●●●●

7.62×25MM ●●●●●

.22LR ●●●●●

1 INCH   BULLETS ACTUAL SIZE

Overkill

Guns don't kill people, ammo does.

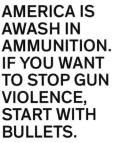

Cost Per Round	
●○○○○	$1.00
●●○○○	$2.00
●●●○○	$3.00
●●●●○	$4.00
●●●●●	$5.00

12 Gauge One of the firearms used in the Aurora movie theater shooting last year was a 12-gauge shotgun made by Remington. A similar weapon was used in the mass shooting at Columbine High School in 1999.

.380 AUTO ●●○○○

.44 MAGNUM ●●○○○

.45×39MM ●●●○○

.50 BMG A standard caliber for machine guns, the .50-caliber Browning was also one of the bullets that the Branch Davidians shot at FBI agents during a siege on their compound in 1993.

Relative Stopping Power
A measure of a bullet's wounding potential, derived from its muzzle velocity, weight, and surface area. The term was coined by major general Julian Hatcher, a military firearms expert and onetime president of the NRA.

.32 AUTO ●○○○○

.38 SPECIAL ●●○○○

AMERICA IS AWASH IN AMMUNITION. IF YOU WANT TO STOP GUN VIOLENCE, START WITH BULLETS.

by Joanna Pearlstein

GUNS DON'T KILL PEOPLE; people don't kill people; *bullets* kill people. As the nation debates, again, the best way to curb gun violence, many of the questions focus on the firearms themselves. But an equally important consideration is ammunition. Roughly 10 billion rounds are manufactured in the US each year, with a weight equal to two *Titanic*s. More to the point, it's enough bullets to pump 32 rounds into every man, woman, and child in America.

From the musket ball to the .45 Colt cartridge to the .223 shells used in the Newtown massacre, the story of ammunition is in many ways a familiar tale of technological progress, as bullets have become cheaper, easier to use, and often more deadly. But this engineering success has become a social and moral crisis. Here's a data-driven examination of the bullet: its variety, its spread, and the policies that might help curb its lethal consequences.

INFOGRAPHIC BY **CARL DETORRES**

0 9 7

ARTISTS Infographic design and illustration by Carl De Torres of Carl De Torres Graphic Design. Art direction by Margaret Swart, contributing art director; editing by Bill Wasik, senior editor; writing by Joanna Pearlstein, senior editor/research, at *WIRED*.

CONTINUED

America the Ammo Dealer (and Buyer)

Our immense appetite for bullets—and expertise in producing them—drives the entire global market, in which the US is the biggest importer *and* exporter. Between 2005 and 2009 alone, US imports quadrupled, in large part because the military, waging wars in Afghanistan and Iraq, was sapping domestic production. This map shows official US exports from, and imports to, its top 10 partners in bullet sales. Unofficially, US bullets also find their way into bloodshed from Mexico (via smuggling to cartels) to Norway (where mass murderer Anders Breivik ordered his online from a US seller).

Senior editor JOANNA PEARLSTEIN *(@jopearl) is* WIRED*'s research chief. Additional reporting by Cameron Bird.*

Total US Exports of Small Arms Ammunition, 2011	$414.3M
Total US Imports of Small Arms Ammunition, 2011	$297.3M

SOURCES Citizens Crime Commission of New York City, Coalition to Stop Gun Violence, Conflict Armament Research, Law Center to Prevent Gun Violence, Mayors Against Illegal Guns, National Shooting Sports Foundation, Norwegian Initiative on Small Arms Transfers, *Small Arms Survey, The Tax Burden on Tobacco*

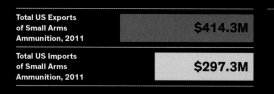

Top 10 Countries Importing US Small Arms Ammunition

Top 10 Countries Exporting Small Arms Ammunition to the US

AUSTRALIA $64.8M
UNITED KINGDOM $11.5M
CANADA $15.6M
MEXICO $10.9M
CANADA $69.9M
BRAZIL $15.6M

THE CASE FOR BULLET CONTROL

If you can't constrain supply, you have to go after demand. Some of the smartest "gun control" proposals are actually about bullets, with the goal of making ammo more difficult to purchase or use in large quantity.

`0` `9` `8`

BAN LARGE-CAPACITY MAGAZINES

Most of the gunmen in mass shootings in the past five years used ammunition magazines that held dozens of rounds—allowing the shooters to fire as many as 100 times without stopping to reload. In January, President Obama proposed banning large-capacity magazines as part of an extensive gun-control plan.

- ■ MAGAZINE CAPACITY
- ■ NUMBER OF FATALITIES
- □ NUMBER OF WOUNDED

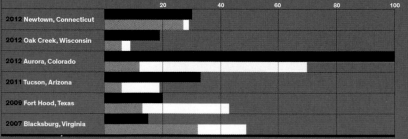

2012 Newtown, Connecticut
2012 Oak Creek, Wisconsin
2012 Aurora, Colorado
2011 Tucson, Arizona
2009 Fort Hood, Texas
2007 Blacksburg, Virginia

STATEMENT Gun violence received a flood of media and political attention in the wake of the December 2012 school shootings in Newtown, Connecticut. But the conversation nearly always focused on the weapons themselves, not the ammunition that is so easy to purchase and that makes guns so deadly. So *WIRED* took a data-driven approach to an examination of the ammunition industry—looking at bullets' manufacture, trade, regulation, popularity, and stopping power.

FEEDING THE FIRE FOUR NATIONS THAT SUPPLY BULLETS TO WAR ZONES

Russia
Both sides in the Syrian civil war—loyalists to President Bashar al-Assad and the Free Syrian Army that opposes him—are armed to the teeth with Soviet-era AK-47 variants and ammunition. And Russia is believed to be selling new arms to Assad's side.

Belgium
Between 2001 and 2010, this tiny country exported more than $300 million in ammo. Its Five-seven pistol and armor-piercing bullets have made their way to Mexican drug cartels; in 2009, Gaddafi's Libya scored more than $16 million in Belgian gear.

Eastern Europe
With a major surplus of ammo left over from the Cold War, eastern European nations such as Albania and Serbia have established privately owned, state-controlled companies to offload it—helping equip the Afghan army and others.

Iran
In December, a state-run munitions maker in Iran was found to be selling Kalashnikov cartridges to warring groups in the Ivory Coast, as well as to al Qaeda affiliates in Niger, DR Congo, Guinea, and Kenya—and the Taliban in Afghanistan.

AFGHANISTAN $39.6M

IRAQ $8.7M

GERMANY $16.8M

$8.3M

ISRAEL $42.7M

SPAIN $23.0M

UNITED KINGDOM $12.5M

CZECH REPUBLIC $22.3M

SERBIA $15.5M

ISRAEL $18.9M

RUSSIA $73.1M

TAIWAN $18.4M

SOUTH KOREA $92.5M

TAX BULLETS

Bullets are cheap: A box of fifty 9mm Luger rounds costs less than $20. One popular proposal, put forward by policy thinkers ranging from the late US senator Daniel Moynihan to comedian Chris Rock, is to tax bullets at a rate that reflects their cost to society. It worked for cigarettes: Since 1990, tobacco taxes have more than tripled, and consumption has dropped 40 percent.

508.7B Cigarettes Consumed

$32B in Taxes Collected

$9.5B in Taxes Collected

307.2B Cigarettes Consumed

1990

2010

TRACK AMMO PURCHASES

In 47 out of 50 states, buyers aren't required to have a license to purchase ammunition. Would it help reduce gun crime if they were? Statistics on gun licensing suggest the answer to be yes: States that don't require purchase permits for guns are far more likely to be the source for guns that are used in crimes.

6.2
Purchase Permits Required

19.2
No Purchase Permits Required

CRIME GUN EXPORT RATE PER 100,000 INHABITANTS

PUBLICATION *WIRED*
(March 2013)

What a Fastball Looks Like

Think fast.

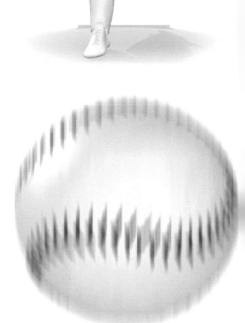

4-SEAM FASTBALL

From the box, the straightest pitch is a reddish, brownish solid without much form. Batters don't really see seams.

2-SEAM FASTBALL

The pitch's downward slide makes the seams look like blurred vertical railroad tracks.

CURVEBALL

The only pitch that moves up after its release has seams that run from 10 o'clock to 4 o'clock and look like lateral railroad tracks.

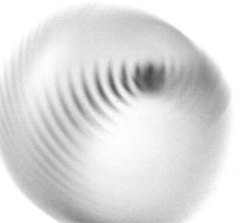

---

^

SLIDER

At first it looks like a
fastball, but as it breaks
down and away (or in, to a
lefty), there's a red dot at
about 2 o'clock.

---

^

CHANGEUP

It's blurry and solid like
a four-seamer. Hitters
need sharp foveal vision
to ID the off-white color
before the pitch drops.

ARTISTS Bryan Christie of Bryan
Christie Design. Munehito Sawada, John
Korpics, Jason Lancaster, Bruce Kelley,
Amy Brachmann, Eddie Matz, Paul Kix,
and Ben Bradley of *ESPN The Magazine*.

STATEMENT With this infographic,
we wanted to show something that
bordered on the impossible: what
players see as different pitches come at
them. How did their eyes distinguish a
changeup from a curveball, or a curveball from a slider, or, for that matter, a
two-seam fastball from a four-seam one?
In answering that question, we hoped
to advance an idea that would fit well in
our annual Body Issue: The eyes are the
most important body part on a baseball
player. We wanted, with this piece,
to demonstrate how hard it is to hit a
baseball and to celebrate those who do
it well.

PUBLICATION *ESPN The Magazine*
(February 2013)

The Truth About T. Rex

Colorful and possibly fuzzy.

ARTISTS Illustration by Emily Cooper, freelance artist. Design and graphics by Jasiek Krzysztofiak, art editor; design and art direction by Kelly Krause, art director; text by Richard Monastersky, editor, at *Nature*.

STATEMENT Even one of the best-known dinosaurs has secrets, such as: why the puny arms? Was T. rex covered in feathers, or even fuzz? Scientists are starting to unravel these mysteries, but questions remain. As T. rex has historically been portrayed as a scaly creature, we thought it was particularly important to give readers a visual nudge toward the possibility that it may have looked vastly different. This consideration drove our choice in style, as we felt that the fuzz and feather possibilities should look as realistic as possible, to compete with the many wonderful scaly depictions commonly found in movies and other media. We gave this brief to artist Emily Cooper, who did an amazing job bringing the fur, feathers, and scales to life with a 3D model that served as the center-piece of the graphic.

PUBLICATION *Nature* (October 2013)

The small tyrannosaur known as *Nanotyrannus* (white skull) may have been a juvenile *T. rex* (skull outline).

IN THE FLESH

Our picture of *Tyrannosaurus rex* has undergone several makeovers since the dinosaur was first described in 1905. Early reconstructions depicted a scaly beast that stood upright and dragged its tail on the ground, but recent research suggests the Cretaceous carnivore had a more agile horizontal posture and may have been covered in some sort of plumage.

Feathers on some close relatives of *T. rex* are more like fuzz than the plumage on birds.

If *T. rex* had a coat of proto-feathers, they may have served as a form of display.

Some researchers contend that *T. rex* and its kin had scaly skin.

Muscle scars on the arm bones suggest that the limbs were not vestigial.

1905 reconstruction
T. rex was originally imagined with a reptilian, tail-dragging pose, but newer reconstructions make it a fleeter, more bird-like dinosaur.

TYRANNOSAUROID TREE

The tyrannosauroid superfamily includes Cretaceous tyrannosaurids, such as *T. rex*, and more distant relatives that first emerged in the Jurassic period. Researchers are trying to trace how tyrannosauroids evolved from small early species to the giants of the Cretaceous.

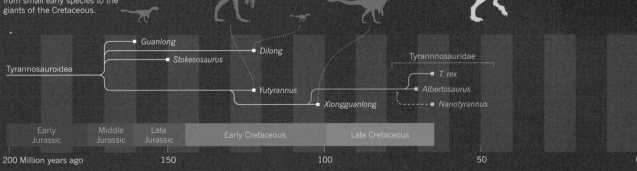

	Guanlong		*Dilong*		Tyrannnosauridae	
	Stokesosaurus					
Tyrannosauroidea					*T. rex*	
		Yutyrannus			*Albertosaurus*	
			Xiongguanlong		*Nanotyrannus*	

Early Jurassic	Middle Jurassic	Late Jurassic	Early Cretaceous	Late Cretaceous	
200 Million years ago		150	100	50	0

THE SIZE OF THE PART OF EARTH'S SURFACE DIRECTLY UNDER VARIOUS SPACE OBJECTS

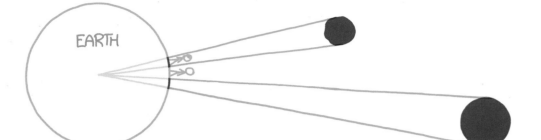

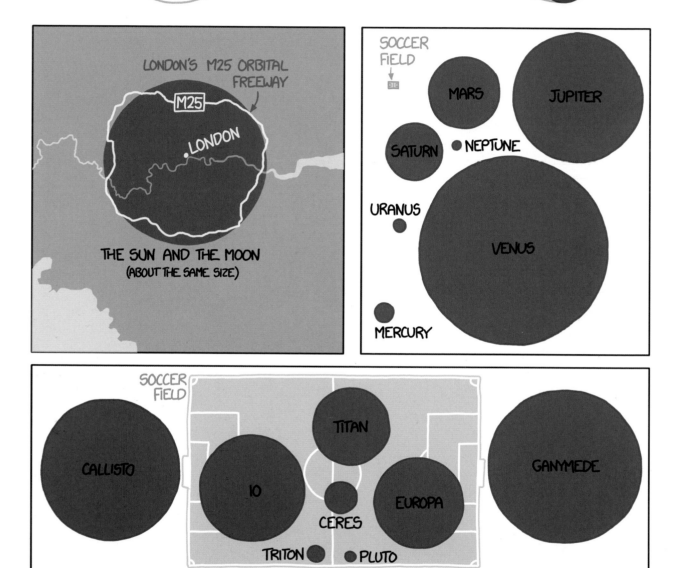

Angular Size

An exposition of angular space, from the Sun to Voyager 1.

ARTIST Randall Munroe

STATEMENT This diagram shows how much of the "celestial sphere" around Earth various stars, planets, moons, and space probes take up. In other words, it shows how small the patch of the Earth's surface is where a line drawn straight upward will hit a given star or planet. The chart also includes a few recently discovered planets orbiting other stars; these are labeled with the ridiculous names suggested for them in xkcd.com/1253.

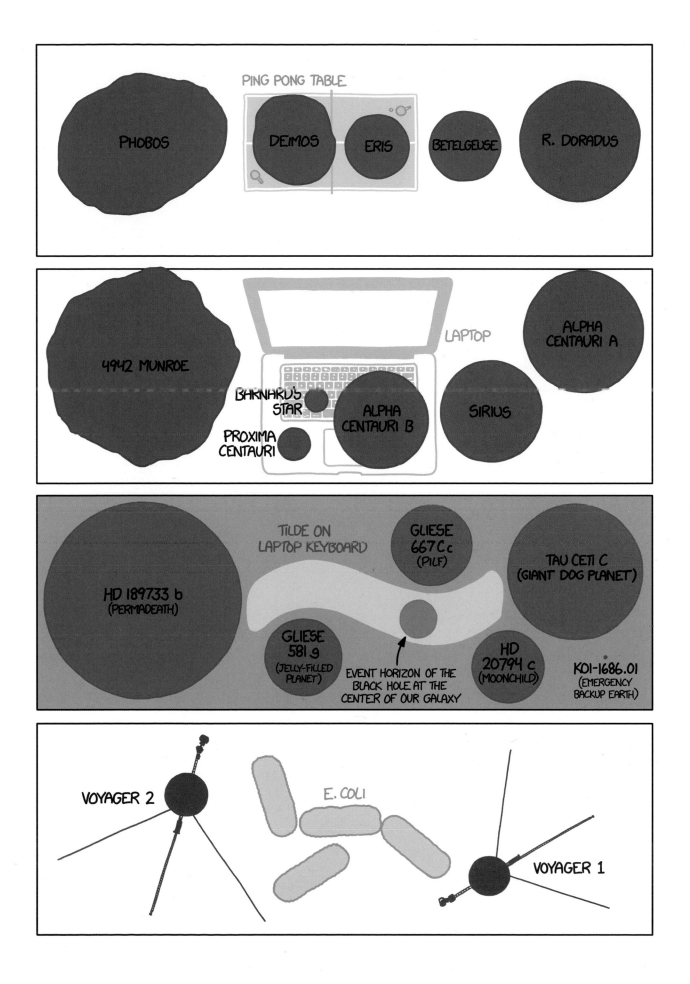

PUBLICATION *xkcd.com* (October 2013)

PERILOUS JOURNEYS

It's an extraordinary feat. Three billion birds of some 300 species—songbirds, waterbirds, raptors—migrate thousands of miles for summer breeding in Eurasia, then return to Africa for winter. They navigate by cues still not fully understood: the sun, the stars, landforms, scents, even Earth's magnetic field. Almost all their numbers are falling, mainly due to habitat loss. The additional toll of illegal and indiscriminate hunting claims hundreds of millions of birds a year.

- Critically endangered
- Endangered
- Least concern

Ortolan bunting
Emberiza hortulana
Length 6.3 inches
Migrates as far as 3,600 mi

A French delicacy, ortolans—now illegal to catch or sell—are netted, fattened up, drowned in brandy, then roasted.

Saker falcon
Falco cherrug
Wingspan 3.5 to 4 feet
Migrates as far as 2,500 mi

One of the rarest raptors, it's captured for use as a hunter in the sport of falconry in the Middle East and Central Asia.

Hoopoe
Upupa epops
Length 11 inches
Migrates as far as 3,000 mi

Named for the sound of its song, it heralds spring in southern Europe and is the national bird of Israel.

Northern bald ibis
Geronticus eremita
Wingspan 4 feet
Migrates as far as 1,800 mi

A few hundred survive in the wild around the Mediterranean. Hunters have shot a third of those that researchers are trying to reintroduce to Italy.

Red-backed shrike
Lanius collurio
Length 7 inches
Migrates as far as 6,800 mi

Abundant overall yet now rare in Great Britain, in part because its patterned eggs were so sought by collectors.

WHY BIRDS DIE

Icons show the chief reason wild birds are killed in a country. Birds hunted for "leisure" may also be eaten, but many are left where they fall.

- ⊕ Human consumption
- 🐟 Illegal trade
- 🌾 Farm protection
- ⊕ Hunting for leisure

→ KNOWN ILLEGAL TRADE ROUTE

WHERE THEY GATHER

Green areas along the migration flyways show where birds mass at favorable crossings or stop to rest and feed. Hunters gather there too.

⇨ MAJOR MIGRATORY FLYWAY

● Congregation areas

✹ Killing hot spots

TOP OFFENDERS

BirdLife International creates these rankings with data from countries that have signed bird-protection acts and from other reports.

REPORTED ILLEGAL ACTIVITY
HIGH | LOW | NO DATA

Red-breasted goose
Branta ruficollis
Length 22 inches
Migrates as far as 3,500 mi

Illegally shot as it flies from breeding grounds on Russia's Arctic tundra to its winter home on the western Black Sea coast.

MAJOR MIGRATION CROSSINGS

A SOUTHERN SPAIN
The shortest route across the Mediterranean attracts large numbers of soaring raptors, which rely on updrafts created by heat rising from land.

B CENTRAL MEDITERRANEAN
Island-hopping migrants suffer most on Malta, infamous for illegal hunting—for trophies, for food, and for entertainment.

C ADRIATIC
"Hardly any bird species is safe," a 2009 study says of this flyway. Illegal hunting in the Balkans is boosted by Italians who come to shoot where enforcement is lax.

D EASTERN MEDITERRANEAN
The most heavily traveled route on this map funnels birds east to the Siberian Arctic and west through the Bosporus.

BIRD HAVENS
Areas vital to conservation are designated by BirdLife International as Important Bird Areas (green).

Important Bird Areas

Major migratory routes

EQUATOR

GREENLAND
ASIA
EUROPE
AFRICA
SAHARA

0 mi 250
0 km 250

FERNANDO G. BAPTISTA, VIRGINIA W. MASON, AND DANIELA SANTAMARINA, NGM STAFF; FANNA GEBREYESUS
SOURCES: BIRDLIFE INTERNATIONAL; IUCN; NATIONAL AGENCY FOR NATURE CONSERVATION (ALGERIA); ENVIRONMENT GENERAL AUTHORITY (LIBYA); LIBYAN SOCIETY FOR BIRDS; NATURE CONSERVATION EGYPT; ASSOCIATION "LES AMIS DES OISEAUX" (TUNISIA); PETER LACK, BRITISH TRUST FOR ORNITHOLOGY; SMITHSONIAN INSTITUTION, NATIONAL MUSEUM OF NATURAL HISTORY, DIVISION OF BIRDS

Great Winged Migrations

What birds endure.

ARTISTS Map by Virginia W. Mason, senior graphics editor, art by Fernando Baptista, senior graphics editor, production by Daniela Santamarina, graphic design specialist, and text by Jane Vessels, senior text editor, at *National Geographic*. Research by Fanna Gebreyesus, freelance researcher.

STATEMENT Three million birds migrate every year between Africa and Eurasia, and many (mostly songbirds) are killed for human consumption, for illegal trade, by farmers protecting their land, or simply for leisure. The map shows the major migratory routes, congregation areas of birds, killing hot spots, and the level of illegal activity recorded in every country. Some iconic species are illustrated, with comments on their status and level of endangerment.

PUBLICATION *National Geographic* (July 2013)

Actual European Discoveries

land unknown by humans* before the Age of Exploration

NOTES

Large Dark Names = currently inhabited
Small Light Names = currently uninhabited
(or only military / scientific personnel)

Stripes indicate ambiguous or shared discovery.

* Islands marked with an asterisk show evidence of prior human inhabitation but were unoccupied at the time of European discovery. (The north coast of Greenland was also previously occupied. The South Shetland Islands may have been as well.)

† Islands in the Indian Ocean marked with a dagger were known to Arab traders but never occupied.

All islands labeled with present-day names, which are often different from the names given at discovery. Equal-area projection (Eckert IV). Map by Bill Rankin, 2013; www.radicalcartography.net

country sponsoring original exploration	date of first discovery	total area discovered (non-continental; km²)	current population of discovered land
Portugal	1418	13,776	3,424,609
Spain	1493	8,938	149,732
Netherlands	1596	73,903	5,642
United Kingdom	1609	10,597	11,436
France	1711	7,627	70
Russia	1712	74,634	613
United States	1796	7,699	3,754
Austria-Hungary	1873	16,134	0
Norway	1878	34	0
		213,342	3,595,856
		(roughly the area of Great Britain; 0.14% of all land) (adding continental land at the poles, ~11% of all land)	(0.05% of all humans)

ARTIST Bill Rankin, Yale University.

STATEMENT This map shows all the land unknown to humans before the European "Age of Exploration"—that is, all the land that was discovered by Europeans and found to be uninhabited. Every Columbus Day, we're reminded of the difference between discovery and "discovery"—and rightly so. After all, the vast majority of the land found by European navigators was already inhabited and had been for centuries. Even in the vast Pacific and the barren Arctic, only a few isolated coasts were truly terra nullius. The extent of the truly unknown areas found by Europeans is perhaps a bit humbling: a scattering of diminutive islands, along with extravagant amounts of ice and snow.

This map offers a few other lessons as well. First, it particularly underscores the maritime expertise of Pacific Islanders. Unlike the islands of the Atlantic and Indian Oceans, nearly all of the Pacific was settled by the fourteenth century. The map also shows the changing geopolitics of exploration. For example, it shows at a glance how the Treaty of Tordesillas split the sixteenth-century world between the Portuguese and the Spanish; it also shows the dominance of the British in Australasia and south of the Antarctic Convergence. Contrast this with the seemingly random color patterns in the Arctic, Pacific, and southern Indian Oceans, where aggressive whaling often led to a free-for-all of destructive competition.

PUBLICATION *RadicalCartography.com* (July 2013)

You can learn a lot about a species by what it leaves behind.

SCATOLOGY | To conservation biologists like Samuel Wasser, an animal's droppings are hardly waste. Each pellet or patty packs a history of its host's diet, territory, and sexual state. Most mammals can sniff out this info; human trackers—with less keen noses—have had to rely on other methods. Enter Wasser. His University of Washington lab has pioneered more advanced means of studying scat, including hormone profiles and DNA extraction. That means less need for dart guns. "Once we had DNA," he says, "we could ID an animal without seeing it. Essentially, we could connect the dots."

For the past decade Wasser has been connecting elephant "dots" across Africa. He collects the animals' dung, genotypes the samples, and adds the information to a growing genetic reference map. By matching DNA from seized tusks with DNA from dung sites, he can even pinpoint ivory-poaching hot spots.

But the map has gaps. In the heart of the Democratic Republic of the Congo, where few elephants remain, Wasser had little data. So in March 2011 he enlisted two National Geographic grantees, Trip Jennings and Andy Maser, for what Maser calls "CSI: Elephant." The duo found fresh samples. More important, they taught locals how to collect dung and send it directly to Wasser's lab.

Now Wasser is picking through their finds. With each new shipment, he gathers hope for elephants—in heaps. *—Oliver Uberti*

ABOUT 7 IN*

Herbivores defecate more than carnivores because they eat more. Large bull elephants consume up to 650 pounds of vegetation a day and defecate more than a third of it.

SCAT FACTS	1	2	3
Animal	*African elephant*	*Lion*	*Large-spotted genet*
Contents	*Leaves, bark, bulbs, seeds, roots*	*Hair, hooves, bones, digested meat, blood*	*Feathers, grass, insect parts, rodent hairs*
Distinguishing features	*Barrel-shaped, fibrous pieces; several per site*	*Tapering, sausage shaped, with hair*	*Sausage shaped, with a point at one end*

Appearance may vary based on habitat, age of sample, and what an individual animal has consumed.
*Drawings are proportional.

What a Species
Leaves Behind

Scat studies.

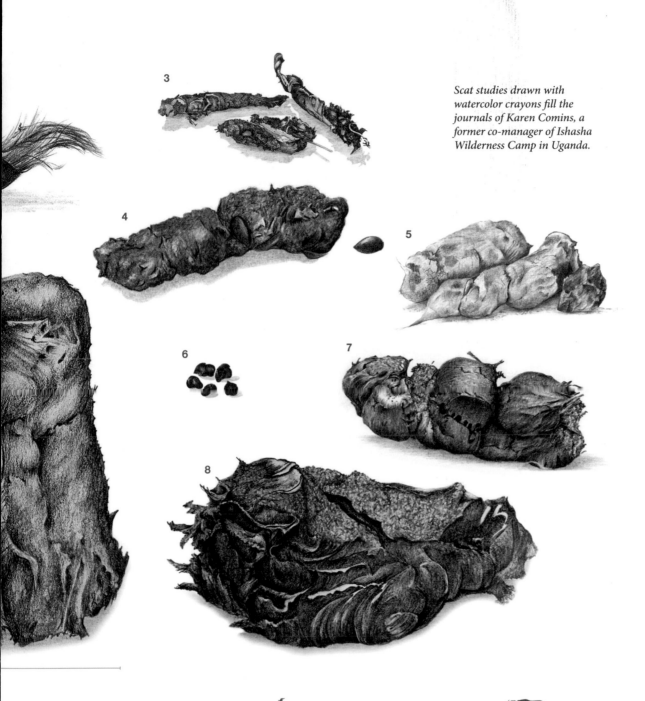

Scat studies drawn with watercolor crayons fill the journals of Karen Comins, a former co-manager of Ishasha Wilderness Camp in Uganda.

4	5	6	7	8
Yellow baboon	*Spotted hyena*	*Topi*	*Warthog*	*African buffalo*
Fruits, seeds, bulbs, insects, digested meat	*Bones, hooves, hair, scavenged meat*	*Grass*	*Grass, roots, bulbs, sometimes leaves*	*Grass, reeds, leaves, other parts of plants*
Segmented, similar to human waste	*White when dry, from digested bones*	*Small heaps of 15 to 30 pellets*	*Kidney shaped, with defined segments*	*Wet patties in wet season, firmer in dry*

ARTISTS Art by Karen Comins and design by Oliver Uberti and Hannah Tak, design editors, at *National Geographic*.

STATEMENT The graphic shows an illustrated gallery of animal droppings based on the studies of conservation biologist Samuel Wasser. Each pellet tells a story of diet, territory, and more. Scientists use the DNA found in elephant droppings and match it with seized tusks to locate ivory poaching hot spots.

PUBLICATION
National Geographic (January 2013)

by FERNANDA B. VIÉGAS

FROM IMPLICIT CONNECTIONS of Chinese officials to recurring jokes in the TV show *Arrested Development,* the best interactive infographics of 2013 cover a wildly diverse set of narratives. This broad range speaks to the sweeping reach of this medium today. But it wasn't always so: Data visualization had previously been accessible only to the elite in academia, business, and government. It used to be "serious" technology, created by experts for experts. In recent years, however, web-based visualizations—ranging from political art projects to news stories—have reached audiences of millions.

The winners here have succeeded in creating visualizations that are accessible to lay users while supporting expert-level analysis. The *New York Times,* for instance, tackled the seemingly dry question of corporate taxes in an illuminating and attractive bubble chart that draws viewers in with its animated transitions. "Bloomberg Billionaires" breaks down wealth by demographics, geography, and industry in an intricate and whimsical dashboard. The result is a complex analysis that deepens readers' understanding of multifaceted financial data.

Half of this year's winners are maps. As it turns out, maps are undergoing something of a revolution, allowing new kinds of cartography. The development of tools and techniques such as APIs, geotagging, and geospational crowdsourcing has considerably democratized mapmaking. Equipped with new data, aspiring cartographers are profoundly expanding the landscape of what maps can accomplish. The "Racial Dot Map" draws a point of color for every US citizen, and Bklynr shows every single building in Brooklyn by age. The level of detail and texture in these interactive maps is something that was hardly possible before.

Digital maps are becoming more artistic too. Stamen's "Map Stack" allows creators to fine-tune the appearance of their maps not only for data legibility but also for aesthetic purposes—watercolor option included. NOAA's Green piece presents a dramatic, breathing portrait of Earth's vegetation over time. It makes you cheer for the lovely—and fragile—shades of green that cover our planet.

The work in the following pages makes me excited for the future of data and visual literacy. As infographics become a part of political dialogue, citizen activism, game playing, and educational exchanges, we can expect the language of data visualization to evolve. It's thrilling to see that, at its best, this language can be deep enough to capture the texture and complexity of the human condition.

Fernanda B. Viégas is a computational designer whose work focuses on the social, collaborative, and artistic aspects of information visualization. She is a co-leader, with Martin Wattenberg, of Google's "Big Picture" data visualization group in Cambridge, Massachusetts. She is also a member of the Best American Infographics brain trust.

TO SEE THE INTERACTIVE WINNERS, GO TO:
WWW.HMHBOOKS.COM/INFOGRAPHICS2014

Out of Sight, Out of Mind.

ATTACKS VICTIMS NEWS INFO

CHILDREN	CIVILIAN	OTHER
175 5.4%	**535** 16.7%	**2453** 76.3%

2004 | 2005 || 2006 |

Drone Attacks

The rise of a new era.

ARTISTS Concept, data analysis, creative and technical direction by Wesley Grubbs; programming by Nick Yahnke; and design by Mladen Balog at Pitch Interactive.

STATEMENT This project visualizes every US drone strike and known fatality recorded in Pakistan. This relatively new military tactic was promoted heavily by the Obama Administration as a surgically precise and wise move in the war against terror. However, with the release of "Living Under Drones," the first independent study of the effects of drones on civilians, and

with the efforts of independent news organizations like the Bureau of Investigative Journalism, we are learning a much different story. Less than 2 percent of all drone strike fatalities are considered to be identifiable high-profile targets. This project's aim was to bring light to the drone campaign and help people on all sides of the debate understand the pattern of strikes and the type of people affected.

PUBLICATION *Drones.pitchinteractive.com* (March 2013)

YOU   US   MATERIAL WORLD   INTERACTIVE

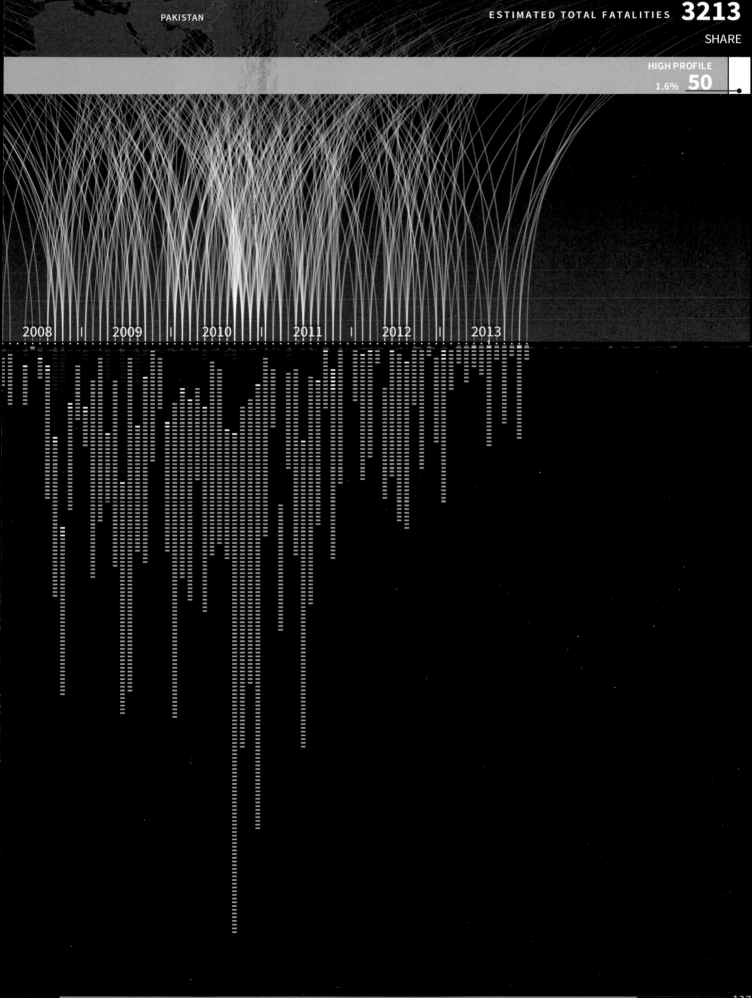

PAKISTAN

ESTIMATED TOTAL FATALITIES **3213**

SHARE

HIGH PROFILE
1.6% **50**

2008 2009 2010 2011 2012 2013

2010 Census Block Data

1 Dot = 1 Person

- ● White
- ● Black
- ● Asian
- ● Hispanic
- ● Other Race / Native American / Multi-racial

THE UNITED STATES
OF AMERICA

Racial Dot Map

Every American is a dot of color.

ARTIST Dustin A. Cable, previously senior research associate for the University of Virginia's Weldon Cooper Center for Public Service, Charlottesville, VA, currently data analyst in the Communications Department at Face-book Inc.

STATEMENT The Racial Dot Map is an American snapshot, an exercise in demographic pointillism that provides an accessible and elegant visualization of the geographic distribution, population density, and racial diversity of the American people in every neighborhood in the entire country. The map displays 308,745,538 individual dots, one for each person residing in the United States at the location they were counted during the 2010 Census. Each dot is color-coded by the individual's reported race and ethnicity.

I drew my inspiration for the map from similar projects by Brandon Martin-Anderson, Peter Richardson, and Eric Fischer. My map combines and expands these works to create the most comprehensive visual of the racial distribution of the United States to date.

PUBLICATION Weldon Cooper Center for Public Service (August 2013)

LOS ANGELES

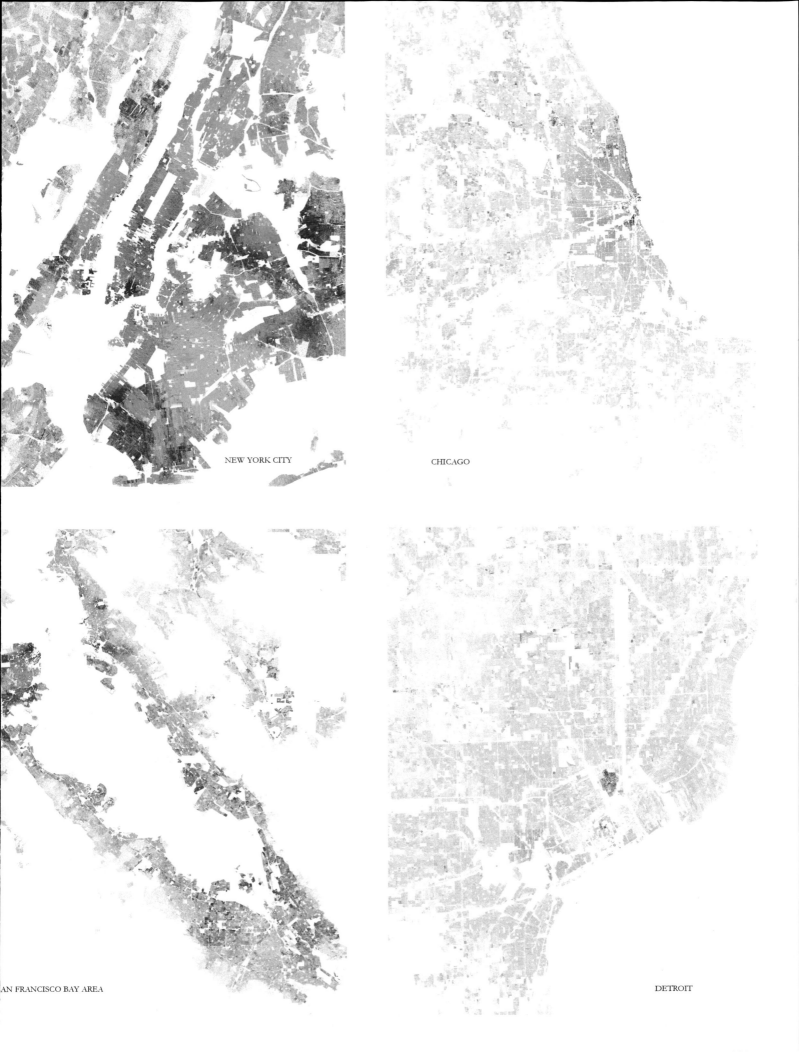

NEW YORK CITY

CHICAGO

AN FRANCISCO BAY AREA

DETROIT

Previously, on Arrested Development

Stop me if you've heard this one.

ARTISTS Adam Cole, Christopher Groskopf, Alyson Hurt, Jeremy Bowers, and Danny DeBelius for National Public Radio.

STATEMENT The recurring jokes of the television show *Arrested Development* densely layer and intertwine over the course of the show's four seasons, visualized in this responsively designed data visualization and episode guide.

Leading up to the release of *Arrested Development*'s fourth season on Netflix, NPR's Adam Cole rewatched the original three seasons. He noticed that many jokes tended to recur, reference other jokes, subtly appear in the background, and even foreshadow themselves. (For example, Cole noticed that one character's major injury is referenced in myriad ways a full season and a half before it actually happens—details that reward longtime viewers and rewatchers, and hint that the show is far more planned and complex than it may seem.) He logged what he saw in a gloriously intricate spreadsheet.

Cole worked with NPR's News Applications (now Visuals) team to visually represent the complicated web behind the show and extend the data he had collected into a full episode guide, pegged to the show's Season 4 premiere.

PUBLICATION *NPR.org* (May 2013)

G.O.B.

... Messes Up A Trick.

G.O.B. kills several doves and showers countless people with lighter fluid over the course of the series. But where did the lighter fluid come from?

■ Occurrence of a joke
■ Joke in the background
■ Foreshadowing

THE BLUTHS
... always leave a note

G.O.B.
Aztec Tomb

trick vs. illusion

"... from whence it came."

... messes up a trick.

"club sauce"

BUSTER
missing limbs

MISCELLANEOUS
Carl Weathers says "No ... I LOVE it."
paint on Michael's shirt

16 episodes feature this joke:

Season 1

2: Top Banana

Dead dove

fireball.

6: Charity Drive

Fireball.

11: Public Relations

G.O.B. loses Earl Milford in the Aztec Tomb.

16: Missing Kitty

G.O.B. paints a card on his chest which rubs off on Michael's dress shirt.

Related Joke: paint on Michael's shirt

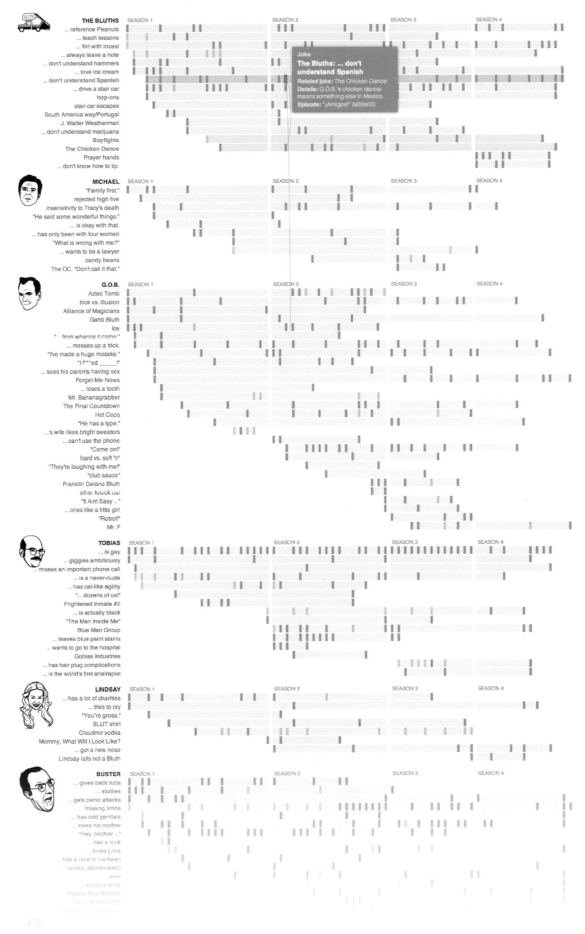

■ Occurrence of a joke   ■ Joke in the background   ■ Foreshadowing   — Combined joke

THE BLUTHS   SEASON 1   SEASON 2   SEASON 3   SEASON 4
... reference Peanuts
... teach lessons
... flirt with incest
... always leave a note
... don't understand hammers
... love ice cream
... don't understand Spanish
... drive a stair car
hop-ons
stair car escapes
South America way/Portugal
J. Walter Weatherman
... don't understand marijuana
Boyfights
The Chicken Dance
Prayer hands
... don't know how to tip.

Joke
The Bluths: ... don't understand Spanish
Related joke: The Chicken Dance
Details: G.O.B.'s chicken dance means something else in Mexico.
Episode: "¡Amigos!" (s02e03)

MICHAEL   SEASON 1   SEASON 2   SEASON 3   SEASON 4
"Family first."
rejected high five
insensitivity to Tracy's death
"He said some wonderful things."
... is okay with that.
... has only been with four women
"What is wrong with me?"
... wants to be a lawyer
candy beans
The OC. "Don't call it that."

G.O.B.   SEASON 1   SEASON 2   SEASON 3   SEASON 4
Aztec Tomb
trick vs. illusion
Alliance of Magicians
Gahb Bluth
ice
" ... from whence it came "
... messes up a trick.
"I've made a huge mistake."
"I f***ed ____!"
... sees his parents having sex
Forget-Me-Nows
... loses a tooth
Mr. Bananagrabber
The Final Countdown
Hot Cops
"He has a type."
...'s wife likes bright sweaters
... can't use the phone
"Come on!"
hard vs. soft "c"
"They're laughing with me!"
"club sauce"
Franklin Delano Bluth
either knock out
"It Aint Easy ..."
... cries like a little girl
"Robot!"
Mr. F

TOBIAS   SEASON 1   SEASON 2   SEASON 3   SEASON 4
... is gay
... giggles ambitiously
... misses an important phone call
... is a never-nude
... has cat-like agility
"... dozens of us!"
Frightened Inmate #2
... is actually black
"The Man Inside Me"
Blue Man Group
... leaves blue paint stains
... wants to go to the hospital
Gobias Industries
... has hair plug complications
... is the world's first analrapist

LINDSAY   SEASON 1   SEASON 2   SEASON 3   SEASON 4
... has a lot of charities
... tries to cry
"You're gross."
SLUT shirt
Cloudmir vodka
Mommy, What Will I Look Like?
... got a new nose
Lindsay is/is not a Bluth

BUSTER   SEASON 1   SEASON 2   SEASON 3   SEASON 4
... gives back rubs
... studies
... gets panic attacks
missing limbs
... has odd genitals
... loves his mother
"Hey, brother ..."
... has a rock
... loves juice
... has a hole in his heart
... curses (abbreviated)
seal
... wants a turtle
Balboa Bay Window
... is a MONSTER

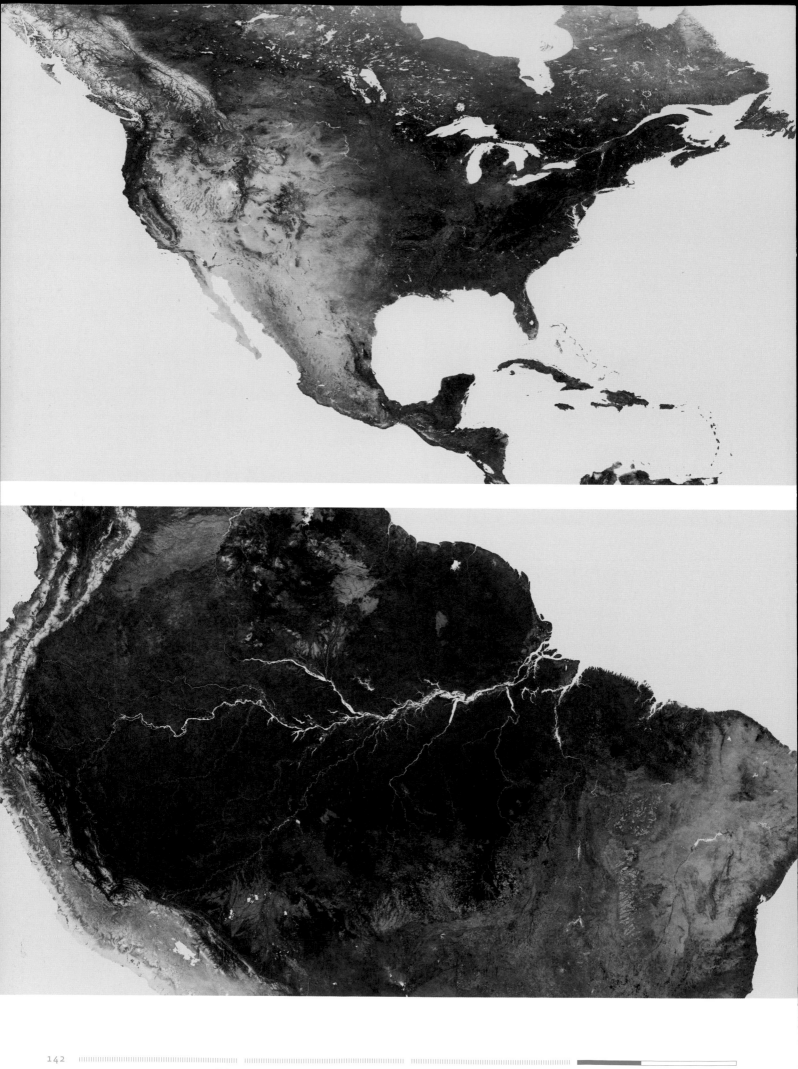

YOU   US   MATERIAL WORLD   INTERACTIVE

Our Green World

When Earth's vegetation is mapped over time, the planet appears to breathe.

ARTISTS Dan Pisut, Tim Loomis, Vivek Goel, and Wei Guo of I.M. Systems Group, under contract to the National Oceanic and Atmospheric Administration.

STATEMENT From its orbit 824 kilometers above Earth, the Suomi NPP satellite, developed by NASA and NOAA and operated by NOAA, looks at our planet not in terms of recognizable objects, but in colors of light (and energy that our eyes cannot see). Data from that satellite allows us to measure the amount of surface vegetation at a location based on what is known about the light plants absorb for photosynthesis.

What did it take to create these maps? Besides a lot of computer storage and processing, it took a team of computer and physical scientists, along with graphic artists. The scientists evaluated and interpreted the data, creating equations that convert how much energy is absorbed or reflected by the planet's surface into an index of global vegetation. The graphic artists worked with the scientists to translate the 1s and 0s of that data into stunning imagery and visualizations. We chose a very simple color scheme. The maps answer a simple question, "Is there vegetation, and if so, how much?" There are no colors detailing cities, or snow, or rock, or ocean. Just green.

PUBLICATION NOAA (June 2013)

Across US Companies, Tax Rates Vary Greatly

Some pay no taxes at all.

ARTISTS Mike Bostock, artist, Matt Ericson, deputy graphics editor, David Leonhardt, columnist and Washington bureau chief, and Bill Marsh, graphics editor, at the *New York Times*.

STATEMENT This interactive graphic allows readers to survey the great variety of effective tax rates imposed on the S&P 500 companies, individually and by sector. The column and graphic were part of a series of reports on how major companies are able to minimize their taxes by complex strategies not available to others. The sector view especially highlights these disparities. Different industries, and companies in the same industries, range from zero taxes owed to very high rates. Readers can also search for individual companies. General Electric, whose successful methods of minimizing taxes were detailed in a *Times* series, had an effective tax rate of 16 percent.

PUBLICATION *New York Times* (May 2013)

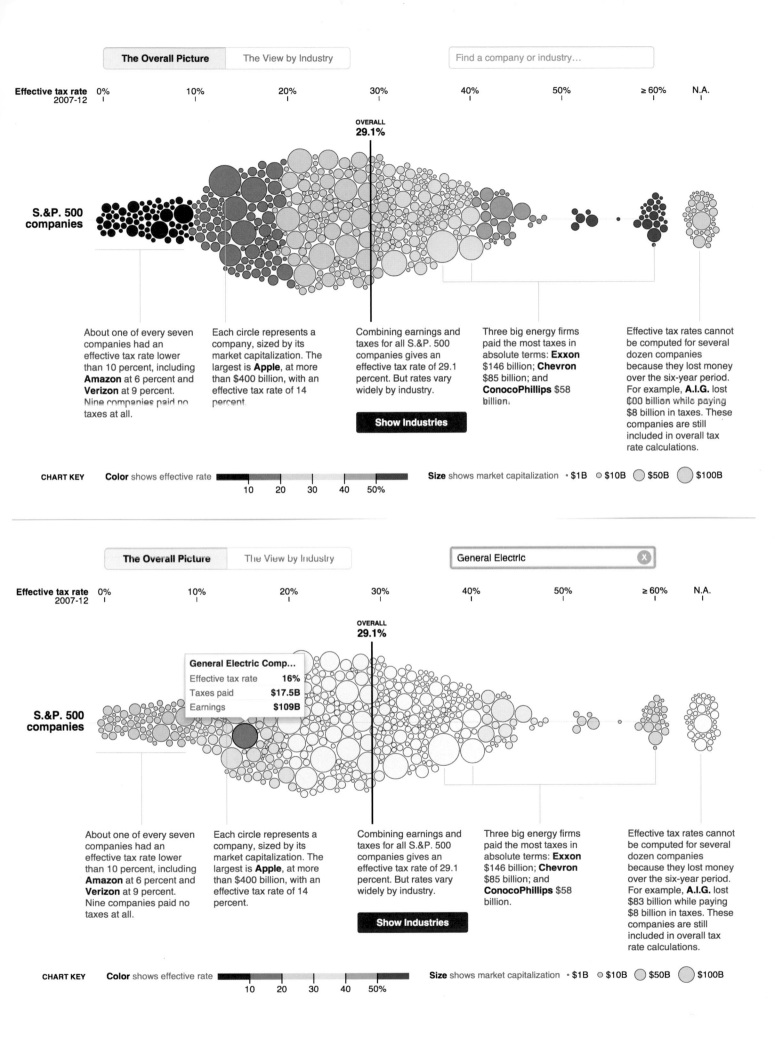

Effective tax rate
2007-12   0%   10%   20%   30%   40%   50%   ≥ 60%   N.A.

OVERALL
29.1%

S.&P. 500 companies

About one of every seven companies had an effective tax rate lower than 10 percent, including **Amazon** at 6 percent and **Verizon** at 9 percent. Nine companies paid no taxes at all.

Each circle represents a company, sized by its market capitalization. The largest is **Apple**, at more than $400 billion, with an effective tax rate of 14 percent.

Combining earnings and taxes for all S.&P. 500 companies gives an effective tax rate of 29.1 percent. But rates vary widely by industry.

Show Industries

Three big energy firms paid the most taxes in absolute terms: **Exxon** $146 billion; **Chevron** $85 billion; and **ConocoPhillips** $58 billion.

Effective tax rates cannot be computed for several dozen companies because they lost money over the six-year period. For example, **A.I.G.** lost $00 billion while paying $8 billion in taxes. These companies are still included in overall tax rate calculations.

CHART KEY   **Color** shows effective rate
10   20   30   40   50%

Size shows market capitalization   • $1B   ○ $10B   ◯ $50B   ◯ $100B

Effective tax rate
2007-12   0%   10%   20%   30%   40%   50%   ≥ 60%   N.A.

OVERALL
29.1%

General Electric Comp…	
Effective tax rate	**16%**
Taxes paid	**$17.5B**
Earnings	**$109B**

S.&P. 500 companies

About one of every seven companies had an effective tax rate lower than 10 percent, including **Amazon** at 6 percent and **Verizon** at 9 percent. Nine companies paid no taxes at all.

Each circle represents a company, sized by its market capitalization. The largest is **Apple**, at more than $400 billion, with an effective tax rate of 14 percent.

Combining earnings and taxes for all S.&P. 500 companies gives an effective tax rate of 29.1 percent. But rates vary widely by industry.

Show Industries

Three big energy firms paid the most taxes in absolute terms: **Exxon** $146 billion; **Chevron** $85 billion; and **ConocoPhillips** $58 billion.

Effective tax rates cannot be computed for several dozen companies because they lost money over the six-year period. For example, **A.I.G.** lost $83 billion while paying $8 billion in taxes. These companies are still included in overall tax rate calculations.

CHART KEY   **Color** shows effective rate
10   20   30   40   50%

Size shows market capitalization   • $1B   ○ $10B   ◯ $50B   ◯ $100B

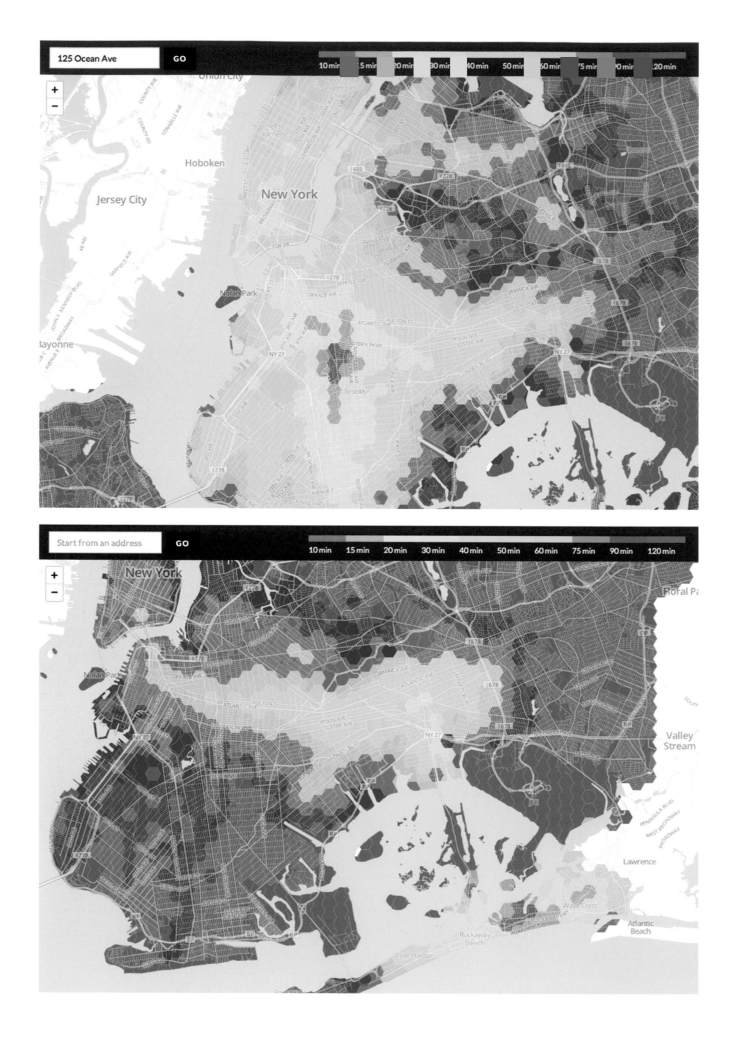

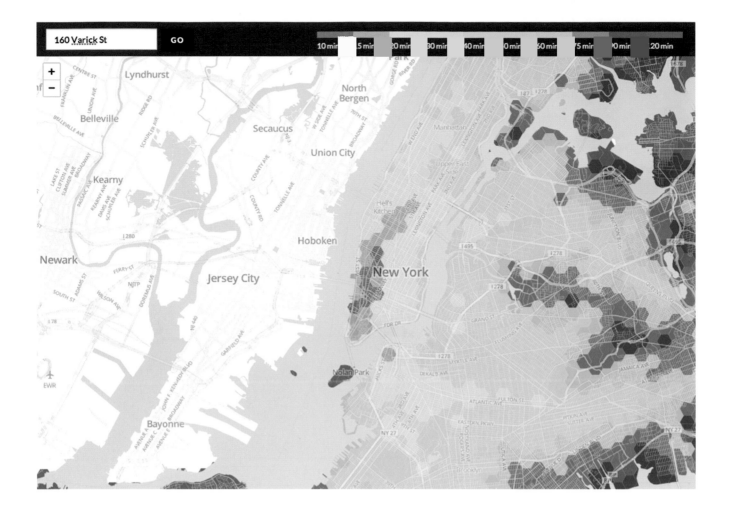

160 Varick St — GO

10 min 5 min 20 min 30 min 40 min 0 min 60 min 5 min 0 min 20 min

Transit Time, NYC

How many minutes it takes to get from A to B.

ARTISTS The WNYC Data News team: John Keefe, editor, Steven Melendez, developer, and Louise Ma, designer.

STATEMENT The Transit Time Map was created as an extension of WNYC's reporting on the legacy of departing Mayor Michael Bloomberg. We wanted to show how his championing of extensive real estate development pushed residents of limited means farther from Manhattan, creating longer commutes for many workers. The map also illustrates how the Manhattan-centric system fails many commuters who travel from one outer borough to another. In searching for ways to represent these dramatic stories, we were inspired by Jonathan Soma's TripTrop project. The WNYC audience is passionate and active, and our listeners avidly participated in discussions about the map's implications and Bloomberg's legacy. That participation validates for us the impact and importance of data-driven news visualization for investigative reporting and readers' understanding of the issues.

PUBLICATION *WNYC.org* (July 2013)

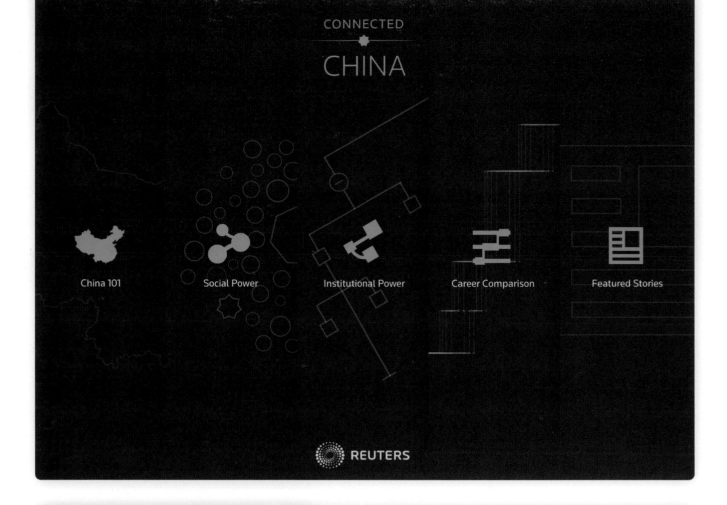

CONNECTED

CHINA

China 101   Social Power   Institutional Power   Career Comparison   Featured Stories

REUTERS

INSTITUTIONAL POWER   HIDE GUIDE ⊗

VISUALIZATION GUIDE
2/3

The Seven

In addition to their roles as leaders of the Communist Party, "The Seven" concurrently hold top titles in state and military organizations, making the Politburo Standing Committee China's de facto governing body.

For example, Xi Jinping ⓘ is Party general secretary and the top-ranked Politburo Standing Committee member. He also serves as vice president of China — a state function — and chairman of the CPC Central Military Commission.

PREVIOUS   NEXT

Party
Communist Party of China

Military
People's Liberation Army

Government
People's Republic of China

7

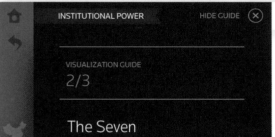

Xi Jinping
习近平

Li Keqiang
李克强

Zhang Dejiang
张德江

Yu Zhengsheng
俞正声

Liu Yunshan
刘云山

Wang Qishan
王岐山

Zhang Gaoli
张高丽

Politburo Standing Committee

Connected China

A country's power structure, in real time.

ARTISTS Irene Jay Liu of Thomson Reuters; Katy Harris and Mark Schifferli of Fathom Information Design, in Boston.

STATEMENT Connected China is a news app that tracks and visualizes the people, organizations, and relationships that form China's elite power structure. During a period of significant political transition—the retirement of Hu Jintao and rise of Xi Jinping as China's top leader—Reuters sought to deepen its coverage by tackling a fundamental question: how does power flow in China? One thing soon became clear: connections, known in Chinese as *guanxi,* were key. So we structured inherently qualitative information about tens of thousands of relationships

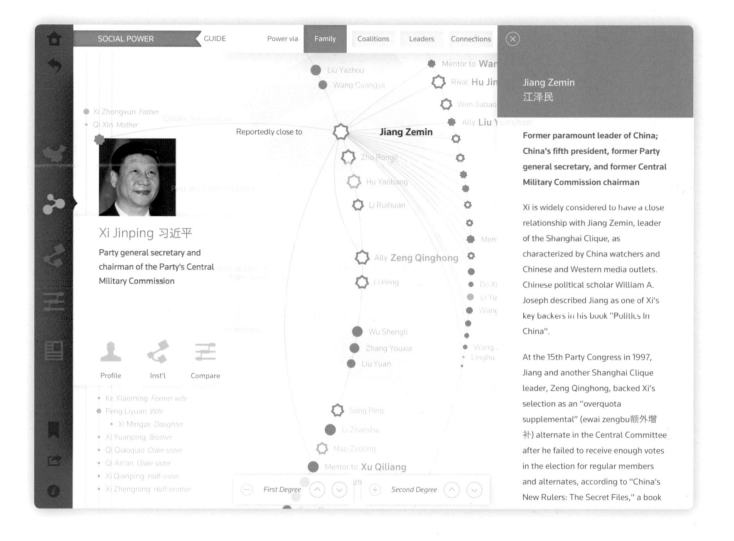

pertaining to China's top leaders—a tightly woven fabric of familial, political and business ties, mentorship, and shared work histories—and put them into a database.

Traditional media could not convey the dense, shifting, and nuanced dynamics of Chinese governance. Our design goal was to find ways to simplify each graphic based on how it would be used, rather than showing visually complex, but mostly useless, tangles of connections. Like wayfinding in a building, we needed to build a universe of information where people could get in, move around, and exit without getting lost or having the world shift around them. Connected China is a "living" app, designed

to support real-time updates, which was crucial during the leadership transition, when scores of officials changed positions in a matter of days. By using the database to drive its complex visualizations, Connected China doesn't just capture a moment in time, but evolves with the news.

PUBLICATION Reuters (February 2013)

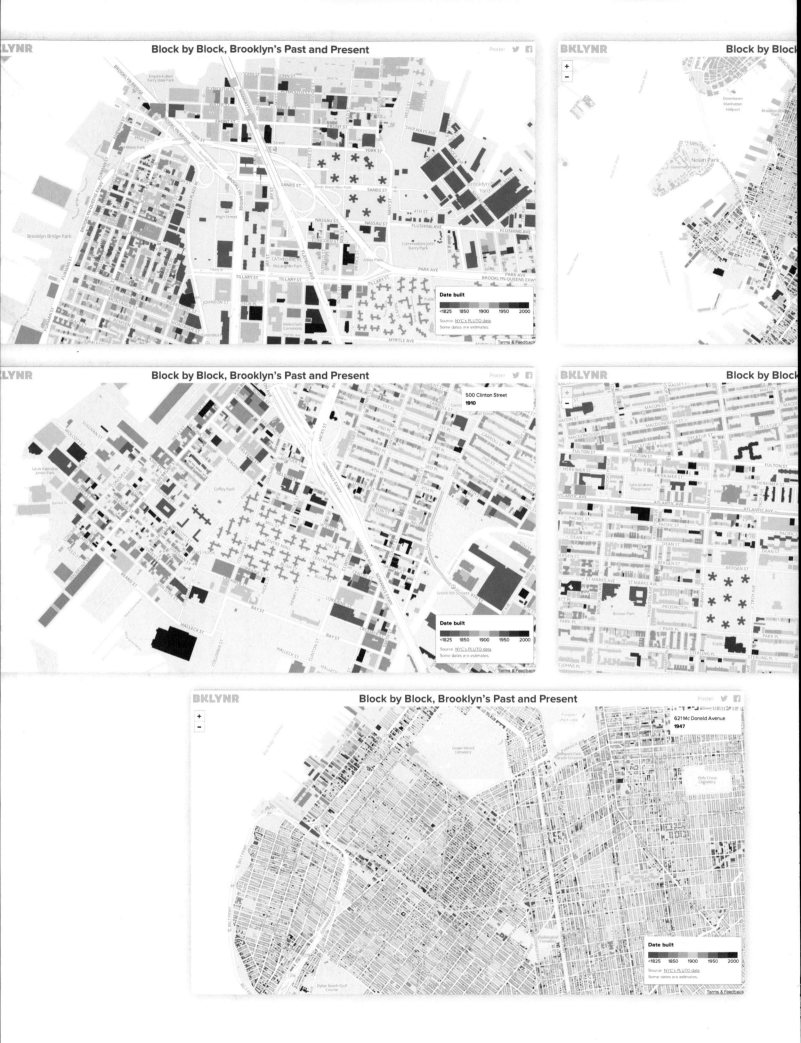

Block by Block, Brooklyn's Past and Present

The age of every building.

ARTIST Thomas Rhiel, founding editor of *BKLYNR*.

STATEMENT The concept of my "Block by Block" map is pretty simple: it shows all of Brooklyn's 320,000-plus buildings and colors them based on their age of construction. I pulled the data from the NYC Department of Planning's PLUTO dataset. Some of the dates are estimates.

On my weekly walk to get groceries, I pass a row of brownstones—some well-kept and majestic, some fossil-like and crumbling—bookended by a gleaming, square-windowed silver tower. It's an architectural contrast of a kind that's commonplace throughout Brooklyn. The borough's a patchwork of the old and new, but traces of its history aren't spread evenly. "Block by Block" is a snapshot of Brooklyn's evolution, revealing how development has rippled across certain neighborhoods while leaving some pockets unchanged for decades, even centuries.

PUBLICATION *BKLYNR.com* (August 2013)

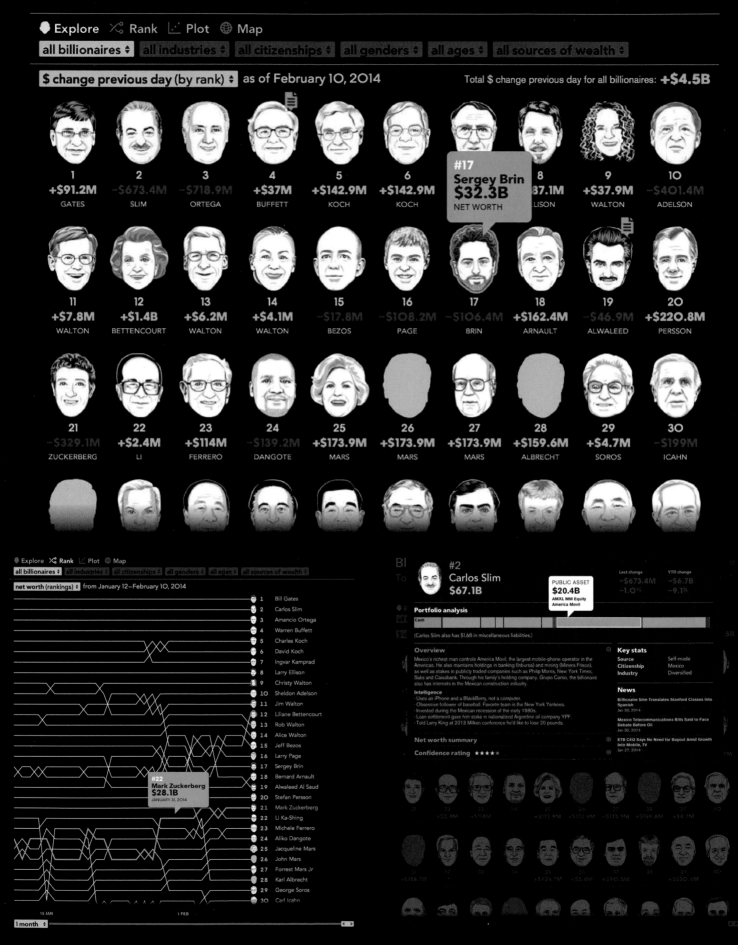

● Explore ✕ Rank ⊵ Plot ⊕ Map

all billionaires ⬦   all industries ⬦   all citizenships ⬦   all genders ⬦   all ages ⬦   all sources of wealth ⬦

$ change previous day (by rank) ⬦   as of February 10, 2014   Total $ change previous day for all billionaires: **+$4.5B**

1	2	3	4	5	6	#17	8	9	10
+$91.2M	–$673.4M	–$718.9M	+$37M	+$142.9M	+$142.9M	**Sergey Brin $32.3B** NET WORTH	37.1M	+$37.9M	–$401.4M
GATES	SLIM	ORTEGA	BUFFETT	KOCH	KOCH		LISON	WALTON	ADELSON

11	12	13	14	15	16	17	18	19	20
+$7.8M	+$1.4B	+$6.2M	+$4.1M	–$17.8M	–$108.2M	–$106.4M	+$162.4M	–$46.9M	+$220.8M
WALTON	BETTENCOURT	WALTON	WALTON	BEZOS	PAGE	BRIN	ARNAULT	ALWALEED	PERSSON

21	22	23	24	25	26	27	28	29	30
–$329.1M	+$2.4M	+$114M	–$139.2M	+$173.9M	+$173.9M	+$173.9M	+$159.6M	+$4.7M	–$199M
ZUCKERBERG	LI	FERRERO	DANGOTE	MARS	MARS	MARS	ALBRECHT	SOROS	ICAHN

● Explore ✕ Rank ⊵ Plot ⊕ Map

all billionaires ⬦   all industries ⬦   all citizenships ⬦   all genders ⬦   all ages ⬦   all sources of wealth ⬦

net worth (rankings) ⬦   from January 12–February 10, 2014

1	Bill Gates
2	Carlos Slim
3	Amancio Ortega
4	Warren Buffett
5	Charles Koch
6	David Koch
7	Ingvar Kamprad
8	Larry Ellison
9	Christy Walton
10	Sheldon Adelson
11	Jim Walton
12	Liliane Bettencourt
13	Rob Walton
14	Alice Walton
15	Jeff Bezos
16	Larry Page
17	Sergey Brin
18	Bernard Arnault
19	Alwaleed Al Saud
20	Stefan Persson
21	Mark Zuckerberg
22	Li Ka-Shing
23	Michele Ferrero
24	Aliko Dangote
25	Jacqueline Mars
26	John Mars
27	Forrest Mars Jr
28	Karl Albrecht
29	George Soros
30	Carl Icahn

#22 Mark Zuckerberg $28.1B JANUARY 31, 2014

15 JAN   1 FEB

1 month ⬦

BI
To

#2 Carlos Slim $67.1B

	Last change	YTD change
	–$673.4M	–$6.7B
	–1.0%	–9.1%

PUBLIC ASSET **$20.4B** AMXL MM Equity America Movil

Portfolio analysis

Cash

(Carlos Slim also has $1.6B in miscellaneous liabilities.)

Overview
Mexico's richest man controls America Movil, the largest mobile-phone operator in the Americas. He also maintains holdings in banking (Inbursa) and mining (Minera Frisco), as well as stakes in publicly traded companies such as Philip Morris, New York Times, Saks and Caixabank. Through his family's holding company, Grupo Carso, the billionaire also has interests in the Mexican construction industry.

Intelligence
- Uses an iPhone and a BlackBerry, not a computer.
- Obsessive follower of baseball. Favorite team in the New York Yankees.
- Invested during the Mexican recession of the early 1980s.
- Loan settlement gave him stake in nationalized Argentine oil company YPF.
- Told Larry King at 2013 Milken conference he'd like to lose 20 pounds.

Net worth summary

Confidence rating ★★★★☆

Key stats

Source	Self-made
Citizenship	Mexico
Industry	Diversified

News

Billionaire Slim Translates Stanford Classes Into Spanish
Jan 30, 2014

Mexico Telecommunications Bills Said to Face Debate Before Oil
Jan 30, 2014

ETB CEO Says No Need for Buyout Amid Growth Into Mobile, TV
Jan 27, 2014

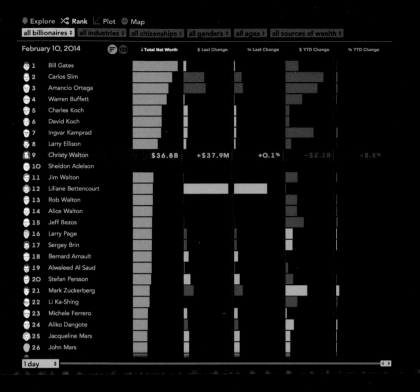

February 10, 2014

		↓ Total Net Worth	$ Last Change	% Last Change	$ YTD Change	% YTD Change
1	Bill Gates					
2	Carlos Slim					
3	Amancio Ortega					
4	Warren Buffett					
5	Charles Koch					
6	David Koch					
7	Ingvar Kamprad					
8	Larry Ellison					
9	Christy Walton	$36.8B	+$37.9M	+0.1%	−$2.1B	−5.5%
10	Sheldon Adelson					
11	Jim Walton					
12	Liliane Bettencourt					
13	Rob Walton					
14	Alice Walton					
15	Jeff Bezos					
16	Larry Page					
17	Sergey Brin					
18	Bernard Arnault					
19	Alwaleed Al Saud					
20	Stefan Persson					
21	Mark Zuckerberg					
22	Li Ka-Shing					
23	Michele Ferrero					
24	Aliko Dangote					
25	Jacqueline Mars					
26	John Mars					

1 day ⬧

Bloomberg Visual Data

Bloomberg Billionaires ⓘ
Today's ranking of the world's richest people ⬠

SEE BILLIONAIRES STORIES ⌄

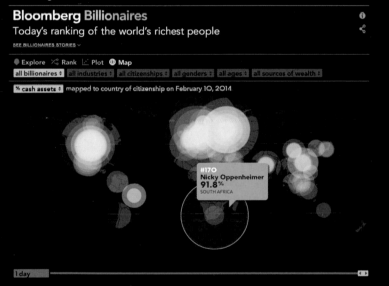

#170
Nicky Oppenheimer
91.8%
SOUTH AFRICA

1 day

Bloomberg Billionaires
Who's who and where they stand.

ARTISTS The Bloomberg Visual Data team for the Billionaires Index: Lisa Strausfeld, head of data visualization, Hilla Katki, design director, Christopher Cannon, senior designer, Jeremy Diamond, interaction designer, Kenton Powell, designer, David Harding, R&D lead, and Alia Shafir, project manager. Freelancers: Christian Swinehart, developer, and Lina Chen, illustrator.

STATEMENT The Bloomberg Billionaires Index visualizes a daily ranking of the world's richest people as reported by a team of Bloomberg journalists. The index is a dynamic measure of the top 200 billionaires based on changes in markets, the economy, and personal assets. Users can sort the list of billionaires by rank (total net worth) or by changes to their wealth in either dollar amounts or percent change. These changes can be tracked over time, placed geographically on a map, or plotted against other variables. Users can also search for a specific individual or filter the list by industry, country of citizenship, gender, age, or source of wealth.

The profile view for each billionaire contains a detailed analysis of how that person's fortune has been tallied, as well as a summarized biography and links to Bloomberg articles and videos related to that individual.

There were a few surprising aspects to interacting with the finished product. One was being able to see just how much money these billionaires stand to gain or lose in a single day. Another surprise was being able to visualize how few of these individuals have the majority of their wealth in cash—most are "paper billionaires" with their wealth tied up in stocks. The third insight was that none of the world's richest women in this list were self-made—they all inherited their fortunes (with the $2.9 billion she has earned, Oprah hasn't made the cut yet).

PUBLICATION *Bloomberg.com/billionaires*
(January 2013)

Map Stack

Maps for all—free, forever.

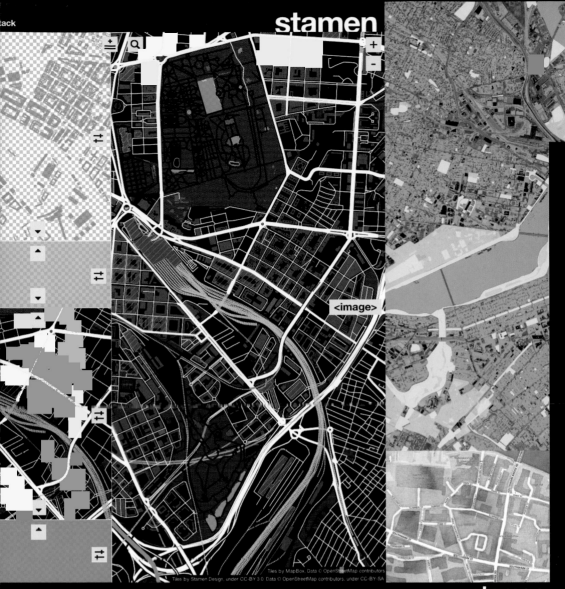

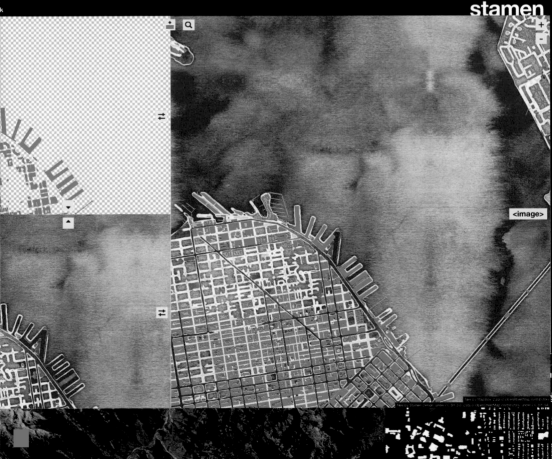

stamen

stamen

ARTIST Stamen Design.

STATEMENT In the summer of 2013, the team at Stamen released a project we had been dreaming of for many years: Map Stack, a tool that allows anyone at any skill level to design their own map image. This web-based tool offers Photoshop-like layering capability with real map data from OpenStreetMap. For the first time, no code or cartography skills are required to create a beautiful, custom map of anywhere in the world.

Map Stack is the most recent example of Stamen giving away free mapmaking resources, which we have been proudly doing for almost ten years. The first few tools we put on-line were open-source software librar-ies like Modest Maps, Tilestache, and Polymaps. Arguably, these were not useful to anyone who doesn't speak in code, but widely used in a small com-munity of geo-nerds. In 2010, we were funded by the Knight News Founda-tion to facilitate the emerging practice of data journalism. The result of that Citytracking grant was two free Cre-ative Commons–licensed worldwide tilesets — Watercolor and Toner — along with Terrain, which is available for the US. These tilesets are available for use by anyone. The free map tool metamorphosed last year into Map Stack. So far, we've seen 199,852 orig-inal maps created, and in January 2014 we served over 240,000,000 map tiles.

PUBLICATION *Stamen.com* (June 2013)

155

Best American Infographics Brain Trust

THOMAS ALBERTY was brought on as the design director at *New York* magazine in 2012. Prior to that he worked at *GQ* for eight years. His work has been recognized by the Society of Publication Designers and the Type Directors Club. He lives in Brooklyn, NY.

SAMUEL ARBESMAN is a complex systems scientist and writer. He is a Senior Scholar at the Ewing Marion Kauffman Foundation and a fellow at the Institute for Quantitative Social Science at Harvard University. He is the author of *The Half-Life of Facts.*

ALBERTO CAIRO teaches infographics and visualization at the University of Miami. He has been a professor at the University of North Carolina at Chapel Hill and infographics and multimedia director at various media organizations in Spain and Brazil. He is the author of *The Functional Art: An Introduction to Information Graphics and Visualization.*

JEN CHRISTIANSEN is the art director of information graphics at *Scientific American.* Previously she was an assistant art director and then a designer at *National Geographic.* She completed her undergraduate studies in geology and art at Smith College, and her graduate studies in science illustration at the University of California, Santa Cruz.

AMANDA COX joined the *New York Times* graphics desk in 2005. She holds a master's degree in statistics from the University of Washington.

CARL DETORRES is a multi-disciplinary graphic designer operating at the intersection of design, illustration, and information graphics. He is a longtime contributor to publications such as *Nature, WIRED, Fortune, Time,* and the *New York Times* and regularly partners with corporations and institutions like IBM, Visa, Facebook, and The Gates Foundation. He has recently partnered with Jeffrey O'Brien to create StoryTK, a hybrid design and storytelling agency.

MARIETTE DICHRISTINA is editor-in-chief and senior vice president of *Scientific American,* which includes oversight of the magazine as well as *ScientificAmerican.com, Scientific American Mind,* and all newsstand special editions. Under her leadership, the magazine received a 2011 National Magazine Award for General Excellence.

JOHN GRIMWADE has his own information graphics business. He has produced infographics for over forty magazines. Before moving to the US, he worked for fourteen years in newspapers in London, including six years as head of graphics at *The Times.* He cohosts the annual Malofiej "Show, Don't Tell" infographics workshop in Pamplona, Spain, and teaches information graphics at the School of Visual Arts in Manhattan.

KARL GUDE is the former director of information graphics at *Newsweek* and the Associated Press. Karl left *Newsweek* after a decade to spearhead the first information-graphics program at Michigan State University's School of Journalism. Karl also teaches a class on creative problem-solving and the creative process.

NIGEL HOLMES is the founder of Explanation Graphics, a design company that helps people to understand complex processes and statistics. He was graphics director for *Time* from 1978 to 1994. The Society for News Design gave him a Lifetime Achievement Award in 2009, and a retrospective exhibition of his work was shown at Stevenson University in Baltimore in 2011. His most recent book, *Instant Expert,* was published by Lonely Planet in 2013. With his son, Rowland, he makes short animated films.

ANDY KIRK is a UK-based data visualization specialist, published author, and editor of the blog *visualising data.* He is a globe-trotting freelance design consultant and provider of training workshops, as well as a visiting lecturer at Maryland Institute College of Arts, teaching in the Information Visualization Master's program. Andy is on Twitter as @visualisingdata.

GEOFF MCGHEE develops interactive media at the Bill Lane Center for the American West at Stanford University. Previously, he spent a decade doing infographics, multimedia, and video at the *New York Times*, ABC News, and France's *Le Monde.* In 2009–2010, he was a John S. Knight Journalism Fellow at Stanford University, studying data visualization, which resulted in the web documentary "Journalism in the Age of Data."

JOHN NELSON is the user-experience designer and cartographer at IDV Solutions. He researches, creates, lectures, and writes on the intersection of design, usability, and mapping. His work focuses on the effective visualization of Earth's systems and elements of risk.

HANSPETER PFISTER is
An Wang Professor of Computer
Science and director of the Institute for
Applied Computational Science
at the Harvard School of Engineering
and Applied Sciences. His research in
visual computing lies at the intersection
of visualization, computer graphics,
and computer vision. He has a PhD
in Computer Science from the State
University of New York at Stony Brook
and an MS in Electrical Engineering
from ETH Zurich, Switzerland. Before
joining Harvard he worked at Mitsub-
ishi Electric Research Laboratories,
where he was associate director and
senior research scientist.

MARIA POPOVA is the
founder and editor of *Brain Pickings*
(brainpickings.org), an inventory of
cross-disciplinary interestingness. She
has written for *Wired* UK, *The Atlantic*,
Nieman Journalism Lab, the *New York
Times*, *Smithsonian Magazine*, and *Design
Observer*, among others, and is an
MIT Futures of Entertainment Fellow.
She is on Twitter as @brainpicker.

KIM REES is cofounder of
Periscopic, a socially conscious data
visualization firm.

ERIC RODENBECK is
the founder and creative director
of Stamen, a leading mapping and data
visualization design studio based in
San Francisco. He's been called one of
Esquire's "Best and Brightest" new
designers and thinkers, and one of *ID*
magazine's top 40 designers to watch.
He sits on the board of directors of
the Kenneth Rainin Foundation and
the Gray Area Foundation for the Arts,
and has been a judge of the National
Design Awards sponsored by First Lady
Michele Obama. His work is in the
permanent collection of the Museum
of Modern Art in New York City,
and he has shown work at galleries
and museums in San Francisco, London,
Chicago, Minneapolis, Los Angeles,
and Shanghai. Eric picked the top
ten interactive infographics for *Best
American Infographics 2013*.

SIMON ROGERS is data editor
at Twitter and former editor of the
Guardian's "Datablog and Datastore."
In 2012, he won the Royal Statistical
Society award for statistical excellence
in journalism.

DREW SKAU is the visualization
architect at Visually, a community
for infographic and data visualization
creators to showcase their work and
get connected with clients. He is
pursuing a PhD in computer science
at University of North Carolina at
Charlotte with a focus on supporting
creativity in visualization design.

ANDREW VANDEMOERE
is an associate professor at KU Leuven
University in Belgium and the author
of the blog *Information Aesthetics*
(infosthetics.com), which showcases
compelling data visualizations,
ranging from data art to scientific
data analytics.

JUAN VELASCO has been
the art director of *National Geographic*
since 2008, and is now the senior
editor, art & graphics. Previously,
Juan worked as a graphics artist for *El
Mundo* and as the graphics art director
for the *New York Times*. In 2001, he
founded his own consulting company,
5W Infographics, which is based in
New York City and Madrid. He is an
instructor for the "Show, Don't Tell"
infographics workshop, part of the
SND-e Malofiej conference at the
University of Pamplona in Spain, and
a visiting teacher of information
graphics at the University of Hong
Kong.

FERNANDA B. VIÉGAS is
a computational designer whose work
focuses on the social, collaborative,
and artistic aspects of information
visualization. She is a co-leader, with
Martin Wattenberg, of Google's
"Big Picture" data visualization group
in Cambridge, MA.

MARTIN WATTENBERG
is a computer scientist and artist
whose work focuses on visual explora-
tions of culturally significant data.
With Fernanda Viégas, he leads Google's "Big Picture" visualization research
group. A particular interest is using
visual tools to foster collaboration and
collective discovery.

BANG WONG is the creative
director of the Broad Institute of
MIT and Harvard and an adjunct
assistant professor in the Department
of Art as Applied to Medicine at
the Johns Hopkins University School
of Medicine. His work focuses on
developing visual strategies to meet
the analytical challenges posed by
the unprecedented scale, resolution,
and variety of data in biomedical
research.

NATHAN YAU has a PhD in
statistics from the University of
California, Los Angeles, and is the
author of *Visualize This* and *Data
Points*. He writes about visualization
and statistics at the blog *Flowing Data*.

DAN ZEDEK is the assistant
managing editor/design at the
Boston Globe, where he leads the design
and infographics teams in print and
online. In 2012, BostonGlobe.com
was named the world's best-designed
website by the Society for News
Design.